A
VALIDATION
OF
KNOWLEDGE

A
VALIDATION
OF
KNOWLEDGE

A NEW,
OBJECTIVE THEORY
OF
AXIOMS,
CAUSALITY,
MEANING,
PROPOSITIONS,
MATHEMATICS,
AND
INDUCTION

RONALD PISATURO

WITH A FOREWORD BY,
AND A CHAPTER ON MATHEMATICS
CO-WRITTEN BY, GLENN MARCUS

PRIME MOVER PRESS
NORWALK, CONNECTICUT

Prime Mover Press
Norwalk, Connecticut

Second Edition
Revised March 25, 2026

ISBN 978-0-9997041-6-5 (Paperback)

To Glenn Marcus, the prime mover of this book

CONTENTS

FOREWORD

I am honored to write the Foreword to Ronald Pisaturo's *A Validation of Knowledge: A New, Objective Theory of Axioms, Causality, Meaning, Propositions, Mathematics, and Induction.*

In 1992, I asked Ron to write a treatise on philosophy, in order to validate explicitly how we know the fundamental truths of philosophy. This book is his validation. In my judgment, Ron presents a methodologically-explicit, step-by-step, logical argument—where no logical step is skipped, and all abstractions are firmly tied to their concretes.

Let me give some advice to readers who want to engage seriously with this work. First, you must know some mathematics to do so successfully. The issue of how mathematics relates to philosophy has been an open question for more than two and half millennia. Mathematics is the science of measurement, and, as such, can be applied to *any* field, helping to make that field's conclusions more precise. Probability measures the certainty of what we know; therefore, philosophy, especially epistemology, can use mathematics to make its conclusions—the certainty of its inductions—more precise. To measure the level of certainty of our inductive generalizations, Ron explicates here his "$n/(n+1)$" method. The mathematics necessary to understand fully Ron's validation consists of about two semesters of calculus and one semester of probability. If you don't already know these two subjects, learning them is certainly within reach if you put your mind to it.

Second, I want to caution readers about potentially misapplying the cognitive method of integration. (I should know, because it was while reading Ron's book that I learned not to make this error.) As Ayn Rand (1971, 173) explained, "Integration is the essential part of understanding." But what kind of integration should an active mind perform when reading, and which integrations are fundamental? In my judgment, before trying to integrate a new logical argument with one's existing context of knowledge, one should focus first on whether the new argument corresponds to the relevant facts. As Ron has stated (in private correspondence), each reader should put aside his own past thinking, follow the book's argument, and judge whether it identifies reality. That is, focus first on existence: does the argument correspond to the facts? If so, then—and only then—integrate the now-validated argument with one's old context, making any needed corrections to ensure that one's new context remains without contradiction. Put existence first, and consciousness second, honoring what Ayn Rand identified as "the primacy of existence."

The epistemological issues covered in this book are difficult, because they require identifying steps in reasoning that have always been implicit. To do that takes substantive effort. I should know. I have been studying philosophy for almost fifty years now, and I have studied Ron's work since he began explaining it to me almost thirty years ago. I try not to think about all the effort I have invested during these decades, and all of the many confusions I have had to overcome. Rather than think about my past effort, I take joy in understanding—to whatever extent I do—what I consider a valid proof that resolves these issues, and in how this understanding has substantively enhanced my life. I wish you—the careful, thoughtful reader—a similar understanding and its resultant joy.

Glenn Marcus
September 2020

PREFACE

This book presents a validation of the corpus of human knowledge, explaining how we know what we know, and how well we know it.

Along the way of presenting this validation, I offer original answers to all the major open questions in epistemology—as indicated by the book's title. These questions and my answers arise organically in the course of my validation, not through dialectic with the ideas of other philosophers, but through first-hand study of reality. I present a positive theory, motivated and directed at every step not by a need to reply to skeptics or subjectivists, but by the need of a rational individual to know the world.

I do embrace and use truths identified by others—most notably, Ayn Rand. I rely heavily on—and suggest that the reader be already familiar with—her theory of concepts as presented in *Introduction to Objectivist Epistemology* (*IOE*) (1990). Her theory of concepts entails a new understanding of the very concept of objectivity. It is fitting that she named her philosophy "Objectivism."

Ayn Rand made other crucial epistemological identifications, regarding axioms and axiomatic concepts (existence, consciousness, and identity), causality ("the law of identity applied to action"), and the relation between existence and consciousness ("the primacy of existence"), to name a few.

But not all identifications made by Ayn Rand, especially regarding causality, were put into writing in the same depth as was her theory of concepts. Moreover, she never wrote a theory of propositions or induction. She never wrote a treatise on epistemology; she wrote only her *Introduction*. Other thinkers—most notably Peikoff

(1991)—elaborate on foundational ideas that Ayn Rand introduced in various written passages or expressed in private communications but did not herself put into systematic writing. But these elaborations, in my judgment, serve more to indicate logical gaps—particularly regarding causality—than to fill them.

In this book, I endeavor to present an epistemology without such logical gaps—not by trying to fill the gaps in Objectivism as written, but by starting fresh and presenting the essentials of my own epistemology. The seeds of my theory of causality and induction are planted throughout my epistemology. Therefore, I cannot merely add ideas on to the end of the work of others; I must start again at the beginning.

In the end, I conclude that many original ideas from Ayn Rand—and Aristotle—are true and crucial to my own epistemology. In accordance with Aristotle (see Gotthelf 1987, 208–211), it is indeed entities that act causally. A proposition indeed "asserts or denies something of something" (Aristotle 1941b, 42, 17a21). In accordance with Ayn Rand (1990, 55–61), the axiomatic concepts of existence, consciousness, and identity indeed are foundational to all forms of knowledge, from the identification of entities to the formation and use of concepts to the formation and use of propositions. The law of causality (Ayn Rand 1957, 1037) indeed is "the law of identity applied to action."

Nevertheless, I do not think that my argument for this last idea, at least, is consistent with Ayn Rand's. For one thing, my position on the epistemological status of perception of entities differs from that of Ayn Rand (as presented by Peikoff 1991, 52–54) and those of other Objectivist philosophers such as Peikoff, Binswanger (2014, 57–96), Salmieri (2013, 48–52), and Ghate (2013).

Also, I present a theory of propositions and a theory of induction, theories absent from the corpus of Ayn Rand. My theory of propositions relies somewhat on an idea about conceptual meaning not contained in the writings of Ayn Rand. Part of my theory of induction relies on probability theory. Although my probabilistic arguments

rely on a philosophical identification made by Ayn Rand, no probabilistic approach to induction is contained in the works of Ayn Rand
or other Objectivists—most notably, Peikoff (2002) and Harriman
(2010, based heavily on Peikoff 2002).

Therefore, although I have been a serious student of Objectivism
for more than four decades, I am not an Objectivist with a capital
"O." My philosophy is mine, not Ayn Rand's.

This book began from notes in the 1990s, then became a rough,
28,000-word draft in 1998, for which I got helpful feedback from several individuals, but encouragement from only one: Glenn Marcus. I
wrote a better, 35,000-word draft in 2002, and received encouragement from Glenn (again) and also from Leslie Kaminoff. But I
thought I would have to write something many times as long in order
to turn the draft into a satisfactory book. The only completed section
of that draft was my theory of propositions, which I self-published
separately.

In 2003, I posted—on HBL (HBList.com), a private, subscription-
based email list moderated by Objectivist philosopher Harry
Binswanger—summaries of several of the new ideas in my 2002 draft.
None of my ideas received encouragement from any of the profes-
sional philosophers on the list. But I take encouragement, because
none of the comments I received give me reason to think that my
ideas are either wrong or unoriginal.

I turned to developing the final part—the probabilistic, mathematical part—of my theory of induction, and made much progress.
Some of that final part was published in *Philosophy of Science* (Pisaturo 2009). The article has been favorably cited in three other top-
ten ranked journals of philosophy—but for my refutation of the so-
called "Doomsday Argument," not for my theory of induction. In
2011, I self-published a short book (Pisaturo 2016) expanding on my
consideration of the Doomsday Argument and related theories, also
correcting a non-critical error in my analysis of Gott's (1994) "delta
t" argument; but I did not expand much on my theory of induction.

I thought it would take me years of uninterrupted work to turn my 2002 draft into a treatise on epistemology. Because I have never had an academic job—my only degree is a B.S. in mathematics—and have usually had to earn a living by doing non-academic work, I thought the project might never get done.

But in 2018, I reread my 2002 draft and was astonished to realize that I could readily turn it into a short book. To do so, however, I had to make three strategic decisions to limit the book's scope.

First, I focused on what I have to state that is new. The book is not a comprehensive treatise or textbook on epistemology. I do not present self-contained accounts of deductive logic, concept-formation, volition, or objectivity, because others have already done so. I do not provide extensive background that would be useful for a layman to understand my work. The book assumes a degree of philosophical maturity, although not academic training (which I myself do not have), on the part of the reader. After the first twenty pages of light reading to set the course, I propose solutions to fundamental and crucial philosophical problems. Moreover, the last third of the book employs mathematics at least at the level of a college upperclassman, although less mathematical explanations are also included to make the general ideas accessible to lay readers.

Second, I confined myself to writing up the conclusions I had already drawn, and did not seek to expand past what I already knew. I am not a scientist or a scientific scholar. I do not presume to theorize on how scientists should create theories or devise experiments. What my book does focus on is this: Given a body of evidence and conclusions, I present a general method for judging the validity and for calculating the reliability of those conclusions when applied to the future.

Third, I mostly refrained from criticism or polemics even after I have presented my positive theory on a given matter. I do sometimes engage critically with Hume and Kant (though only to the extent of helping to explain my own philosophy). Those two philosophers engineered what I consider the major wrong turn that mainstream

Western philosophy made to end the Enlightenment. If I present a positive, reality-based theory immune to their attacks, then I render irrelevant most of contemporary philosophy.

Near the end of the project, in May 2020, I inserted a chapter and appendix on mathematics, because I use much mathematics in the chapters on induction.

Most philosophers today devote a whole book to subject matter that I treat in a single chapter. They are not wrong to do so. But there is also something to be gained in integration by making a wide sweep of the subject of epistemology in a single, short volume.

This book is primarily for a specialized readership—familiar with epistemological ideas in general, Ayn Rand's theory of concepts in particular, and mathematics somewhat beyond basic calculus. I hope that such readers will find the book worthwhile.

* * *

A few stylistic conventions are worth noting.

The style that I use for citations in this book is the author-date system recommended by the *Chicago Manual of Style, 14th Edition*. In this style, each source is cited briefly in the text by the author's name (usually just the last name), date of publication, and (where applicable) page numbers. The reader can use this brief citation to look up the source's full bibliographic information in the References section at the back of the book, just before the Index. The citation "Ayn Rand (1975, 45)," on the previous page, refers to page 45 of a work by Ayn Rand, published in 1975. The list of references at the back of the book identifies this work as "Art and Cognition", reprinted in *The Romantic Manifesto*. This publication is a reprint of a work published in 1971, and so "[1971]" appears before "1975" in the reference entry.

Relying on an option described in Section 6.74 of the 14th Edition of *The Chicago Manual of Style*, I use single quotes for philosophical terms and their meanings. This convention subtly calls special attention to important concepts.

In the text, I always write out the name "Ayn Rand," because that name is a pen name.

* * *

I am thankful to Jeffrey Perren for numerous valuable suggestions on the manuscript. Ed Powell helped me clarify some important points and maintain scientific accuracy. Ed also re-did all the figures in the chapter and appendix on mathematics. Robert Bidinotto did an able job of copyediting, although some awkward expressions may have crept in from later revisions I made. Maureen Thompson ably answered my questions about how, as a visual artist, she sees the world. Alexandra York caught some missteps in late revisions, and suggested that much of the book is indeed accessible to readers with little background in mathematics. Brad Thompson helped me explain what is distinctive in my approach to epistemology. Leslie Kaminoff gave helpful feedback on early chapters before being called to write a new edition of his own book. Shortly before press time, Ray Cole also gave helpful feedback on early chapters. Robert W. Stubblefield edited the mathematics article in *The Intellectual Activist* that became the chapter on mathematics. Robert Tracinski edited the mathematics article in *The Intellectual Activist* that became the appendix. Robert Stubblefield also reminded me of numerous new ideas in the book—by disagreeing with most of them, always thoughtfully and with abundant good will. Johann Gevers made helpful comments on early chapters of the first edition. After publication of the second edition, James Ellias made helpful suggestions to Section 3.3, "Existence, Consciousness, and the Causal Relation Between Them"; these suggestions motivated me, in 2024, to insert a new passage (about how we can discern the conscious self) and to correct an unclear formulation.

My greatest debt by far is to Glenn Marcus, who first suggested that I write such a book, and then read numerous drafts across decades, offering many thousands of notes—and many arguments—on both content and presentation, from small to extremely large. I know from Glenn's own writing that his standards are higher than mine. Striving to approach his standards has made for a far better book than I could have made otherwise.

Shortly before the publication date of the first edition, Glenn became ill and was not able to review the final draft. Glenn is well again, and the second edition is the result mainly of my incorporating his feedback on the first edition.

1 INTRODUCTION TO METAPHYSICS AND EPISTEMOLOGY

Epistemology is the branch of philosophy known as the theory of knowledge. Epistemology addresses how to take the evidence of your senses and form concepts, statements, sequences of statements, and a corpus of knowledge that is true, organized, readily applicable to new situations, and conducive to the discovery of new knowledge.

Metaphysics is generally understood to be the study of the fundamental nature of existence and of man's relationship to existence. Metaphysics and epistemology taken together are considered the two fundamental branches of philosophy. Whereas metaphysics identifies fundamentally what is, epistemology identifies fundamentally how we know it.

However, I think it is better not to divide the study of these two matters—what we know fundamentally and how we know it. Under such a division, metaphysics usually is completed before epistemology is even begun. This division seems fitting for a philosophy of two worlds, such as Plato's, but artificial for a philosophy of *the* world. For Plato, metaphysics was a description of his made-up world, the World of Forms, for which a theory of knowledge could not be relevant until the whole made-up world was described. Hence, for Plato, a method of knowing (covered in epistemology) was an afterthought to a metaphysics that was "known" by revelation.

A better approach is to have metaphysics and epistemology proceed concurrently. Each identification of fact in metaphysics should be accompanied by an identification of how the fact is known. That is how I will proceed.

Metaphysics, as I conceive of it, consists of the basic knowledge implicit in all further knowledge, indeed in the very concept of knowledge. Metaphysics begins with identifying the base of knowledge, and encompasses ideas pertaining to the basic nature of the world. These ideas include existence, consciousness, and their relation; entity, identity, attribute, change, and action; and the nature of causality. Metaphysics ends when we know enough to know what knowledge is. Equipped with this knowledge of what knowledge is, epistemology continues with identifying a method for acquiring more knowledge.

Indeed, the foregoing indicates that metaphysics should be incorporated as part—the essential beginning part—of epistemology.

This book presents my epistemology—my theory of knowledge—including my metaphysics. But how do I start metaphysics and epistemology? The next chapter begins a search for a starting point by reviewing the history of starting points in philosophy.

2 HISTORY OF STARTING POINTS IN PHILOSOPHY

To begin our search for a starting point of metaphysics and epistemology, let us see how these subjects started historically.

The first philosopher is generally recognized to be the ancient
Greek named Thales of Miletus, who flourished in the sixth century
B.C. But let us go back to before the beginning of philosophy, that is,
before philosophy was understood as an explicit subject of study. Let
us try to understand how primitive man's thinking about the world
culminated in metaphysics and epistemology. That way, we will understand most clearly what questions these subjects are intended to
answer.

By the dawn of history, man had already come far in his ability to
satisfy his material needs for survival. Consider his obtaining food.
For hunting, he possessed well-conceived tactics for stalking and at-
tacking his prey; knife-type and spear-type weapons for piercing his
prey; and even the bow and arrow, which vastly increased the safety
(for him) and effectiveness of his hunting. He controlled fire, and
thereby could cook his food. He had begun raising animals as a sup-
ply of food. Most remarkably, he had begun agriculture. All these
achievements required forming abstractions and making inferences
that gave men knowledge far beyond what they could perceive directly with their senses.

Take a primitive example: If a hunter saw a certain kind of footprint in the soil, he could tell that, for instance, a small herd of buffalo
had come by a few hours before, was heading west, and was probably
a short distance ahead. (How would he know? He would know that

the buffalo caused the footprints.) He would know that if he walked quickly west, he would probably see this herd, and could make a kill. He would know all these things even though he had not actually seen any buffalo. He would know what he would probably see and what would probably happen if he took certain actions.

Examples from agriculture follow the same pattern, only along a more complex chain of reasoning and action. A farmer knows that if he tills the soil a certain way, plants a certain kind of seed, and cares for the seed a certain way over the course of months at a certain time of year when the weather is a certain way, a plant will probably grow; if he harvests the plant a certain way, the plant will serve well as food. A man knows these things before he actually perceives the grown plant. He knows what will probably happen to him if he takes a certain series of actions.

A man can also foresee—that is, infer before literally seeing—certain dangers that could thwart his actions. For example, a different kind of footprint tells the hunter or farmer that there is a different kind of cause: instead of buffalo, there is a pack of wolves nearby. He knows this fact without actually seeing the wolves. The wolves might eat his stored food. But he can protect his food by taking certain actions: he can build fences that he knows the wolves cannot climb.

Let us identify some characteristics of the thinking method used by the men in these examples. In all the examples, the purpose of each man's thinking is to deal with the future. He wants to know what will happen if he does nothing, and what actions he can take to change the future to make it good for him. But how can he know the future? The thinking tools available to him include a rudimentary knowledge of causality, which tells him that certain entities acting in a certain way will lead to certain effects or results. But because every new situation is different, how does he generalize from past situations to future ones? He does so using concepts. A concept is, in general terms, a certain kind of mental grouping of specific, concrete things and instances. A man groups some animals (and their footprints) under the concept "buffalo" (and buffalo footprints), and others under the concept "wolf." Then, when he sees a wolf footprint, he knows (because the wolf print is caused by a wolf) that a wolf is near, and he knows (by knowledge of the concept "wolf") how the wolf probably will act.

Thus man acquires knowledge for the purpose of foreseeing and causing certain outcomes in the future.

But there are some events that man knows he does not foresee. When he confronts the buffalo that made the footprints, he can use his best fighting tactics; but he does not know exactly what the buffalo will do every time, and the buffalo might kill him. Or a lion might confront him even when he saw no footprints. Or, though he knows there are certain predictable patterns of climate and weather, a sudden storm might kill his crop.

But man is ambitious, and he tries to expand the realm of what he can foresee. After all, there was a time when he did not know to look for footprints, and every new animal he saw was a surprise. But then he learned that animals cause footprints. He also learned how to make fire, instead of having to stumble on it by chance; he learned that sparks on dry leaves cause fire, and rubbing certain stones causes sparks. He also strove to understand what causes storms, wind, and all the other events he could not yet foresee.

Some men, however, tried to explain what they could not foresee, not by trying to learn more, but by imagining or making up explanations. In other words, they did not base their explanations on facts they observed. Some such explanations became religion.

Let us briefly examine early religion, because it was a primitive form of, or precursor to, philosophy. Religion began well before the start of recorded history, so we can only conjecture how it actually started. But such conjecturing could still shed light on the practical motivation for religion, and hence the practical motivation for philosophy and for epistemology in particular.

Suppose a man were confronted by irregular, seemingly unpredictable events such as the ignition of fire, before he understood fire. In trying to predict and deal with fire, a man might conjecture that, just as animals cause footprints, some other kind of entity causes fire. He might conjecture further that, just as human beings make inconsistent or unpredictable choices, so some other volitional consciousness does the same regarding the creation of fire; that is, some kind of unseen consciousness or spirit sometimes chooses to ignite a fire. The man might draw a similar conclusion about another spirit, in the sky, causing storms and changes in weather, and another spirit in the earth causing floods, and another spirit causing animals to be easy or difficult prey. These spirits are 'gods'.

Therefore, such a man would believe that a way to predict or influence the occurrence of fire or of storms would be to understand, in order to influence or even to control, these gods. Hence the beginning of religious rites.

But how does one know how to influence these gods? One can proceed by trial and error, offering a gift and observing whether a storm occurs or not. Men must have proceeded in this way. Because they could not observe the gods as they could observe animals, they used their imaginations instead; they probably interpreted their dreams and imaginings as having a basis in reality. But still, they probably were (justifiably) uncertain and uneasy about the truth of their imaginings, especially when the imaginings clashed with each other. What to do?

Let us review what methods the man in our example has used thus far. He has observed similarities among unpredictable events in nature; he has also observed choices that men make. He has tried to integrate, or at least group, these examples under the hypothesis that all these events are caused by willful spirits. Notice that he looks for causes. In summary, he uses, among other things, observation, a rudimentary process of integration (analogous to the integration used in forming simple concepts), and a rudimentary knowledge of causality. But the kind of causes he looks for are entities other than the ones he observes. Just as he knows that the buffalo causes footprints, and that he causes himself to take a step forward, so he concludes that another entity, a god, causes the storm.

But though he eventually sees the buffalo that made the foot-prints, and he sees himself as the one who stepped forward, the man does not ever see the god. If he saw the god, his knowledge would be anchored; he would know he was right about the existence of the god and what the god was like, and he could then proceed to figure out how to influence the god. In other words, his observation—of the god—would serve as a starting point for further knowledge and action. But without observation as a starting point, he must find a different starting point before he can trust his conclusions. So he uses his other tools: integration and causality. He tries to find causes (causality) common to all (integration) of the gods. Because he thinks of causes as entities apart from the affected entities, he imagines other, higher gods as the causes of his first gods. Eventually, he constructs a whole hierarchy of gods, each level in the hierarchy bringing the next level into existence. The beginning of the hierarchy is the starting point of the entire universe.

This starting point is not as good as observation as the starting point, but is what many primitive men accepted as a substitute. This starting point does not give men as much of a sense of security as observation would, but gives them *some* sense of security. This starting point becomes the starting point of their philosophy.

To this day, scientists do not know the starting point of the universe, in the sense of knowing what was the first action of the first entity that acted. Yet man's understanding of nature is now so great that we enjoy marvelous material lifestyles inconceivable to earlier men. Evidently, man must be using a different, extremely fruitful starting point.

Over time, man increased his knowledge. Man discovered the cause of fire. He learned how to predict changes of season. He developed irrigation, making him less dependent on unpredictable rains. Eventually, man saw a regularity regarding regularity: phenomena that had once seemed irregular and explicable only by the existence of willful gods could now be seen to be regular and explicable by causal relations among observed entities. The whole motivation for hypothesizing gods was becoming obsolete in more and more fields. In contrast, the reverse progression was not happening: phenomena that had seemed regular were not becoming unpredictable. A new hypothesis was formed: perhaps all events are regular and predictable if we just have enough knowledge; perhaps, after all, no gods exist at all.

Barnes (1965, 41) applies this idea even up to modern times:

> Supernaturalism has been outgrown when and as technological progress made possible control in terms of fact instead of fiction. …
>
> This may be illustrated by many ready examples. The irrigation engineer killed more rain gods and rain magic than all the skeptical philosophers of history. The telescope, spectroscope, and the like have been the destroyers of the astronomy of primitive man, of Genesis and Joshua, by providing factual rather than fictional conceptions of the astral regions. The microscope, the test tube, and pathology have revolutionized our ideas of the nature and origin of disease. We need no longer attribute disease to the wrath of God, malicious magic, or the violation of a taboo. Nor need we have recourse to sorcerers to effect a cure. The increasing technological control of our environment has rendered many theologies obsolete. When the further development of industrialism makes possible the complete factual control of our social life, other forms of supernaturalism will disappear.

Of course, many people still believe in gods. But some independent individuals must have looked for a new starting point. They must have sought an alternative answer to a question religion claimed to answer; that question was, "What is the starting point of the universe." These thinkers may have postulated the existence of non-spiritual entities, arranged in a causal chain, as a substitute for religion's spiritual entities. But, by and large, there was little more evidence for the existence of these non-spiritual entities than there was for the spiritual ones. (A later, known example of this kind of thinking is Aristotle's idea of a prime mover. See 1941, *Metaphysics* Book XII, Chapters 6 and 7, 1071b4–1073a13).

Then came Thales. Thales made discoveries in a wide variety of fields. He figured out how to measure the height of the pyramids, by proportions of shadows. He used the same method to deduce the distance of ships at sea. He picked out a stable constellation—the Little Bear—by which seamen could navigate. And, according to Herodotus ([449 B.C.] 2004, 27–28, [Book I, Sections 73–74]), Thales predicted a solar eclipse in 585 B.C.

Thales found predictable patterns of action by entities close enough to touch, and by entities in the distant sky. All of these entities could be understood—at least to some degree—by man, using the same process of thought. This fact highlights another remarkable fact: that there must be something in common to all of these entities, to all the entities we perceive, that makes them all perceivable and knowable by the same means. What is this something in common? Thales's answer was this: they are all made of the same material. He thought that all entities were created out of this common material. He had conceived *of a new kind of starting point: a common material.* This starting point was not some entity external to or apart from the entities we observe, but rather something that underlies them.

This new kind of starting point became the basis for science.

Thales thought this common material is water, but the main significance of his theory is not what he chose as the starting material, but two other characteristics: that he thought of a *material* as his starting point, and the thinking he used to support his conclusion. He relied on observation, the factual evidence from his senses, from which he tried to reason to his conclusions. Although men for many thousands of years undoubtedly had used the evidence of their senses and a process of reason, Thales was the first to use these means to justify a starting point.

Though Thales was wrong that water was the basic element, he was right that there is an elemental material (or a few elemental materials), and that an elemental material is a very fruitful starting point. Subsequent thinkers hypothesized different elemental materials, such as fire, air, and earth. Then Democritus hypothesized that the starting material was atoms—tiny particles too small to perceive directly, which constitute all things we do perceive (Laertius 2018, 457). The perceivable differences among entities, according to Democritus, are due to different combinations and arrangements of these atoms. All change is due to changes in these combinations and arrangements, through the physical motion of the atoms.

This atomic theory was an extremely remarkable and monumentally valuable idea. When it was developed more fully two millennia later, it led to great advances in the field of chemistry and physics, and a flood of scientific and technological breakthroughs. At the time of Democritus, however, an ironic carryover from religion—even though atomism is an atheistic theory—caused the atomic theory to be, for the most part, rejected. That carryover was the search for the first motion of the universe as a starting point. The atomists thought—correctly—that the atoms behave mechanistically, and that each new motion is caused by collisions with others atoms, analogous to collisions of billiard balls. Thus, when an atom changes its motion, the change is caused by another atom hitting it. But then the question is, what caused the first motion or the first change in motion? In other words, what was the starting point of all the motion in the world? The atomists' answers were implausible (see Laertius 2018, 457), and the whole theory therefore was undermined at the root.

There was a second ironic error in atomism. The atomists generalized too far and tried to use their theory to explain consciousness as well as physical change and motion (Laertius 2018, 457). Some modern ideologies, such as communism and behaviorism, continue this same error today.

The solution to the atomists' philosophical problem related to a starting point came in two parts, two millennia later. (Of course, the scientific validation of the atomic theory came in many parts—that is, through a long sequence of experimentation and conceptual identification.)

The first part of the solution to the problem of a starting point was this: Inanimate entities exert forces on each other even when they are not in motion—at least, not in motion perceptibly—and even when they do not collide. In short, even without perceptible motion, there is force, and the force comes from the entities that we perceive. That is, there are forces, such as gravitation and electrical and magnetic attraction and repulsion, that are exerted by the very entities we perceive. Therefore, the entities we perceive do not require the existence of unperceived and unknown (and unknowable) entities as the ultimate cause of action. The cause of action of the entities we perceive is these very entities. These entities are not merely *recipients* of forces; they are also *sources* of force. *That is, the starting point of forces is entities, the very entities we perceive directly or have perceptual evidence for.*

(This idea that entities exert forces on each other does not, of course, preclude the idea that these entities exert these forces through intermediaries, such as electromagnetic and gravitational fields.)

This understanding freed thinkers from the misguided task of inventing an unperceivable ultimate source of force and motion.

The second part of the scientific solution was this: Even if we do not know the first actions, the interactions between inanimate entities are much more regular and predictable than was realized in ancient times. The fact that storms sometimes occur and sometimes do not occur does not imply two completely different kinds of events; the events are different in degree. The same forces are at work; only the degrees, or measurements, differ. Likewise, Newton showed that the same forces of the same kinds of entities are at work causing the motion of a rock when dropped, a ball when thrown, or a planet in orbit; again, only the measurements differ. (For more on this issue, see my later section on the use of mathematics in integration—"9.1.3 Integration Through Lawful Quantification of Differences.") If we apply mathematical measurement to our observation of events, we

discover more and more action (leaving aside, for now, human volitional action) to be regular and in principle predictable. Therefore,
we do not need to know the first cause or the first motion in order to
know a great deal about the physical world. Granted, it does not hurt
to trace events back billions of years, and maybe even to the first motion; such knowledge might turn out to be very useful. But our vast
amount of current scientific knowledge does not rest on that starting
point. Newton made his momentous discoveries regarding motion
and gravitation based on the starting point that everything is made
of the same kind of matter that exerts and reacts to the same forces
in the same way to the same degree. All of his scientific explanations—which still hold today within certain ranges of measurement—start with this matter and these forces, then trace a causal
chain of matter and events, and end with the events we observe or
predict. Newton did not have to know the first motion of the universe. Nor did he have to know the most elemental particles that constitute the universe. He did not have to know the most elemental particles or most basic forces that cause the forces of motion and gravitation, which he did know, although knowing more basic things
would certainly be valuable.

Scientists today disagree about precisely what all these forces are
and what causal chains they follow. Even more often, although they
may agree on the basic forces, the causal chains are so long and complex that no one yet knows how to trace them. We know the laws of
motion, but we still cannot calculate how countless particles of matter will exert those forces to cause a specific weather condition next
week. We still do not know the causal pathways in the progression of
many diseases, though they too follow known laws of force and motion. How does one go about identifying causal chains to explain
more phenomena and predict more future events? How does one go
from one's current knowledge to new knowledge?

Moreover, how does one know that one's current corpus of
"knowledge" is really knowledge? We know that man is capable of
making errors. How can we *validate* our knowledge, to distinguish

knowledge from erroneous ideas? The present book focuses on this question.

How, for example, does a doctor know that his prescribed treatment is the right one, leading to a cure? He knows because the treatment conforms to his medical principles. How does he know those principles are right? He knows because he has observed many other cases that conform to those principles. But each case has differences; how does he know he has the right principles by which to characterize this new case? He knows because his principles follow from biological laws. How does he know that the laws of biology are right? He knows because of his observations. But how does he know that his observations in fact prove the laws of biology? And how does he best proceed to discover *new* laws of biology? Moreover, how does he even know his observations are accurate? And when he explains his observations in terms of some other premise, how does he know that the premise is right? In short, where does he start? He needs *a starting point of his knowledge.*

Notice that this is another kind of starting point!

Similar questions faced the ancients. There were many conflicting ideas, many conflicting theories, such as monism, pluralism, atomism, theism, skepticism. How does one know which theory, if any, is true? And how does one arrive at the truth in areas in which there are not yet even theories to choose from?

In addition to illustrating the need for a starting point of knowledge, the above examples show further that we need to understand a new kind of causal chain. In the physical sciences, we dealt with a causal chain of entities exerting physical forces on other entities, causing changes in motion, changing the orientation of forces, and so on. Now, we seek a starting point for a mind with certain mental abilities, and which acquires its first knowledge by some means, making it possible for the mind to acquire more knowledge by some means, and so on.

Finding the starting point of knowledge, and finding also the means by which knowledge progresses in a step-by-step order or

hierarchy, with each step validated, is the subject matter of epistemology. This subject was originated by Socrates, Plato, and Aristotle.
Thanks to Aristotle, men know a great deal about logic, definitions,
observation, and other principles of how we acquire and validate
knowledge. Other thinkers, such as Enlightenment scientists and,
above all, philosopher Ayn Rand (1990), have discovered much
more. Over the course of my inquiry in this book, I will make use of
these discoveries after I validate the underpinnings of each, and I will
seek to discover more.

Epistemology—in which I include, contrary to common practice,
metaphysics as a concurrent branch or sub-branch—is the most fundamental branch, the starting point, of philosophy. It is the starting
point we will use in order to give an account of our entire hierarchy
of knowledge.

But how will we begin epistemology? What is epistemology's
starting point? To help us find the answer, we will again look at history—not the history of mankind this time, but the history of an individual human being.

In addition to seeking a starting point of knowledge, we will seek
to understand the methods needed to build and validate a hierarchy
of knowledge. We will especially be on the lookout for the methods
we have already encountered above; these methods include observation, the search for causes, and integration of specific things and observations into concepts and general statements.

In this chapter, we have traversed a sequence of starting points:

- A conjectured primary causal entity distinct from the entities
  we observe.
- An elemental material common to all entities.
- The entities we observe, along with the forces these entities exert.
- A starting point of knowledge, which is also the starting point
  of epistemology.

In the next chapter, we will seek this starting point of epistemology. Once we identify this starting point, we will proceed from there to develop the essentials of an entire epistemology.

3 STARTING THE SUBJECT OF EPISTEMOLOGY

3.1 A BRIEF CHRONOLOGY OF KNOWLEDGE

To start our study of epistemology, it is useful to articulate our working idea of what knowledge is. A person has many experiences throughout his life. Which of these experiences are instances of knowledge?

Some examples of knowledge are these: recognizing the object before us as our car, knowing how to drive the car, knowing what a steering wheel is, knowing words and rules of grammar in English, knowing what to do on our job, knowing facts of history, knowing the cause of the Civil War.

Some things that are not knowledge are these: a sneeze, a knee-jerk reflex, a tree we have not seen, thinking that Abraham Lincoln was the first President.

By the end of our study, we will have a better idea of what knowledge is than we can have at the outset. But for now we can say this: knowledge is some kind of awareness of something about the world. With this working idea, let us proceed.

Just as our goals are arranged in a hierarchy, with goals dependent on other goals and all ultimately dependent on our ultimate goal, so it is with knowledge. When we ask ourselves how we know something—when we try to prove something—we base our proof on prior knowledge, on knowledge more basic in our hierarchy. But our most basic knowledge cannot be proved; it is what we rely on to prove other things. Nevertheless, we must understand *how* we know our most basic knowledge.

How do we identify our most basic knowledge and how we know it, and then how do we identify the hierarchy that we can build from our basic knowledge? A useful approach is to try to figure out the chronology of the hierarchy we have already built throughout our life. It is reasonable to conjecture that the most basic knowledge in our current hierarchy perhaps came first chronologically, and that the rest of our current hierarchy may also be very similar to the original chronology. Therefore, inferring—or even hypothesizing—this chronology is a good way to start our inquiry. If our conjecture turns out to be wrong, or partially wrong, then we can either discard or modify it.

Let us start when a baby is born. The baby's senses are functioning at birth, even before birth. The baby has sight, hearing, touch, smell, and taste. But, at birth, the baby does not yet seem to perceive specific things; or at least he does not recognize specific things as objects that persist through time, that act on all his senses in a coordinated way, and that maintain continuity of spatial location. (See, for example, Johnson 2010.) The baby looks at objects before him, but probably cannot yet distinguish the specific objects, at least not until the objects move, and he certainly does not know they would feel solid. Rather, he possibly just sees one big mass taking up his entire visual field and changing its pattern before him. An analogous kind of experience may occur with his sense of touch and his other senses.

A few days or weeks or months or hours into life (the precise duration is an open scientific question), the baby probably begins to perceive specific objects—that is, entities. The baby then progresses to recognizing those objects when he sees them again.

After about a year of life, the baby begins to speak words. His first words are usually names for specific things, such as Mommy and Daddy. Soon after, the baby learns words that stand for concepts— such as a word for the mother's breasts and the feeding/drinking process, bottle (possibly denoting some combination of the physical bottle and the process of drinking from it), ball, and dog—after perceiving numerous specific things and/or actions referred to by these concepts. Months later, he begins to speak in basic sentences using the concepts he has learned. Concurrently, he learns additional, more abstract concepts.

When the child is a few years old, he is able to put sentences together into a sequence to make an overall point. He learns to reason from one thought to the next. This ability is facilitated greatly when he learns to write. He writes whole paragraphs, then longer works. (Some adults never get this far.) He formulates entire theories. Eventually, he may even formulate a theory of philosophy, and then reformulate many of his past ideas in light of his newly-explicit philosophy. During this whole process, he continues to make many new perceptual observations, he continues to form additional concepts, and he continually enhances his understanding of the concepts he already holds.

The order described above is always the order in which knowledge develops. No one recognizes specific objects right out of the womb, nor does any new-born know any words or speak sentences. Children with impaired senses may be delayed in their ability to form concepts; if the impairment is very great, as in the case of Helen Keller, they may never do so.

There is much still to discover about what an infant and young child knows and when he knows it. Nevertheless, it is clear that perception of specific objects depends first on prior sensory data, the forming of concepts depends on prior perception of objects, and the forming of sentences, or propositions, requires prior experience with concepts. We are already discovering a general order or hierarchy of knowledge by noticing this universal chronological progression.

3.2 A PHILOSOPHICAL HIERARCHY OF KNOWLEDGE

Now that we have observed this chronological progression of knowledge, we are ready to improve upon it.

We are ready to go back to the beginning of our hierarchy of knowledge. But instead of going back to the chronological beginning, we are ready to make a new beginning—to find a new starting point from which we will rebuild our whole hierarchy.

Why do we want to do this? We want to because our old hierarchy was built before we were philosophers. We cannot even remember where we actually started, because we were mere babies at the time. We cannot go back and validate that old starting point, whatever it may have been. We cannot remember, and do not know for sure, the steps we took to build from that starting point; therefore, we cannot validate those steps. The steps we took back then may have been in error, or they may have been based on plausible assumptions instead of knowledge, and we cannot go back to check these steps. Yet we want to have a body of knowledge that we know is true—that starts with something we know and builds from there, using methods we know are valid. Therefore, we must start again.

One may ask, "How can we say we are starting now? We have just gone through several pages of studying epistemology, and we plan to use that study in our next step. Haven't we already started? Isn't the next step a continuation of our inquiry, and therefore not a starting point?"

Here is my answer: Simply, we are starting again. But we are not now looking for the old, chronological starting point. We are looking for a philosophical, logical starting point that will begin a new hierarchy. We want to start with something we know without reference to anything else that we assume. We want this starting point to consist of the facts we refer back to when we judge whether anything else is true.

One may ask, "But however we try to start, aren't we relying on knowledge we already have, developed over the course of many years—knowledge in the form of memories, words, concepts, and sentences?"

Here is my answer: Memories, words, concepts, and sentences denote things in the world, and direct our attention to those things. I will be using words to direct our attention to certain things, but it is up to us then to consider those things afresh. Our consideration of those things afresh is our starting point.

One may ask, "Does this mean that we will have to throw out everything we know and then try to relearn it all from scratch?" No, we will not have to do that. In some important cases, we will be able to validate whole categories of knowledge at a time. For example, we will be able to validate all of our perceptual knowledge in one reasoned argument; we will not have to consider separately every single perception that we ever had.

One may ask, "How can a logical or philosophical hierarchy of knowledge be different from the original, chronological one? Isn't the chronological hierarchy the only logical one?"

No. Let me illustrate. Suppose a petroleum engineer tries to figure out where there are oil deposits underground. Suppose he concludes that there is oil at latitude x and longitude y. Suppose you ask him how he knows. His answer might be that his conclusion is based on his knowledge of science, engineering, and all of the many measurements he has taken concerning soil composition, seismology, sonar, etc. Therefore, his knowledge that there is oil at this location is dependent on all of these other constituents of his current hierarchy of knowledge.

Now suppose the oil company drills for oil at this location, and— sure enough—the company strikes oil. Now how does the engineer know that there is oil at this location? He knows it for a simple reason: he observes the oil. His knowledge that there is oil at this location no longer depends on his advanced knowledge of science and engineering and all of his scientific measurements. He has rearranged his hierarchy of knowledge.

Similarly, we do not need to retrace our old hierarchy of knowledge and try to validate it. All we need to do is to establish a hierarchy that is valid now. We will use our general knowledge of chronology as a heuristic source of clues, but not a precise requirement. We will discover that our new hierarchy is similar in overall outline to our chronological hierarchy: beginning with awareness of the world (covered in the remainder of this chapter), and then progressing to perception of entities (Chapter 4), then to concepts (Chapter 5), and then to propositions (Chapter 6). But we will form some concepts—such as existence, consciousness, and entity—along the way, as the need for them arises.

Also along the way, I will introduce elements of my theory of induction as they arise logically. In the final two chapters, I will complete my validation of that theory.

3.3   EXISTENCE, CONSCIOUSNESS, AND THE CAUSAL RELATION BETWEEN THEM

From observing the chronological development of our hierarchy of knowledge, we know that knowledge given to us by our senses precedes conceptual knowledge. Therefore, let us look out at the world, and begin our investigation from there.

We might hypothesize that we are looking out at the world as a baby does, but we do not know how a baby sees the world. When I look out at the world in my customary way, I see entities. That is, I see objects that I assume have a shape that is not fully evident just from my seeing, objects that I assume also will act on my sense of touch in a certain way. But with a little bit of mental effort, I can direct myself to look at the world as an illustrator might when he wants to draw precisely what he sees without his assuming that what he sees will act in a certain way on his other senses. For example, I can see a cup without assuming that the cup is actually cylindrical in shape, actually solid to the touch, and actually separate from its background. I must use my conceptual faculty to guide me to see in this way. However, even in being so guided by my conceptual faculty, I am conscious of reality directly by this careful way of sensing. It is reality as we are conscious of it by this careful way of sensing, devoid of assumptions, that we will take as the infallibly veridical base of our philosophically validated corpus of knowledge of reality.

In looking out at the world in this way, we can make some imme-diate differentiations. For one thing, we differentiate parts from a whole. For example, we see a tree (without having to know that it is a tree), and we can distinguish this thing from the entire visual field before us. The tree is a part, and the visual field is the whole.

Another differentiation we can make is to distinguish various parts from each other. For example, we see a tree, and we distinguish that part from other parts such as a car, a dog, and a ball.

A part, such as a tree, may be much easier for us to see than it is for new-born babies, but the difficulty faced by newborns does not concern us now. The fact is that we see these parts now, and we should take this part as a fact. We know this fact because we observe it. Indeed, our concept of observation is more basic than our concept of knowledge. The concept of knowledge is a later generalization we make once we realize that there is, besides observation, another way—namely, reason—by which we can be aware of the world.

Another word for 'world' in this sense is 'universe'. 'Uni' means 'unit' or 'one'. 'Versus' is the past participle of 'vertere', which means 'to turn'. 'Universe', etymologically, means 'turned into one'. The concept 'universe' differentiates the whole from its parts. It differen-tiates everything from every thing.

We can make another differentiation. We can differentiate any one state of the visual field—the visual field we perceive at a given moment—from the visual field grasped as a persisting thing. We can grasp that, while the visual field changes, there is something persist-ing: the visual field itself. Using our conceptual faculty, we can broaden our idea of this visual field and conceive the whole of what we sense now plus the whole of what we have sensed in the past plus the whole of what we might ever sense. We can integrate this con-ceptualization of the persisting visual field with the perceptual 'fields' given to us by our other senses to form an even broader conceptual-ization, and we can call this broader conceptualization "the persist-ing whole," or 'the world'.

Let us review and be more precise about our knowledge, at this stage, of the world as a persisting whole. In order to be precise here, we face a challenge. We have just formed a concept, "the world." But an understanding of the general method of concept formation comes later in our hierarchy of knowledge. Therefore, what I present here is, more narrowly, the method I use to form this specific concept. The careful reader, after reading the chapter on concepts, could return to the present passage and see that I was applying the general method of concept-formation to this specific case.

To form this basic concept of the world, we first introduce three subjects:
- Similarity and difference.
- Abstraction.
- The basics of concept-formation.

We do not yet know that the world persists or will persist *when we are not conscious of it*. But we are conscious of the similarity of the whole at one moment to the whole of a later moment, as compared to the parts at any given moment and across moments.

By similarity, I mean less difference. Of course, the whole that I see changes from moment to moment; that is, the whole I see now looks different from the whole I saw earlier. But this difference between the wholes is less different from the difference I see between part and whole.

In order to grasp explicitly the degrees of difference noted above, I perform a process of *abstraction*. That is, among all the characteristics of the parts and wholes—characteristics such as hue, shape, and overall extent—I select one of those characteristics: overall extent. Then I perform a process of *measurement* to determine that, in regard to the characteristic of extent, the differences between the wholes is measurably less than the difference between parts and wholes.

(I will go into more depth about similarity, difference, abstraction, and measurement in the chapter about concept-formation. For much more depth still, see Ayn Rand 1990.)

The human mind possesses another faculty that makes concept-formation possible. That faculty is the ability to treat existents we are conscious of as existential *units*. (For the concept of 'unit', see Section 5.1 and Ayn Rand 1990, 6–7.) Using our memory, we can then form mental units referring to the existential units that we have been directly conscious of. Then, through an act of volitional mental effort, we can rearrange and organize those mental units in our mind. For example, we can form mental units of the parts we see (such as a tree or a rock) and of the wholes we see (such as an entire visual field), and we can—by the volitional exertion of mental effort—rearrange those mental units so that all the parts are in one mental group, and all the wholes are in another mental group. (I do not subscribe to the representationalist idea that *perception* of entities consists of perception of mental units instead of direct perception of entities. Rather, we can form mental units—such as memories of perceived entities—that can be manipulated and grouped in our mind in the process of *conceptualizing*.)

After forming these groups of units, we can conceive of each of the groups as *open-ended*. That is, we can give our mind the standing order to put all future parts we see—or even don't see—into the group of parts, and to put all of the wholes into the group of wholes. (See Ayn Rand 1990, 17–18 for this meaning of being open-ended.)

In this way, we have broadened our knowledge of a single whole, seen in a single moment, to a grouping of all wholes that we might ever see. We can do another kind of broadening. In our visual field at any given moment, we see a certain collection of parts. At another moment, we may see some of the same parts along with some new parts. We can broaden our conception of the whole to mean the full collection of all the parts that we might ever see or know of, or even never know of. This broadened conception is our concept of *the world*.

Thus we have begun our hierarchy of knowledge. We have identified facts we know; and we know these facts directly, without reference to other facts. We can state these facts in propositional form as follows: (Pointing to the tree:) This is a part of the world. (Waving our arm across our entire visual field:) This is the world.

Moreover, we have stated *how* we know these basic facts. We know these facts because we *observe* them and are able to *conceptualize* them. Thus, in addition to having identified some facts at the base of our knowledge, we have also identified a *means* of knowledge. That means of knowledge is observation combined with conceptualization. (Conceptualization will be covered more generally and in depth in Chapter 5.)

Finally, the knowledge identified above will serve as a *standard* for all the rest of our knowledge. All other candidates for knowledge will be compared to this standard. All subsequent candidates for knowledge in our hierarchy will be considered knowledge if they are identified in the same kind of way, or in some kind of related way, that we identified the above knowledge.

Merely from observation of parts of the world such as a tree, a car, a dog, and a ball, we cannot yet say that we know that the part before us is a tree (for instance); to do so would require forming and validating the concept "tree." In the exposition above, I called that part a "tree" merely to direct your attention to it, because you the reader knew the part to be a tree in your previous hierarchy of knowledge and could thereby choose to look at it now.

Moreover, merely from our visual observation of these parts, we cannot yet state that the part before us is an *entity* in the full respect of that term (such as that the part is solid to the touch), though the part is an entity in the looser respect that the part is a part in our visual field. Our inquiry has not yet gotten as far as entities in the stricter sense. But the fact remains that we perceive these parts *qua* parts even if not yet *qua* entities.

Let us now address a concept that we have used above in implicit form: the concept of existence.

"There is" means "there exists." Where is "there"? "There" means "in the world." "There is a planet Earth" means "In the world exists a planet Earth." A similar, although not identical, statement would be "The world includes a planet Earth." That is, to exist is to be included in the world, to be a part of the world.

From this meaning of 'exist', it follows that whenever we notice a thing, whether it be a tree or a rock or a planet, we notice that it exists. In this sense, the most basic fact we can state about a thing is that it exists, that it is included in the world.

For the term 'existence', note two different usages. One usage is for the nominalization of 'exist'. That is, existence in this sense denotes the fact or state or attribute of existing. To state that the earth exists is to denote the existence of the earth.

There is another, very important usage of the term 'existence': as a synonym of 'the world' or 'the universe'. In this usage, 'existence' is a collective noun subsuming all things—all existents—as does the term 'universe'. The difference between the term 'universe' and this usage of the term 'existence' is as follows. Whereas the term 'universe' places emphasis on the fact that the world is parts considered together as a whole, the term 'existence' places emphasis on the fact that the world persists. The emphasis on persistence is, in my judgment, more fundamental to the rest of the development of epistemology, and therefore I will usually refer to existence instead of the universe. But it is good to keep in mind that the concept of existence entails both the whole and the persistence of the whole.

Now let us identify some further facts. The order in which we proceed is somewhat optional. We can proceed next with consciousness (even though consciousness was known later in the chronological hierarchy), or we can proceed next with entities. Let us proceed next with consciousness.

I have described our knowledge of existence and of parts of existence—parts such as the tree and the ball. I have focused on that of which we are aware. But now let us focus on, and thus be aware of, that which *is* aware—that is, our conscious self. Focusing on that which is aware is called 'introspection'. When we introspect, we are aware of our self being aware of existence. We are aware of awareness of existence. By abstracting, we can isolate that which is aware: our self. Thus we know our conscious self.

It is important to clarify something at the outset. By 'consciousness', I do not mean the senses, the brain, or even the subconscious; those things, which we will address as they arise from observed evidence in the due course of our inquiry, are part of existence. I use the term 'consciousness' literally, meaning only consciousness.

It may take several years of life before a child becomes aware of his own conscious self. But again, we are not here concerned with chronology. Now that, as adults, we are aware of our conscious self, we are aware of it directly, as we are aware of existence directly. We need not rely on any other knowledge to be aware of our conscious self. Nevertheless, let me state some more words to guide our awareness to this thing I am calling the conscious self, to help make sure my meaning is clear.

As we did to guide our grasp of existence, let us consider several different instances of our experiencing a visual field, or an array of sounds, or a touch. Notice that there is something in common in these instances: a self having these experiences. Consider also the instances of us attending selectively to some aspect of the visual field, etc. Again there is this self exercising the selective attention. In the same way that we can observe a persisting visual field, we can notice a persisting thing having all these experiences. Moreover, then we can notice this persisting thing—the self—in each new experience. Sometimes this persisting conscious thing is seeing, sometimes hearing, sometimes focusing on some thing in the world or aspect of a thing in the world, sometimes focusing on what is in common with various things, and sometimes focusing on itself and only peripherally aware of the external world. In every case, there is this same, one persisting thing that is aware of something. This one persisting thing is what I am calling an individual's conscious self.

Note that there is a certain kind of relationship between the world we are conscious of and our conscious self. We can understand this relationship without even having to perceive specific entities in the world. Try this exercise: Feel something touch your arm; hear some sounds, feel the wind (without having to know specifically that it is wind) on some parts of your body (without having to know specifically that it is your body). Then, using sight, consider your whole range of vision as one big object that is in turn part of the world as we conceived of the world a few pages ago; see each patch of color as a patch, or part, of the field of vision, which is in turn part of the world. Visual artists often look at the world in this way in order to draw or paint. If one does this exercise, one should find that one is indeed aware of the world without even having to be aware of entities.

Let us now employ our ability of abstraction to these cases of awareness. What parts or aspects of these instances of awareness can we distinguish here? We can distinguish two parts or 'things': the world we are aware of, and the self that is aware of the world. Moreover, we know that the self is not only a thing, it is a persisting state; we call that state 'consciousness'.

When we are not introspecting, how do we know that the world we are conscious of—what we can call the *external world*, the world external to our consciousness—and our consciousness itself are two different things? How do we know that the external world we are conscious of is not our consciousness? Simply, we introspect to discern what our consciousness is, and we discern that the external thing we observe is not a state of our consciousness.

(To avoid misunderstanding of my theory, and to avoid any conflating of my theory with a kind of theory of perception known as 'representationalism', let me underscore the following. By "external world," I do not mean a world distinct from some "internal world"— or from some Kantian 'phenomenal world'—known more directly by our senses. Rather, by 'external world' I simply mean the world except for an individual's own consciousness.)

To put the point another way, one might ask, "Is your consciousness making up the world?" Well, are you conscious of making up the world? No? Then your consciousness is not making up the world, because there is nothing to consciousness other than being conscious.

There is more that we know. We can also discern a relation—indeed, an inter-action—between the (external) world and consciousness. The world acts on us, exerts a force on us, makes itself felt by us, is sensed—felt, seen, heard, etc.—by us. When something touches us or hits us, it gets our attention. Something that is not our consciousness, that is external to our consciousness, gets the attention *of* our consciousness. The world does something to us. The world *causes* us to be conscious of it, and our being conscious of it is the *effect* of this cause. Thus we have knowledge of *causality*. We have knowledge of a causal relation between the world and our consciousness of it. The world acts on us, and that action makes us aware of the world.

The world as a cause, and our awareness as an effect, is most readily apparent in our sense of touch, especially when something gets our attention via touch. When we feel something touch us or carry us, it is unmistakable that the world is doing something to us, changing our state of consciousness, making us conscious of the world in a changed form. Indeed, when we say "I feel it," we could just as well say "It makes itself felt to me"; that is, it causes my feeling of it; it touches me, it acts on me.

Thus knowledge of the existence of causality is a corollary of the knowledge that we are conscious of existence. Without causality—specifically, without cause-and-effect interactions between certain things that exist—there could be no such thing as consciousness. Ayn Rand (1957, 1015) explains that consciousness without existence is a contradiction in terms; now I am adding the following: consciousness without causality is a contradiction in terms—also meaning, in this case, a contradiction against fact.

Note that the fact, identified by Ayn Rand (1984a, 32–33), of "the primacy of existence"—the fact that existence has primacy over consciousness, that consciousness is dependent on existence—is a consequence of the fact that any state of consciousness is *caused* by existence. The primacy of existence over consciousness is a *causal* primacy.

Thus, our knowledge of causality is not based merely on "constant conjunction" (such as the repeated conjunction between the striking of a billiard ball and the ball's subsequent motion) as Hume (1902, 34 [Section 59]) would have us believe. Our knowledge of causality, in this rudimentary form pertaining to the relation of existence to consciousness, is an inescapable corollary of the identification of the facts of existence and consciousness.

According to Hume (1902, 11–43 [Sections 22–74]), we have no evidence of causal interactions. The exact opposite is true. We have no evidence of the *absence* of causal interactions. Every moment of our consciousness is an instance of many causal interactions. We have never experienced, and could never experience, anything that had no effect on us. Our very experience is an effect. Moreover, there is no basis in any of our experience to support the notion that something can act without thereby acting on something else.

Philosophers as divergent as Descartes (1984, Third Meditation, 26–27) and Locke (1975, II.xxxi.12) have addressed the issue of existence causing consciousness. Here I have presented my own position on this causal relationship, a position that should not be conflated with others.

I will state much more about causality, and some more about Hume, throughout the remainder of the book.

3.4   MULTIPLICITY, IDENTITY, AND DIFFERENCE

As we have established, the external world we perceive and our consciousness that perceives are two different things. Thus the whole of existence, by which we include both the external world and consciousness, *consists of parts*—at least these two. We also observe that the external world consists of parts of a whole.

I will call this fact, that the world consists of parts, the Law of Multiplicity. When we discuss entities in the next section, we will see why this law—as well as laws that follow—is important to make explicit.

We also know another law: the Law of Identity. At this early stage in building our corpus of knowledge, this law states that each of the multiple parts of the world is recognized by the ways it characteristically and distinctively acts on our consciousness. We identify the external world because of the ways it characteristically acts on our consciousness: the external world causes our consciousness to sense it in the form of sights, sounds, tastes, smells, and touches. We identify our consciousness by the ways *it* characteristically acts on our consciousness: it causes our consciousness to be aware of it in the form of introspections. The characteristic and distinctive way that each part acts on our consciousness is that part's *identity*. (Later, we will expand our understanding of identity and the law of that name.)

We also know the Law of Difference, which is another perspective on the laws of Multiplicity and Identity. This law states that the world and our consciousness are two *different* parts, each part acting differently on our consciousness.

The importance of all of these laws will become evident as we continue to develop our hierarchy of knowledge.

Let us introduce another concept that is similar to 'existence', 'world', and 'universe': 'reality'. The concept of reality distinguishes between what exists and what consciousness might project or imagine.

Sometimes the phrase 'physical reality' or 'external reality', referring to all of existence except consciousness, is used to emphasize that consciousness is non-physical, and internal to the self that is conscious.

So far in our new, philosophical hierarchy of knowledge, notice that we have formed concepts—such as 'existence' and 'identity'—even before identifying physical entities—such as rocks and tables—in physical reality. Also note that we have identified our own consciousness before identifying physical entities. Though such an order of knowledge could not have been the chronological order of our first learning these concepts, we can make this order occur now. We do not now need to rely on our knowledge of rocks and tables as a basis for some degree of explicit knowledge of existence, identity, our own consciousness, and a basic form of causality.

However, once we identify entities, our knowledge—even of existence, identity, consciousness, and causality—will take a colossal leap. Entities are the subject of the next chapter.

3.5   RECURRING THEMES

At this point in our inquiry, it is useful to be more explicit about a concept we have been using: integration. To integrate is to organize—in a specific way—parts or elements of some kind to make a whole that we can understand as a new kind of single unit, enabling us to go beyond our understanding of the parts when considered individually.

For example, a machine such as an automobile is an integration of various specialized parts including an engine (itself an integration), chassis, passenger compartment, etc. If we place the engine on a seat in the passenger compartment, we still may have all the parts of an automobile, but we don't have an automobile, because the parts are not integrated in the way required by an automobile.

A logical argument is an integration of individual statements. The statements must be organized into a logical order, proceeding from premises through a chain of reasoning to a conclusion.

In some cases, the parts of an integrated whole are not so specialized as the parts of an automobile or argument. All the bricks of a brick wall may be so similar as to be interchangeable (unlike an engine versus a chassis, or a premise versus a conclusion), but they nevertheless must be combined in a specific way in order to form a wall. Four lines, though interchangeable, must be organized in a certain way in order to make a square.

In our inquiry, we will encounter important integrations made from parts that are similar—like bricks in a wall—but that nevertheless must be combined in a specific way in order to produce a certain kind of integrated whole. A crucial integration of this kind is a *concept*. All the cats that go into the forming of the concept "cat" are similar, but the actual forming of the concept requires a specific way of understanding and relating the individual cats to each other in contrast to other things, and a specific way of forming a new kind of single unit—a *mental* unit that refers back not to a combination or collection of cats (as a wall is a combination of bricks), but rather to each individual cat *as a member of a collection* of cats, thereby enhancing our understanding of each individual cat.

We will also encounter integrations made from parts that are specialized. As mentioned above, one such kind of integration is a logical argument. Another such kind of integration is an entire corpus of knowledge.

To further the end of being able to hold the entire contents of this book as an integrated whole, we will highlight three recurring themes throughout our inquiry:

1. Axiomatic concepts and their role in cognition.
2. Similarity, difference, and range of measurement.
3. The very concept of integration itself.

4 PERCEPTION OF ENTITIES

Let us again focus our attention on differentiations that we can make regarding the external world, the world external to and not including our consciousness.

We have established that we see separate parts of the external world, such as a tree, a car, a dog, a ball, a stick. But we have not yet established that these parts are entities. At this point, it is useful to define 'entity'. Doing so will begin to illuminate why the concept of entity is fundamental to our hierarchy of knowledge.

It is often most difficult to define the most foundational concepts, because there are few other concepts to use in such a definition. It often helps first to identify concretes subsumed by the concept (ball, stick, etc.), what is being differentiated by the concept, and what is our cognitive purpose for the concept.

We seek to differentiate entities from their attributes (such as the roundness of a ball and the long and narrow shape of a stick), and from existence as a whole.

Regarding our cognitive purpose, we can at least state at this stage that we seek a concept that captures more of our understanding of trees, cars, dogs, balls, etc. than the concept "part" does. As we will see throughout the remainder of the book, the concept 'entity'—as I define and explain it—will reveal a great deal of information about causality.

4.1 Definition of Entity

An entity—what we can also call an object, such as a tree, a car, a dog, a ball, a stick—is a persisting part of the world that acts as a distinctive whole on our senses in an integrated way across sense modalities, and in a way distinctive from the way its surroundings act on our senses.

An entity is a physically localized source of sensory information. An entity is not all of the world, but rather some localized part. This localized part is physically separate in some way from each other part. Indeed, we are aware of some entities partly by the fact that we can get our hands around them, and we are aware of some entities partly by the fact that we see them as a self-contained pattern against a background.

Every entity is perceived to be of equal sensible status with every other entity, and of equal sensible status with the world as a whole. In other words, no part is perceived to be an attribute of another distinct part. Each part is self-contained. Each is perceived to be a kind of "microcosm" of the whole world: Like the world as a whole, each entity acts—at least potentially—on all or most of our sense modalities. Whatever constitutes the world we sense as a whole also constitutes entities. An entity is a piece of the world.

Each entity is perceived to have an ongoing existence beyond the duration of a single moment. An entity persists through time and through change, even when we are not perceiving it. This persistence is another way in which an entity is a physical microcosm.

Gotthelf (2000, 40) offers a useful initial description of an entity (which we will work on to flesh out):

> In the concept's primary sense an *entity* is a solid object
> with a perceivable shape, which acts or resists action as
> a whole.

This description implicitly adds another important fact about entities: not only does an entity act on all our senses in a distinctive and persistent way, but an entity also acts in a distinctive and persistent way in relation to other entities.

To restate the thoughts above, the characteristics of an entity include the following:

- An entity acts on our senses such that both our sight and touch sense distinctive action and distinct boundaries (implying a distinct shape) of the entity. We can call this characteristic 'distinctiveness'.
- An entity acts on our senses such that our sight and touch of the entity are consistent with each other (as in opaqueness and solidity). We can call this characteristic 'consistency across sense modalities'.
- An entity acts on our senses in a persistent way. We can call this characteristic 'persistence'.

In Section 4.6.1, we will introduce a very important fourth characteristic of entities, and in Chapter 8 we will identify additional characteristics, but the three characteristics stated above are enough for us to make our first observations of entities. The next section will describe in depth how we detect these three characteristics.

4.2   SENSORY EVIDENCE OF ENTITIES

4.2.1   Sight

Sight and touch are the main senses that give us clear knowledge of physical extension. Let us first consider sight.

Let us return to looking at the world as an illustrator might in order for him to draw precisely what he sees, without his assuming that what he sees will persist or act upon his sense of touch in a certain way. Again, it is the world as we are conscious of it by this careful way of sensing—not by perception of whole, solid, persisting entities—that is the infallibly veridical base of a philosophically validated corpus of knowledge of the external world.

To make my approach clear in the context of the history of philosophy, I reiterate the point of the previous paragraph by contrasting my approach to other approaches, as follows. To arrive at
knowledge of entities, I do not start with atomistic sensations, such
as individual specks of light and individual sensations on each nerve
ending. Nor do I start with perception of entities in the sense of
things that feel as they look. Instead, I start with what we see and
what we sense in the form of touch (and also sounds, smells, and
tastes), and I show by inference that what we see and what we touch
are the same things—that is, entities.

Let us then begin to understand the sensory evidence for entities
by trying this simple experiment. Follow your moving finger with
your eyes. The finger stands out plainly as a stable part against the
whirling blur of the background.

We get evidence that what we see is an entity when we see an unchanging part—or a less-changing part—amid the changing or
more-greatly-changing world or field of vision.

Paradoxically, the unchanging or less-changing part—such as my
moving finger, or a stick held in hand and moved from left to right—
is first seen by me when it as a whole is in motion (changing its position) against the rest of the visual field. During this motion, the
world is changing simply in virtue of the change in location of the
moving entity. When we notice the moving entity to be unchanging
or less-changing during its motion, we have simplified—that is, reduced the complexity of—the overall change we see.

Recall our discussion, in Section 3.3, of similarity as "less difference" in connection with the formation of the concept of existence.
The idea of "less-changing" is essentially the same idea as the idea of
"less difference." If we were to measure the differences, from one moment to the next, in distance among all the parts of the finger (such
as the distance between the nail and the most distal joint), we would
find that these differences are much less than the difference in the
distance, from one moment to the next, between the parts of the
background occluded by the finger. That is, the parts of the finger

might not change their relation to each other by more than a tenth of an inch, but the part of the background occluded by the finger might change by six inches.

A similar process of recognizing an entity occurs when the observer moves while looking at a stationary object such as a tree. The observer's visual field changes, but the tree is seen as a part that is changing its effect on me in a systematic, delimited way. As Gibson (1986, 180–192) explains, the "occluding edges"—the edges of objects in the foreground in front of changing edges of objects in the background—change in a gradual, systematic, and reversible way.

Gibson 1986 is an in-depth treatment of the process of seeing entities. What I have called "unchanging" or "less-changing," Gibson often calls "persistent" or "invariant." He summarizes the process as follows (1986, 235–236):

> The perceiving of persistence and change (instead of color, form, space, time, and motion) can be stated in various ways. We can say that the perceiver separates the change from the nonchange, notices what stays the same and what does not, or sees the continuing identity of things along with the events in which they participate. The question, of course, is how he does so. What is the information for persistence and change? The answer must be of this sort: The perceiver extracts the invariants of structure from the flux of stimulation while still noticing the flux. For the visual system in particular, he tunes in on the invariant structure of the ambient optic array that underlies the changing perspective structure caused by his movements.

When we lock our focus onto the moving part, follow the moving part with our focus, and thus more clearly see the moving part to be unchanging, we have further simplified our awareness of the unchanging part and further distinguished it from its background. The background in such cases is much less noticeable, becoming almost an indistinguishable blur.

To state the overall point again in other words: Looking at a field that we eventually recognize as an entity in motion against a background, or as an entity that is stationary as we move in relation to it, we see an unchanging or less-changing part of the world amid the changing or more-changing world. That is, we see a combination of similarity and difference. What are different are spatial position, shape, and what Gibson calls "occluding edges" from moment to moment. What is similar is the integrity of the entity from moment to moment.

Of course, this grasping of similarity and difference, in order to perceive entities, occurs automatically and implicitly, without the need for conceptual awareness. However, by explicitly identifying similarity as "less difference" according to some objective measurement, I am establishing the conceptual, objective basis for placing cognitive value in such automatically-perceived similarities. In the next chapter, on concepts, I will develop further this factual basis for similarity and difference, and I will use this understanding of similarity and difference in completing my theory of causality and induction.

4.2.2   Touch

Consider the example of your hand moving along an object such as a stick. You experience an unchanging kind of sensation over a range of motion of your hand; that is, you feel something that acts on you in a similar or unchanging way over some of the stick's length. Then—and this is what gives you a sense of a boundary of the stick— you feel something different at some point of your movement; or, even more dramatically, you feel nothing—meaning that you have gone past the end of the stick. Yet each time you move your hand back over its past path, you feel what you felt before. Thus, you experience an unchanging or less-changing pattern of touch over the extent of the stick—and a greater change or end to the pattern somewhere, which is the end of the stick. As in the case of sight, these lesser and greater changes are measurable as such. For instance, the squeeze of your hand on the stick might cause your skin to deform by between .02 and .03 inches throughout the length of the stick, and by less than .001 inches when you squeeze your hand where there is no stick. Beyond the entity, the pattern is not as predictable as on the entity: the stick might be against the wall, on the floor, held by you, etc. But within the boundary of the stick, the pattern remains un-changing, or less-changing in some discernible respect.

Moreover, the stick feels rigid. That is, its shape remains the same, and the stick is resistant to your touch. Your hands do not pass through the stick.

4.2.3   Sight and Touch in Combination

Next, note how our sense of touch of an entity coordinates with our sight of the entity. For example, you see a stick. You also see your own hand. When there is no visible space between your hand and the stick, you feel something. This combination of sight and touch is al-ways coordinated. What you feel when you touch the stick is always similar, just as what you see is always similar. Again, you feel an un-changing or less-changing part of the changing world—this time changing in how it feels to your hand.

Thus the world acts on our sight and our touch in some unchang-ing (or less-changing) and coordinated way within some specific spa-tial extent. That is, this part of the world is acting on us as an entity.

When we twist and tilt our hands as we hold the stick, the stick feels the same. But the stick does not look the same, although it looks similar. The shape of the visual appearance of the stick transforms in a systematic way, getting longer or shorter depending on the angle at which we hold it.

When we extend our hands away from our source of vision (what we will later identify as our eyes) as we hold the stick, the stick feels the same. But the image of the stick gets smaller in comparison to the rest of our visual field. When we bring the stick close to our eyes, it looks bigger in comparison to the rest of our visual field, blocking out most of our visual field. But the stick continues to feel the same size.

Our sense of touch tells us that the size and shape of the stick do not change even though the visual image changes as the stick moves in relation to our self. We realize that the changes in our sight of the stick pertain to the position of the stick in relation to our self; the stick is not changing in size and shape. (This realization is later confirmed when we discover the laws of optics.)

Consequently, when the visual image of an object grows, and we are not touching the object, we generally assume that the object is approaching. Knowledge of an approaching object is important because, as experience indicates, an object that comes into contact with us makes an impact. Sometimes, however, this assumption that an object is approaching can be mistaken. For example, a growing image on a screen can be mistaken for an approaching object. Animals also make this mistake. (Gibson 1986, 175–176.) But with more sensory information, such as our touching the screen, we can correct this mistake and realize that the image on the screen is not an entity; the entity involved is the screen.

Most of the time, however, when we see something that looks as though it has the characteristics of an entity, our touching the thing confirms that it indeed has those characteristics. When your hand moves to where you see the stick in your field of vision, what you touch is that specific part of the external world that is the stick. That is, when something looks like an entity, it usually turns out to be an entity.

Recall the three characteristics of entities we identified earlier: distinctiveness, consistency across sense modalities, and persistence. We have identified sensory data—the combination of sight and touch—that tell us that a part of the world has acted as an entity, fulfilling these three characteristics, in the past. We have not addressed how we know that the entity will continue to fulfill those three characteristics in the future. For that knowledge, not merely assumption, we will need induction, which we will cover beginning in Chapter 8.

4.2.4 The Other Senses

Next, consider how our senses of sight and touch coordinate with the senses of hearing, taste, and smell. Consider these examples:

- We see a baby's rattle and hold it. When we shake the rattle, we hear a sound. The sound is coordinated with our action of shaking, with our feeling (through changes in force felt by our hand) of something about (inside) the rattle moving, and with our sight of the rattle moving.
- We hear a dog when we see and/or touch it. The apparent spatial location of the sound coordinates with the location indicated by our sight and touch. Each entity we perceive through sight and touch seems to carry a distinctive range of sounds with it. Again, the sounds of entities are less-changing patterns amid a more-changing cacophony.

Once we perceive entities with the senses of sight and touch, the other senses readily provide correlated information. The sense of taste is easy to correlate with perceived entities, because we taste what we already feel in our mouth. The sense of smell is also easy to correlate because the smell that correlates to a perceived entity is strongest when the entity is near our nose. Likewise, an entity's sound is loudest when near where we see and feel our ears to be.

Thus the other senses add evidence for consistency across senses.

4.2.5 Our Senses as a Causal Factor in Our Sensing

That we sense the world with various senses, and that these senses give us consistent information, imply some very important conclusions.

The world we see is the same world as the world we hear. Yet our experience of seeing the world is very different from our experience of hearing the world. Therefore, the identity of each sense is an important factor in the causal relationship between the world and our consciousness of it. The world causes our consciousness of it, but the nature of our senses is an indispensable factor in the *form* in which we are conscious of the world. Our consciousness of the world is an effect of the world, but also an effect of each of our senses. We come to discover that each of our senses themselves consists of entities in the world, entities such as eyes, hands, and nerves.

Nevertheless, each sense gives us consistent information about the world. Therefore, the difference between one sense and another, or the difference between the state of one sense at a given moment compared to the state of that same sense at a different moment, does not detract from our ability to know the world as entities acting in a regular way. Similarly, the difference between the senses of one person and of another person does not detract from the ability of both people to know the same one world in a consistent way.

Indeed, the differences among the various senses of a given person, or among the senses of different individuals, serves to enhance our knowledge of the world greatly, by offering a greater number of coordinated dimensions of evidence. Finding the consistency in what we see, hear, touch, taste, and smell gives us much more specific information, as well as a wider array of information, than we could get from any one sense alone.

We even come to discover that, as our sight and hearing give us two different simultaneous perspectives on the world, each of our two eyes gives us a slightly different simultaneous perspective on the world. The combined information from these two perspectives is not merely additive, but also more specific. For instance, the degree of difference between the two visual perspectives provides information on how far away an object is.

4.2.6   The Contextual Nature of the Concept of Entity

In one respect, one can say that something that merely looks like an entity is an entity even if it does not feel like one; for example, a spot on a leopard is in one respect an entity. But usually, what we mean by an entity is something that is physically separate to the touch as well as sight. That is, the concept of entity usually includes the characteristics of distinctiveness and consistency across sense modalities.

It is generally recognized that the concept 'entity' distinguishes entities from attributes, actions, etc. But the concept also, and more fundamentally, distinguishes entities from the world as a whole.

Note the objective, contextual nature of the concept 'entity'. A chair is an entity. So is a removable leg of the chair, and so is a screw that holds a leg of the chair to the seat. A part of a part is also a part; a part of an entity is also an entity. Inversely, a whole that is composed of entities is an entity. The world as a whole is a kind of entity in a certain respect. In most contexts, however, an entity means a part whose physical extent can be perceived directly.

Why is it important for the concept of 'entity' to be contextual in this respect? The answer is that we will be able to gain knowledge about each entity we perceive: the chair, the leg of the chair, the screw, etc. The more entities we recognize, the more knowledge we can build.

But what entities will we recognize first: the chair or the leg of a chair; a hand or the fingers of the hand?

Recall our experiment of following our moving finger with our eyes. In that case, we noticed the finger as an entity. If we follow our whole moving hand with our eyes, then we will notice the hand, because the hand—though moving—is what is unchanging amid change. If we wiggle our fingers, then we will notice the fingers, because it is the fingers that are unchanging or less changing amid the changing shape of the hand (which includes the wiggling fingers).

Recall Gotthelf's statement: "In the concept's primary sense an *entity* is a solid object with a perceivable shape, which acts or resists action as a whole." The entities that we perceive are those that move as a whole; they act causally—distinctively and regularly—as a whole on our senses, and will therefore act causally as a whole on other entities.

Similarly, we will notice the chair as a whole when the chair moves as a whole, or when we move around the chair. If we see a leg removed from a chair and moved separately from the chair, then we will readily notice a leg of any chair.

Of course there are variations to the general method described above for recognizing entities. For example, it might be argued that a baby recognizes his mother's nipples as entities, mainly from the senses of touch and taste—the feel of the nipple and the taste of the milk—and little from the sense of sight. But whatever the exact pattern in each case, we have explained the means by which sensory information is differentiated and integrated so that we perceive entities. Not every kind of differentiation and integration is needed in each case. In the example of the nipple, the repeated patterns of touch and taste are enough even without correlating patterns of sight and sound; the nipple is still perceived to be a persisting part of the world.

And, of course, a blind person can come to be aware of entities.

4.2.7   Remarkable Consistency of the World's Causal Action on Our Senses

An entity's effect on our consciousness, although consistent and unchanging in general, is not unchanging in precise detail from one moment to the next. The entity's effect is relatively unchanging in relation to the changing effects around the entity. For example, the pen looks different as its position changes relative to our eyes. There are changes in perspective, color, brightness, etc. That is, the precise form of our perception of an object changes with the relation of the object to our self. But the rules describing these changes—rules such as principles of geometry and optics, causing familiar patterns of appearance—are unchanging. Moreover, the very changes in perspective, hue, brightness, etc., tell us even more information about the entity—information that correlates with the information provided by our other senses. For example, when the projection of a pen in our field of vision is shorter, we have information that the pen is oriented more perpendicular to the plane of the front of our face. Indeed, if our sight were such that our visual perception of an object were always the same (as a bunch of blips on a radar screen), our sight would give us much less information than it does now; and this diminished information would be much less evidence for the remarkable consistency of the world's causal action on our senses.

Thus we have reached a second extremely important idea about causality. The first idea was that existence causes our consciousness of it (of existence), and that causality therefore exists in all of our sensory awareness of existence. The second idea is that this causality has been observed to have a remarkable consistency in terms of distinctiveness, consistency across sense modalities, and persistence of entities.

In order for us to recognize entities, we must experience millions or even billions of instances of regular sensory information. By "regular," I mean "taking repeated actions that are so similar to one another that they adhere uniformly to a given mathematical rule." Though I have not yet presented the method of inductive reasoning that takes this sensory evidence and validates the conclusion that causal interactions will be regular in the future, we will see that this sensory evidence is the most important evidence for this conclusion. The fact that we perceive entities is the most basic and most extensive evidence for our full, philosophically validated knowledge of causality. Indeed, if an entity did not act in regular ways—"in accordance with its nature" (Peikoff 1991, 14)—we would never perceive it in the first place. And if the world does contain things that do not act regularly, then we never will perceive them either directly or indirectly.

In this context, these words from Bacon (2014, I.CXIX) are apt:

> But I, who am well aware that no judgment can be
> passed on uncommon or remarkable things, much less
> anything new brought to light, unless the causes of
> common things, and the causes of those causes, be first
> duly examined and found out, am of necessity com-
> pelled to admit the commonest things into my history.
> Nay, in my judgment philosophy has been hindered by
> nothing more than this, that things of familiar and fre-
> quent occurrence do not arrest and detain the thoughts
> of men, but are received in passing without any inquiry
> into their causes; insomuch that information

concerning things which are not known is not oftener
wanted than attention concerning things which are.

In the present context, the common things are the objects of our perception.

In Chapter 8, we will prove the third and final important idea regarding causality: We should expect this remarkable consistency to continue in the future. More generally, we will validate a method of induction that goes from a large number of observed instances to a conclusion about future instances.

I am postponing this validation because it relies on an account of concepts that I will present in the next chapter. Also, the validation is somewhat mathematical and would interrupt the overall flow of the current exposition. For the purpose of my current exposition, therefore, I am following somewhat the usual chronology of knowledge. For millennia, man has had a general understanding of the Law of Causality along with a strong idea of its plausibility, even while lacking a full validation. In these earlier chapters, I am providing context and motivation for this validation. I am showing that the law is highly plausible even in the absence of a full validation, and I am illustrating how immensely valuable it is to know the law.

Without a more advanced, philosophical knowledge of causality, what do people do when they encounter irregular actions of entities, such as a ball catching fire and burning up? Generally, they get frightened, startled, or surprised. Babies get startled the first time the jack-in-the-box pops out. Primitive men get scared at an eclipse or their first view of fire. Fear is what they feel, but what do they *think*? What do seemingly irregular events do to their expectations of the future? What most people tend to do is develop an expectation proportional to the relative number of past occurrences of each outcome. If a man has looked in a thousand caves, and there turned out to be a bear in the cave five times, the man would expect that next time he looks in a cave there is a small but real chance (say, five in a thousand) that a bear will be in it.

As we will see later, this probabilistic approach to predicting the future is not a bad start. But, for scientific knowledge, we can greatly improve the probabilities, and validate the probabilistic reasoning.

So far in this book, I have used the word 'perception' as part of the phrase "perception of entities" or "object of perception." Hereafter, when I use the word 'perception' alone, I mean perception of entities. Such perception is based on sensory information from sight, touch, etc., as discussed in this section.

4.3   ACTION, FORCE, CHANGE, MOTION, AND ATTRIBUTE

Now let us define and explain further the other basic concepts that we have been using. Because these other concepts are contrasts to 'entity', understanding them will also further clarify our understanding of 'entity'.

Force, change, and motion are three different kinds of action. Let us consider each of them.

4.3.1   Force

Our first clear experience of force is through the sense of touch. The doctor or our mother touches us, lifts us, slaps us. We are feeling the world exert force on our self. The world is causing an effect on us—moving us, making us feel pain, or just making us feel the world or a specific entity.

We experience force even before we perceive specific entities; we experience it as soon as we feel the single, largest 'entity'—the whole world. But of course our experience of a force is much more informative when we can attribute the force to a specific entity.

Force is an action, or that attribute of an entity, whereby the entity initiates or causes another action—change, motion, another force, or awareness.

When the world acts on our senses other than our tactile sense, it still is exerting force on us; but this exertion of force is not as obvious as it is with touch. This exertion of force is least obvious with the sense of sight. The force of a slap is usually more obvious than the force of a flashing light, unless the light is very bright.

4.3.2   Motion and Change

Motion and change generally are different aspects of the same action understood from different perspectives. Change occurs within an entity. Motion is a change in an entity's spatial relation to other entities; therefore, motion occurs between or among entities.

Consider this example:

> A bottle of unhomogenized milk is sitting on the table. The particles of fat are gradually moving to the top, but each particle of fat is not changing significantly within itself. Therefore, each particle, as a separate entity, is moving but not changing. On the other hand, the whole bottle full of milk, as a single entity, is changing but not moving. There is internal motion, but no motion of the whole relative to entities external to it.

Now let us consider these concepts through the hierarchical stages of knowledge we have examined.

At the basic level of sensing the world as the object of awareness making its effect on us, these are the ways we know the world to be acting:

- The world is acting on us, exerting forces on us by which we feel it, hear it, etc.
- The world is changing. We sense its changes by sight and by the other senses.
- The world as a whole is not moving, because it is just one (big) thing.

At the level of perceiving distinct entities, we generally perceive an entity when we perceive something unchanging (or changing less) within the whole, more-changing world.

4.3.3   Attribute

As we have established, an action is an action of an entity. An attribute of an entity is a regular, or characteristic, action of that entity. When we perceive an attribute, we are perceiving the entity in action, exerting a force on our senses. For example, a thing with the attribute of redness acts on our sense of sight in such a way that we see it as red. All attributes are characteristic actions, and vice versa; each of these two terms merely has a different focus and emphasis. Therefore, what we usually refer to as a characteristic action, such as the way an object falls through our field of vision, is just as much an attribute of the object as is its shape, color, etc.

4.3.4   Action and Interaction

If an entity acted but never interacted with any other entity, we could never know about this entity, nor would we need to. We know the actions of an entity by the interactions of that entity with other entities, including ourselves. The *interaction* between existence and consciousness—in particular, the action of existence on our consciousness—is our introduction to *action*.

4.4   The Payoff of Perceiving Entities

We have traced the process by which our basic knowledge of the world progresses to perceptual knowledge of specific entities, which are parts of the world. What is the benefit of this perceptual knowledge over mere knowledge of existence as a whole? What is the payoff?

Recall what we observed to be the purpose of primitive man's thinking. He wanted to deal with the future. He wanted to know what would happen in the future if he did nothing, and what actions he could take to change the future to make it good for him. We can presume that even a baby has a purpose of this kind. When he feels hunger, he wants to make the hunger subside.

But before the baby knows any entities, how does he know how to make the hunger subside? Actually, at birth he does not know how to do so; he does so by reflex. When his mother's nipple or breast grazes or touches his cheek, his head and mouth reflexively turn toward the nipple, and he reflexively sucks.

Imagine if a grown person had to rely on this method to satisfy his hunger: he would stumble around the world, and every time some part of the world brushed or bumped against his cheek, he would turn and suck on that part. Of course, this method would fail. And the person's knowledge of the world only as a whole would give him little guidance beyond his reflexes. He might notice that sometimes when he sucks, he gets milk. But most times, he would not get milk. The plain fact is, one must suck on the right part of the world in order to get milk, and one must bite the right part of the world in order to get food. In order to know which parts to suck on or bite, one must discern the parts—the entities.

Now we can understand the great benefit of perceiving entities. Once a child perceives the nipples, he knows—or at least concludes based on evidence—they are what to suck on. When he perceives a bit of apple sauce, he knows that is what to swallow. He knows what will happen in the future when he swallows his milk or his food, because the same kind of thing has happened every time in the past. Recalling an earlier example, a primitive man knows that a buffalo, a wolf, and a bear are different kinds of entities that will each act in a distinctive way.

But we have jumped ahead a little. Although we have explained how a child or an adult perceives entities, we have not fully explained how we know so much about what to expect from those entities— though we have dropped clues such as "because the same kind of thing has happened every time." How exactly does the child know that if he sucks the nipple or swallows the apple sauce he will get milk or food? To begin to answer that question, we must examine what we learned along with our perception of entities.

4.5 MULTIPLICITY, IDENTITY AND DIFFERENCE REVISITED

Before we perceived entities, the world must have been a mysterious thing. It acted on us in so many ways. And there was little discernible pattern to those ways beyond that there would always be a field of vision, a cacophony of sounds, etc. One moment the world might jostle us, then make a loud, coarse sound, then a soft, soothing sound. The world might look bright, then dark; it might swirl quickly, then look almost unchanging. The world was, in a word, chaotic.

However, the way we came to discern entities was that we noticed, amid the chaos, a regularity. Though the world when regarded as a whole affects our senses seemingly chaotically, each part affects our senses regularly. And this regularity is not on the order of something like a repetitive drumbeat that goes on for five minutes; this regularity is, compared to other regularities we often notice, an *astounding* regularity. If we turn our senses on some object, such as a person walking and talking before us, in five minutes we may receive millions or even billions of sense impulses perfectly coordinated, ordered, regular—obeying laws of motion, optics, acoustics, to every discernible degree of precision, in every detail from eyelashes to fingernails to the way the person's clothing hangs on his body. Imagine the number of details that a sculptor/painter/animator would have to get perfectly right in order to generate the same convincingly consistent combination of visual sensations alone that the world gives you in five minutes.

This regularity of sensory information is noticeable to us only when we regard the world in parts, the parts that we recognize as entities.

But there is one thing we must do to maintain our knowledge of this amazing regularity: We must not confuse the parts with one another. We must be aware that each part is different from each other part. Our knowledge of what the ball does to our senses must be kept distinct from what we know the table does to our senses. If we regard

both the ball and the table as a single part, then our awareness is back
to chaos.

In short, we have learned the following:

- The world consists of parts. I call this fact the 'Law of Multiplicity'.
  We call these parts 'entities'.
- Each entity is recognized by the ways it characteristically and dis-
  tinctively acts on our senses. I call this fact the Law of Identity.
- Each part is distinct and different from each other part. I call this
  fact 'The Law of Difference'.

Knowledge of these laws leads in turn to a fuller knowledge of
causality, as we shall see.

By regarding each perceived entity in a manner consistent with
these laws, we take a great stride in being able to deal with the future.
Consider the Law of Identity. When we recognize the ball before us,
it is the ball that continues to act on our visual sense in a regular way:
we perceive the ball as having round shape and blue hue. At the same
time, we may be experiencing many other visual sensations that are
not from the ball, but we do not let those other sensations obscure
the pattern that makes us recognize the ball. We remember that, in
the past, the ball has acted on us to give us the tactile sensations of
smoothness and a characteristic degree of heaviness. Therefore, we
expect those characteristics to persist; we expect that, if we reach out
to touch the ball, we will experience the characteristic tactile sensations of smoothness and heaviness that the ball has given us in the
past. (We have yet to *validate* those expectations, though we are as-
sembling the evidence we will use to validate them.) Thus, we successfully predict the future!

Thinking in accordance with the Law of Difference, we do not
expect entities other than the ball to feel like the ball, and we do not
expect entities other than a cup to feel like a cup. We know that each
entity is different, and an attribute of one entity is not necessarily an
attribute of another.

In reconsidering the Law of Identity after considering the Law of
Difference, we can see a further implication of the Law of Identity:

Though each entity is distinct and different from each other entity, it is not distinct and different from itself. This principle is the Law of Non-Contradiction, which is the basis for the method of deductive logic. Along these lines, Locke (1975, 57, I.ii.18) writes,

> ... *It is impossible for the same to be, and not to be*, or that which is the Foundation of it and is the easier understood of the two, *The same is not different:*

I will return to the Law of Non-Contradiction in Section 5.6.

4.6   DEVELOPMENT OF AWARENESS OF SELF AND CONSCIOUSNESS, AND IMPLICATIONS

4.6.1   Perception of Self as an Entity, and Causal Interaction of Entities

We have already explained that one introspects in order to be aware of one's consciousness. One's consciousness can be considered a kind of entity, even though it is not solid and shaped, because it is a persisting part of existence.

We see our limbs, our torso, and—as Gibson (1986, 104–112) explains—our nose, cheek, lips, and brow on the periphery of our field of vision. We become aware that sensory information impinges on specific parts of our body. We notice that our perception of our own body is of the same nature as are our perception of other entities. Just as we feel the stick with our right hand, we feel our left hand with our right hand, and vice versa.

In addition to all the kinds of evidence that we get of the entity-ness of other entities, we get additional evidence in regard to the entity-ness of our self:

- Our sense of touch extends exactly as far as does our body as sensed according to our feeling and seeing our body in space.
- We have control over our body, in contrast to our surroundings.
- We feel our body move as a single entity.

- As we move, we notice a concomitant change in our point of reference for sight, hearing, and our other senses. The precise form of our perception of an object changes in a coordinated way with the relation of the object to our self.
- Just as we recognize entities, other people recognize us.
- We perceive other people, who are entities, and those people resemble us in contrast to other kinds of entities.

Thus we learn that our body is a part of the external world, that is, a part of the world external to our consciousness! We are within the world, and are also a part distinct from other parts of the world. There are important ramifications to this knowledge.

For one thing, understanding one's body as an entity enhances the grasp of other entities *qua* entities. Those other entities exhibit the same entity-like qualities as does one's body.

More importantly, knowledge of the self as an entity sets the stage for a further development of knowledge of causality, because causal relations between external entities and the self can now be understood as causal relations between two entities in the external world. That knowledge further establishes the possibility that causal relations can exist between two entities that are both not us. Just as the wind knocks us over, so the wind can knock over the chair. Just as a mother lifts her child (and the child feels the force of his mother), so his mother lifts the chair. Just as I fall when I step over the ledge, so a rock falls when I drop it from a ledge. Just as a horse carries me, so the horse apparently carries a saddle.

Indeed, the apparent causal relations between external entities are perceived to be just as regular as the relations between an external entity and oneself. We have just arrived at a fourth characteristic of entities: interaction. That is, in addition to acting on our senses in a distinctive and persistent way, an entity acts in a distinctive and persistent way in relation to other entities. We have just generalized the Law of Identity.

Again, in Chapter 8, I will present a method of induction that goes from observation of distinctive and persistent action of entities to the conclusion that entities act causally on each other. It is not just a co-incidence that the chair falls over when the wind blows, or rises when the mother lifts it; the chair receives the force of the wind or the mother just as the child does. And it is not just apparent that the horse carries the saddle.

4.6.2 Awareness of One's Own Consciousness and the Independence of Existence

Awareness of one's body, and even of oneself, is not yet awareness of one's faculty of consciousness *qua* consciousness. When one is aware of oneself, one perceives one's self as an object, a physical entity. To be aware of one's consciousness *qua* consciousness, another step is required. One must introspect. In Section 3.3, we followed a scenario of introspection that led us to validate the existence of our own consciousness. Now let us follow a second scenario. In this scenario of being aware of consciousness, we will reinforce our understanding that existence exists *independent* of our consciousness.

Suppose you hold a ball in your hands. If you close your eyes or turn your head away, you still feel the ball in your hands; thus you know the ball still exists—that is, the world still contains the ball—even when you do not see the ball. Likewise, if you keep your eyes open and set the ball down, you see that the ball still exists even when you do not feel it. Thus you realize that the mere facts of the existence of the ball and the existence of your self are not enough for you to be aware of the ball. Your self must be in a certain relationship to the ball; for example, your eyes must be open, or you must be touching the ball. When your self is in that specific relationship, a relationship we have earlier explained to be causal, your self is then in a certain state: a state of consciousness of the ball.

Thus, when one is aware of the fact that one is perceiving, one is aware of one's consciousness in a certain state and in a certain relationship to the rest of the world.

Of course, consciousness is in fact not merely a state, but a process. We recognize this fact when we become aware of our own *thinking,* in contrast to our sensing; but we eventually learn that sensing is a process too.

From the above experiences, we also realize that things continue to exist even when they are not being perceived. For example, the ball exists even when you don't see it, don't feel it, don't sense it in any way.

The following example illustrates something further that can be learned from awareness of one's own consciousness. If a bat strikes a ball, we generally hear the event at the same time—as far as we can discern—that we see it. However, if we are watching a baseball game from the outfield bleachers, we hear the bat strike the ball a split second later than when we see it. What is happening is that there is a whole causal sequence of events, a chain reaction over time, of the sound traveling from the bat and ball through the air and eventually to our ears. We learn that causality works in this way, in chains of one entity acting on a second entity, which reacts and then acts on a third entity, and so on over a duration of time. We have arrived again at the fourth characteristic of entities: In addition to acting on our senses in a distinctive and persistent way, an entity acts in a distinctive and persistent way in relation to other entities.

The most important causal chains include oneself as one of the entities being affected and/or causing an effect. Elaborating on a previous example: Just as the applesauce causes us to see and taste it as a distinct and distinctive entity, eating the applesauce initiates a distinct and distinctive causal chain that acts on our body and eventually satisfies our hunger.

As our knowledge becomes advanced, we learn that there is a causal chain even in the functioning of our senses. For example, light travels from an object to the lens of our eye, and then to the retina, and then information travels to our brain, with many causal steps in between these. All of these causal steps, with all of their regularities, provide even more evidence for causality.

Similarly, we discover more evidence of causality when we discover that seeing the visual field is an integration of sensory data across many individual sensory receptors on our retina, and when we discover a similar kind of integration for our other senses.

However many causal steps there are from an entity acting to our perceiving the entity, there is always the regular, knowable causal sequence that goes from something that is not our consciousness to our consciousness of that something. Indeed, the object we see, the light that travels from the object to the eye, the eye itself, the retina, the optic nerve, the nerve impulses, the brain, the subconscious mind—none of these things is consciousness. Whatever the detailed process, something that is not our consciousness makes us conscious of it.

4.6.3   The Spiraling Development of Our Starting Point of Knowledge

Note how our awareness of self progresses in stages from
- awareness of self as an entity, to
- awareness of self as a part of the world, like other entities, to
- awareness of the faculty of consciousness as the faculty of experiencing states of consciousness, to
- awareness of a state of consciousness as a process.

Our knowledge of the world (first as parts, then as a whole, and then as entities) also goes through a series of spiraling steps that, as we shall see, continues through to the conceptual stage of knowledge. So too, as we shall continue to see, do the concepts of identity and causality go through a series of spirals.

The development of these four concepts—existence, consciousness, identity, and causality—is inextricably linked to the development of knowledge. This fact should not be surprising once we look more carefully at our working definition (which will not be our final definition) of knowledge, as stated at the beginning of the previous chapter: "Knowledge is some kind of awareness of something about the world." Thus knowledge entails a world (existence) that is known, a mind (consciousness) capable of knowing, and some kind of relationship (causality) between the world and the mind whereby the mind processes and organizes (identifies) its awareness of entities and their attributes in the world.

I consider these four concepts axiomatic because they are based on facts underlying the very concept of knowledge. As such, these four concepts constitute the main subject matter of metaphysics, which is the subject at the base of epistemology. (See also Ayn Rand 1990, 55–61 for a discussion of axiomatic concepts.) Along with our direct sensory awareness of the world, these four axiomatic concepts constitute the starting point we set out to find. They constitute the starting point of knowledge.

4.7 THE UNIVERSALITY OF THE UNIVERSE

Let us spiral back to a point I made in the first chapter of this book, when I wrote, "Thales found predictable patterns of action by entities close enough to touch, and by entities in the distant sky. All of these entities could be understood—at least to some degree—by man, using the same process of thought. This fact highlights another remarkable fact: that there must be something in common to all of these entities, to all the entities we perceive, that makes them all perceivable and knowable by the same means."

Taking into account that we perceive entities, we can state this point even more strongly: The fact that we can perceive entities in the distant sky means that these distant entities are acting on our senses in a regular way, just as closer entities do. This fact suggests strongly that distant entities are made of the same kind of materials and obey the same physical laws that closer entities do.

In short, our perception of entities provides a strong factual basis for the conclusion that our fundamental ideas are indeed universal, applicable to the entire universe that we perceive.

That is, all entities we perceive are similar in some fundamental way, by the very fact that we perceive them.

4.8   THE EPISTEMOLOGICAL STATUS OF PERCEPTION OF ENTITIES

It is now time to revisit another important fact about our perception of entities: Sometimes we make a mistake.

We have already considered the example of an image growing on a projection screen, giving the impression that the image is an approaching object. Such an example is an optical illusion, an automatic perceptual integration or association of an unusual combination of sensory information, leading to a mistaken assumption. Another example of an optical illusion is the proverbial straight stick looking crooked when partially submerged in water. But the stick feels straight when I run my hands over it.

Here is another kind of perceptual mistake. Suppose one of a child's toys is a green ball. The child knows much about the ball: It is green in hue, smooth in texture, light in weight, round in shape, of a size the child easily remembers, and it has a distinctive brown mark on one side. The child readily recognizes his ball in contrast to the other entities in his surroundings. But suppose one day at his friend's house he sees a green ball that, from his vantage point, looks just like his. He assumes that this green ball is his, but when he picks it up he notices that it does not have the distinctive brown mark. He then sees his own ball across the room, and he realizes that the ball in his hand is a different one—one that belongs to his friend.

Another example of this type is seeing a man from behind and mistakenly assuming it is your father.

Thus it is possible to be mistaken about a perception of an entity. You may think you are perceiving a certain entity, but you may really be perceiving another. Or you may be fooled by an optical illusion. Even animals, which do not have a conceptual faculty, make such mistakes. (See Gibson, 1986, 175–176.)

This possibility of mistaken perception is in contrast to the fact that one cannot be mistaken about one's sensing the world as a whole, or about one's sensing aspects of the world. The object of our sensing is unmistakably the world, and our sensory experience is unmistakably the experience it is. But when one ascribes the source of a collection or integration of sense data to a particular entity, one sometimes—albeit rarely—does so mistakenly.

Mistaken perceptions are possible because of the following fact: Perceptions are of something under a certain set of conditions, but not of every attribute of everything under every set of conditions.

Two important consequences of this fact are as follows:

- Two different entities might yield the exact same single perception. That is, although the same cause will always lead to the same effect, two different entities may cause indistinguishable effects. The danger in this case is that we might identify two different entities as the same entity. For example, a second green ball might, from one angle, look exactly like the green ball that you own. You might mistake the second ball for the ball that you own.
- The same thing under different conditions might be perceived differently. The danger here is twofold. We might identify the same entity as two different entities. For example, your green ball might in red light look black, and you might not recognize the ball as your own; you might think it is a different ball. Or we might identify the same entity as having contrary characteristics. For example, we might identify a stick as straight when it is on the ground, but crooked when it is partly submerged in water.

A typical person might not think of these consequences explicitly, but he treats his perceptions in a manner consistent with these consequences. When he makes his first mistakes, he probably is extremely confused, but he devises a method to deal with them. He knows that he is sometimes mistaken, but his mistakes are rare. For "everyday" identifications of entities, he trusts that he is right; for important identifications, he makes sure that he has enough correlating perceptual data, thereby greatly lessening the chance of error. For example, when he picks up his luggage at the airport, he looks at the identification tag and even may open the luggage to make sure someone has not swapped name tags. In effect, he is implicitly using a primitive method of induction—a volitional, conceptual method to override his automatic, perceptual faculty.

But someday, when his body of knowledge is great, mistakes seemingly small in isolation might lead to a disastrous sequence of mistakes. At that time, he will need to make this method of induction more explicit. (In Chapters 8 and 9, I will do just that.)

The process of using our conceptual faculty to override automatic perceptual integrations or associations is analogous to how a doctor, knowledgeable about medical science, might conceptually override the sometimes-inaccurate automatic detections of a patient's immune system. The process is also analogous to how a child or primitive man follows the guidance of his pleasure-pain mechanism, but how, with a grasp of ethics and other conceptual knowledge—such as medical knowledge—a man may override the usually-reliable but sometimes-misleading guidance of pleasure and pain. The process is also analogous to how we can use our conceptual faculty to override our emotional responses. The main difference with emotions is that, because they are based on evaluations, they are much more prone to mistake than are perceptual integrations, which are almost always accurate. But the principle is the same.

In Section 8.5, after we have covered concept-formation and other relevant considerations, we will revisit the issue of perceptual and conceptual mistakes.

4.9 SUMMARY REGARDING PERCEPTION OF ENTITIES

The cognitive stage of perception of entities is a great advance over the stage of mere awareness of the world as a changing whole. Only with the recognition of entities do we recognize the regularity by which the world causes effects on our consciousness. From this regularity, we become able to predict and affect the future to our advantage.

This kind of ability is mature for animals, but primitive compared to what man can do beyond the perceptual level. We have already touched on what man can do beyond the perceptual level, because we have already used various concepts and propositions. I have introduced the axiomatic concepts of existence, consciousness, identity, and causality. Also, I have introduced a conceptual, objective basis consistent with the similarities and differences that our perceptual faculty recognizes automatically and implicitly in the perception of entities. And everything I have written so far has been in the form of sentences, which express propositions. Through these concepts and propositions, we have been able to formulate knowledge that goes far beyond what an animal could grasp merely from the perception of entities.

But we can go much farther still by identifying explicitly the nature of concepts and propositions. After we have done so, we will be able to spiral back to our understanding of entities and provide inductive proof for our plausible assumption that entities will continue to act regularly, according to causal law, in the future.

Let us proceed then with a study of *concepts.*

5 CONCEPTS

In her *Introduction to Objectivist Epistemology* (*IOE*), Ayn Rand presents her theory of concepts. In the foreword, she writes (1990, 1),

> The issue of concepts (known as "the problem of universals") is philosophy's central issue. Since man's knowledge is gained and held in conceptual form, the validity of man's knowledge depends on the validity of concepts. But concepts are abstractions or universals, and everything that man perceives is particular, concrete. What is the relationship between abstractions and concretes? To what precisely do concepts refer in reality?

The remainder of her book answers those questions and more, explaining how concepts (symbolized by words) are formed, and how they must be used to serve cognition.

For the present book, I will expect the reader to have read *IOE*. I will rely on Ayn Rand's theory of concepts as explained in that book. I will, however, use this chapter to remind the reader of certain aspects of Ayn Rand's theory, because I will make heavy use of them. I will also make my own observations that may help clarify subsequent sections of the present book.

As in the previous chapters, I will continue to develop the threads regarding axiomatic concepts and similarity, difference, and range of measurement.

5.1   The Concept of 'Unit'

Essential to understanding concept-formation is understanding Ayn Rand's concept of 'unit'. (This concept is different from, though related to, the mathematical concept of a unit of measure.) Ayn Rand (1990, 6–7) writes,

> A unit is an existent regarded as a separate member of a group of two or more similar members. (Two stones are two units; so are two square feet of ground, if regarded as distinct parts of a continuous stretch of ground.) Note that the concept "unit" involves an act of consciousness (a selective focus, a certain way of regarding things), but that it is not an arbitrary creation of consciousness: it is a method of identification or classification according to the attributes which a consciousness observes in reality. This method permits any number of classifications and cross-classifications: one may classify things according to their shape or color or weight or size or atomic structure; but the criterion of classification is not invented, it is perceived in reality. Thus the concept "unit" is a bridge between metaphysics and epistemology: units do not exist *qua* units, what exists are things, but *units are things viewed by a consciousness in certain existing relationships.*

This concept of unit will be of particular importance in the chapter on propositions (Chapter 6), especially regarding my theory of meaning (Section 6.4.5) and regarding Ayn Rand's idea of "unit-economy." (See Ayn Rand 1990, 62–65, 69–74.) On unit-economy, Ayn Rand (1990, 63–64) writes,

> Whether the units with which one deals are percepts or concepts, the range of what man can hold in the focus of his conscious awareness at any given moment, is limited. The essence, therefore, of man's incomparable cognitive power is the ability to reduce a vast amount of information to a minimal number of units .... .

A concept substitutes one symbol (one word) for the enormity of the perceptual aggregate of the concretes it subsumes.

5.2 CONCEPT-FORMATION

Ayn Rand (1990, 83) summarizes concept-formation as follows:

The process of concept-formation consists of mentally isolating two or more existents by means of their distinguishing characteristic, and retaining this characteristic while omitting their particular measurements—on the principle that these measurements must exist in *some* quantity, but may exist in *any* quantity. A concept is a mental integration of two or more units possessing the same distinguishing characteristic(s), with their particular measurements omitted.

Ayn Rand (1990, 10) characterizes this mental integration as

a blending of the units into a *single* new *mental* entity which is used thereafter as a single unit of thought (but which can be broken into its component units whenever required).

Ayn Rand's idea of "measurement-omission" (1990, 11–18, 21–26) is fundamental to her theory of concepts, and therefore merits reiteration. Ayn Rand (1990, 12) writes,

Bear firmly in mind that the term "measurements omitted" does not mean, in this context, that measurements are regarded as non-existent; it means that *measurements exist, but are not specified.* That measurements *must* exist is an essential part of the process. The principle is that measurements must exist in *some* quantity, but may exist in *any* quantity.

When measurements are omitted in this process, a *range of measurement* is thereby specified (though not necessarily explicitly). Ayn Rand states her agreement with an unnamed colleague who says

(1990, 138), regarding the forming of the concept "blue" (a concept of a single characteristic),

> You see the blue of this object and the somewhat differ-
> ent blue of that other object; both have specific meas-
> urements, but those measurements fall into one cate-
> gory, as opposed to the measurements of some red ob-
> ject, which fall outside that category. So that the omis-
> sion of measurements is seeing the measurements as
> falling within a given range or category of measure-
> ments—.

The same colleague also says (Ayn Rand 1990, 138) that "you see blueness as a range or category of measurements" (within a broader range of colors). Indeed, any characteristic can be understood as a range of measurement. This understanding will be crucial to the theory of induction presented in the final chapters of this book.

5.3 KEY ASPECTS OF A CONCEPT

Before one can form a given concept, one must be aware of aspects of reality in the following forms:
1. A "pool" of units. (This word is my terminology, not Ayn Rand's.) This pool will later come to be grasped as the *genus* of the concept's definition. For a first-level concept (a concept formed directly from perceptual concretes, not other concepts) of a kind of entity (such as "stick"), this pool is either all entities in existence or all entities in one's perceptual field.
2. Individual units that constitute the pool. For a first-level concept such as "stick," such units are entities.
3. A conceptual common denominator (CCD). A CCD is an attribute shared by each unit in the pool. For a first-level concept of a kind of entity, all we know about each unit in the universe is that it is an entity, perceivable through its basic physical characteristics; therefore, the CCD is some basic physical characteristic such as shape, color, texture.

4. A distinguishing characteristic (DC). A DC is that attribute shared by the units subsumed by the concept but not by the other units in the pool. The DC is a range of measurement within the CCD. The DC will later come to be grasped as the *differentia* of the concept's definition.
5. The concept's units. This is the group of existents referred to, and to be subsumed by, the concept.
6. The sum of all the attributes of the concept's units. This sum is the content of the concept's "file folder," using Ayn Rand's (1990, 66–67) metaphor.

These six elements related to the first-level concept "stick" are as follows:

1. Pool: all entities, that is, all of existence.
2. Units in the pool: each specific entity in existence.
3. CCD: shape (some, but any, shape) and rigidity.
4. DC: a specific range of shape (long and thin to such an extent as to be graspable by the hand and to be used to extend one's reach) and rigidity (rigid enough to retain its shape when handled).
5. Concept's units: each entity with the shape and rigidity of a stick.
6. All the attributes of the concept's units: the range of shape, range of weight, range of rigidity, etc.

5.4   THE ROLE OF AXIOMATIC CONCEPTS IN FURTHER CONCEPT-FORMATION

As in our treatment of perception of entities, the axiomatic concepts of existence, identity, and consciousness are extremely important in our understanding of concepts, as we now shall see. Later, we will apply this understanding of axiomatic concepts in our treatment of propositions and induction.

Ayn Rand (1990, 58) writes:

> Since axiomatic concepts are not formed by differentiating one group of existents from others, but represent an integration of all existents, they have no Conceptual

> Common Denominator with anything else. They have
> no contraries, no alternatives. The contrary of the con-
> cept "table"—a non-table—is every other kind of exist-
> ents. The contrary of the concept "man"—a non-man—
> is every other kind of existents. "Existence," "identity"
> and "consciousness" have no contraries—only a void.
>
>   It may be said that existence can be differentiated
> from non-existence, but non-existence is not a fact, ...

In this section, I will discuss some ways in which axiomatic concepts do, in my judgment, have conceptual common denominators
and do differentiate one group of existents from others.

5.4.1   Existence and Identity

Note the implicit use of the concepts of existence and identity in
forming first-level concepts. Before first-level concepts such as
"stick" or "tree" can be formed, the world must be understood (at
least implicitly) to be not just a single whole, but also a group of all
its parts. That group of parts is existence. Further, all parts in that
group must have a characteristic that makes them mentally interchangeable and therefore capable of being mentally manipulated and
rearranged as units; these units must be kept track of as they are manipulated mentally. That characteristic is that they each have a specific and distinctive identity, an identity that one can remember
throughout one's mental manipulation—an identity that allows one
to grasp the same entity as the same, and a different entity as different—throughout the mental process.

    The Law of Identity is usually stated as "A is A", or a thing is what
it is. This kind of statement may seem to go without saying. One may
ask, "What fact in the world is this statement referring to, or what
fact requires me to state this?" One such fact was just described
above. That fact is based on the relation of the world we perceive to
our conceptual faculty. When we perceived entities, we were able to
do so because they persisted: they had a persisting identity that we
could distinguish and recognize. Now our volitional, conceptual

faculty requires that we process mental units—formed from memory—referring to those entities; in the course of this processing, it is possible for us to alter the mental units in ways that would ascribe a different identity to the same entity. The Law of Identity in this context tells us that we must not so alter the mental units, because entities in reality have only one, persisting identity. For example, the dogs we remember must be remembered as having paws and claws, not the hooves possessed by the horses we remember.

The concept of existence is the widest integration, subsuming every individual part. The concept of identity is the finest differentiation, in this respect: Each part is different from each other, but it is not different from itself—it *is* itself. After forming the concepts of existence and identity, we have the largest open-ended group (or conceptual common denominator)—existence—differentiated into its finest level of difference (or distinguishing characteristic)—each individual entity with its distinct identity. All further concepts classify entities at some intermediate level of differentiation and integration between these two.

5.4.2   Existence, Consciousness, and Objectivity

Existence differentiates existence (in the sense of a collective noun) from the faculty of consciousness, and it differentiates the state or an instance or the fact of existence from the state or an instance or fact of consciousness.

The importance of this differentiation of existence from consciousness is identified by Ayn Rand (1990, 57) when she writes:

> It is axiomatic concepts that identify the precondition of knowledge: the distinction between existence and consciousness, between reality and the awareness of reality, between the object and the subject of cognition. Axiomatic concepts are the foundation of *objectivity*.

Do not be confused by a slight variation between two usages of 'existence': Existence is differentiated from consciousness, and also subsumes consciousness. Existence is seen to subsume consciousness when we are conscious of our consciousness (either our faculty of consciousness or a particular state or instance of consciousness), when consciousness is the *object* of our cognition, when we perceive that consciousness *exists*.

The CCD for the distinction between existence and consciousness is 'role in cognition'. The two possible measurements of this CCD are 'object of cognition' and 'subject of cognition'. All objects of cognition are subsumed by the concept 'existence'. All subjects of cognition are subsumed by the concept 'consciousness'.

Note how Ayn Rand relates existence, consciousness, and objectivity in the passage quoted above. As epistemological or cognitive terms, "objective" does not refer to an object apart from a subject, and "subjective" does not refer to a subject apart from an object. Instead, both "objective" and "subjective" are relational and volitional terms; each term refers to a different kind of relation that an individual can choose to have between object and subject.

To be objective is to recognize that the causal interaction between existence and consciousness, for the purpose of cognition, depends on the nature of both. As Ayn Rand puts the matter on the final page of *IOE* (1990, 82),

> Objectivity begins with the realization that man (in-
> cluding his every attribute and faculty, including his
> consciousness) is an entity of a specific nature who
> must act accordingly; that there is no escape from the
> law of identity, neither in the universe with which he
> deals nor in the working of his own consciousness, and
> if he is to acquire knowledge of the first, he must dis-
> cover the proper method of using the second; that there
> is no room for the *arbitrary* in any activity of man, least
> of all in his method of cognition—and just as he has
> learned to be guided by objective criteria in making his
> physical tools, so he must be guided by objective criteria
> in forming his tools of cognition: his concepts.

5.4.3   Existence vs. Objects of Awareness

This differentiation of existence from objects of awareness, alluded to earlier, is derived from the differentiation of existence from consciousness, but is a crucial further differentiation and has two aspects.

'Existence' differentiates existence (in the sense of a collective noun) from (a) that which is perceived, and (b) that which is perceived at a certain time.

Let us consider differentiation (a) first. Existence is more than merely that which we perceive; it is more than merely the object of our perception. Existence is *independent* of our perception of it. It *exists*. In other words, if we are not perceiving it, it still exists. Moreover, if there are parts of existence that we have *never* perceived, those parts nevertheless exist. Existence includes *all* parts, whether perceived now, only in the past, or never.

This distinction of existence from that which is perceived is crucial to understanding the primacy of existence, which I discussed in Section 3.3. Not only does consciousness depend on existence, but existence does *not* depend on consciousness. Existence exists whether consciousness perceives it or not.

Of course, if we perceive something, then it exists. But the converse is not true. There exist things that we do not perceive at this time, that we have never perceived, and that we will never perceive. Grasping the distinction of existence versus that which is perceived enables us to hold the concept of existence as *open-ended*.

It is this differentiation made by the concept of existence that enables us to hold all other concepts as open-ended in the first respect identified by Ayn Rand: that a concept refers to an open-ended group of units. "For instance, the concept 'man' includes all men who live at present, who have ever lived, or will ever live." (Ayn Rand 1990, 17–18.) Without holding 'existence' to be open-ended, we would not be able to hold other concepts to be open-ended; the concept "man" could not mean anything wider than the men we perceive or have perceived.

Analogously, it is the realization that the concept of identity is open-ended in this first respect that makes possible our understanding that concepts are open-ended in the second respect identified by Ayn Rand (1990, 66–68): that a concept includes an open-ended set of its units' characteristics.

For the differentiation of existence from objects of awareness, the CCD is 'conceptual extent'. The conceptual extent of 'existence' is all of existence, whether perceived or not. The conceptual extent of 'objects of awareness' is less: merely those existents of which we are aware.

Let us now consider differentiation (b). The axiomatic concept of existence tells us that the existence we perceive at this moment and the existence we perceived at previous moments are *the same existence*. In other words, existence persists through time. Not only is existence a whole composed of parts, but it is a *persisting* whole. (See Ayn Rand 1990, 56–57).

The CCD for this distinction is 'inclusion or omission of psychological time measurements'. For existence, the psychological time measurements are omitted. For existence as perceived in a given moment or a limited duration, the psychological time measurements are included.

To summarize distinctions (a) and (b): Existence is the whole that exists in virtue of the fact that it *exists*, not in virtue of the fact that it was perceived at a particular time or perceived at *any* time.

5.4.4   Demonstrative Pronouns

A baby's first words are usually some kind of proper nouns—such as Momma, Dada, and maybe a specific object/process such as "bottle." But another kind of early word is a demonstrative pronoun, such as "this" or "that." The baby usually does not use the word "this" or "that"; rather, he might let out some vehement grunt while pointing anxiously at some object. But the grunt does mean "this" or "that."

The concept 'this' means some *one* (identity) of *all* (existence) to which one is pointing.

The concept of the demonstrative pronoun relies only on existence, identity, consciousness, causality, and unit (which includes volition), thusly: "This one (identity) of all (existence, or all in my field
of awareness), which I now perceive (consciousness and causality)
and (volitionally) isolate mentally (unit, which can be rearranged
mentally) by looking or pointing."

All first-level concepts of entities start with the same first two elements of a concept described earlier—namely, the universe of all
entities, that is, existence composed of units with their own identity,
or the pool of units in one's perceptual field. That is why the units of
a first-level concept can be identified ostensively, that is, by pointing,
that is, by the implicit use of a demonstrative pronoun—for example,
"these ones of all." Indeed, this fact is what makes first-level concepts
first-level; these concepts are the first step beyond the axiomatic concepts. Second-level concepts (such as "mongrel," compared to the
first-level concept "dog") refer to units that are not perceived units;
such units cannot be identified merely by pointing. Moreover, second-level concepts, even when they are widenings of first-level concepts (as is "furniture") often start with a *narrower* pool delimited by
some concept narrower than existence. (For example, for "furniture," the pool is all man-made objects, not all objects.)

5.4.5   A Derivative Differentiation: Existence vs. Non-
Existence

As this section will explain, the differentiation of existence from non-
existence is not a primary, but rather is derived from the primary
differentiations discussed above.

The differentiation of existence from non-existence is not a differentiation of existence as a collection of entities. There is no such
thing as non-existence to be differentiated from all the things that
exist.

Nor is non-existence an *attribute* of any thing. Things *exist*.
Therefore, a thing cannot have an attribute of non-existence. (See
Ayn Rand 1990, 58–59).

Consciousness cannot *sense* or *perceive* something that does not exist, but a human consciousness can *conceive* of 'something' that does not exist external to the conception itself. An object of perception must exist, but an object of *conception*—actually, a *projection* or *specification* of conception—might *not* exist. That is, one's conception might entail specifications that are not met by any existent. (I am using the term 'conception' to mean a product of my conceptual faculty that might or might not be a legitimate concept.)

One of the most important passages in this book is this passage from Section 3.3:

> How do we know that the external world we are conscious of is not our consciousness? Simply, we introspect to discern what our consciousness is, and we discern that the external thing we observe is not a state of our consciousness.

But when I introspect to discern what a conception is, I discern that the conception itself is indeed a state of my consciousness, a state that my own consciousness creates. I look out my window and see an automobile. I also recall memories of horses. I then form a conception, "horse-car," that is some kind of hybrid of an automobile and a living horse. I am aware of my own consciousness having formed and now holding this conception, as I am aware of my own consciousness holding the concepts "car" and "horse."

Of course, I could not have formed the conception "horse-car" or the concepts "horse" and "car" without having first been conscious of something that was not my consciousness, that is, of existence. And, in the future, if I recall this incident of having created the conception "horse-car," even the recollection and the word "horse-car" will be a memory recalled to my consciousness by something—my memory—that is not my consciousness.

The statement "Horse-cars do not exist" does not mean that the existents, horse-cars, do not exist; horse-cars are not existents. The statement means that the specifications entailed by the conception "horse-cars"—that some existent is both an automobile and a live horse—are not met by any existent. (Binswanger 2014, 180–181 makes a similar point.)

In normal usage, the statement "Jesus Christ existed" means that Jesus Christ, *qua* specification of conception, was also an existent.

In English, there is no way to distinguish this normal usage from the usage that means that Jesus Christ, who was an existent, was an existent. Therefore, in English, the statement "Existence exists" could mean either (1) that existence, *qua* specification of conception, also exists, or (2) that existence, which is that which exists, exists. I am stating that normal usage would imply the former meaning. (Nevertheless, in her statement "Existence exists" as the first philosophical axiom, Ayn Rand clearly intended the latter meaning. See 1990, 3–4, 59 and the next section.)

When we distinguish the fact or state of existence of some particular from non-existence, we are not directly characterizing existence external to consciousness; we are directly characterizing contents of consciousness. We are differentiating whether or not a certain conceptual content of consciousness specifies an existent.

Thus the distinction between existence and non-existence is based on the fact that a conception, whether a single concept or a combination of concepts, can entail specifications that might or might not be met by any existent.

But how can we know that the specifications entailed by a conception are not met by any existent? We can look at a specific entity and determine that it—its identity—is inconsistent with the specification, such as the specification "horse-car." But in order to determine that horse-cars do not exist, we must determine that *every* entity is inconsistent with the specification "horse-car."

Thus the statement "Horse-cars do not exist" means that the combination of specifications entailed by the conception "horse-car" is not met by any part in the whole of existence.

In other words, the statement "Horse-cars do not exist" is synonymous with the statement "Existence—the whole of existence, including everything we have or have not perceived—does not contain any existent whose characteristics are named by the conception 'horse-car'."

Thus the differentiation of existence from non-existence relies on the three primary differentiations of "existence":

- Existence vs. Consciousness (in the respect of existence vs. "projections or specifications of conception").
- Existence (The Whole) vs. Specific Parts, and Existence vs. Identity.
- Existence vs. Objects of Awareness.

To reiterate: In distinguishing existence vs. non-existence, we are not differentiating existents that exist from existents that do not exist (because all existents do exist). Moreover, we are not differentiating whether or not some instance or state of consciousness exists (because if a state of consciousness exists, it exists), nor whether or not some content of consciousness exists *qua* content of consciousness. Rather, we are differentiating whether or not the content of consciousness *corresponds to an existent specified conceptually by* the instance or state of consciousness.

Thus the concepts 'existence' (in this respect) vs. 'non-existence' are measurements of contents of consciousness, and their CCD therefore is 'measurement of content of consciousness'. If some content of consciousness does specify an existent in existence, then the measurement is 'existence'; otherwise, the measurement is 'non-existence'.

That existence vs. non-existence is not the primary distinction made by the concept 'existence' can be seen by noting how existence is defined ostensively—by how we point to it or indicate it. To indicate a particular existent, such as a chair, we point right at it and say, "I mean this." To indicate all of existence, we do not point with our left hand to a place to the left beyond existence, and point with our right hand to a place to the right beyond existence, and say, "I mean everything between these two places." Rather, we sweep our arms across our whole range of vision and say, "I mean this." In other words, the sweep across all is in contrast to the pointing at one particular.

5.4.6   Existence exists.

Finally, let us note what Ayn Rand meant by "Existence exists." She writes (1990, 59),

> The concept existence does not indicate what existents it subsumes: it merely underscores the primary fact that they *exist*. ...
>
> This underscoring of primary facts is one of the crucial epistemological functions of axiomatic concepts. It is also the reason why they can be translated into a statement only in the form of a repetition as a base and a reminder): Existence exists—Consciousness is conscious—A is A.

5.5   SIMILARITY AND DIFFERENCE

For an excellent discussion of Aristotle's conception that "things which differ may differ from one another more or less" (1941, *Metaphysics* Book X, Chapter 4, 1055a4–5), see Salmieri 2012, 41–44. For an excellent discussion of Ayn Rand's conception of similarity and difference, see Binswanger 2014, 110–117.

Section 5.5.1, directly below, draws on my understanding of Ayn Rand's conception of similarity and difference as explained by Ayn Rand and by Binswanger. The subsequent section contains my own additional thoughts.

5.5.1   The Objectivity of Similarity and Difference

As discussed in the previous chapter (Section 4.2.1 in particular), our perceptual faculty recognizes similarities and differences automatically. But it is important that we are able also to classify similarities and differences conceptually, and in a way that is consistent with the automatic classifications made by our perceptual faculty. We will see the importance of this consistency later, when we consider a full validation of the method of induction. Therefore, let us see how we identify a *conceptual* basis for similarity and difference.

Consider the following simple example. A man perceives a short stick (maybe a foot long), a longer stick (maybe a foot and a quarter long), and a still longer stick (maybe three feet long). He holds the short stick alongside the medium stick so that their left ends line up, and then the medium stick's right end extends past the short stick. He sees that for the common extent of both sticks, both sticks look and feel the same. But then for the remaining extent of the medium stick, there is no corresponding part of the short stick. He then lines up the right ends of the sticks. But then the left end of the medium stick extends past the short stick on the left. No matter how he tries to line up the sticks so that they are identical for the extent of the short stick, the medium stick will always extend past the short stick with nothing from the short stick to match it. The only ways for the short stick to match the medium stick would be for the short stick to be extended—that is, to be made longer—or for the medium stick to be cut and made shorter. If the short stick were made longer or the medium stick were made shorter, then both sticks would behave the same in terms of their lining up on both left and right.

Thus the man concludes that the two sticks are different, because one stick would have to be changed in order to be the same in length as the other stick.

The man detected a difference between these two entities by trying to make them the same, then seeing an unavoidable difference. In order to perform this mental procedure, he had to find a *commensurable characteristic* (in this case, length), by which he could see what it would take to make the entities the same. Then he saw that it would take a change to one of the entities. The short stick having the length it has (a foot long) precludes it from having the length of the medium stick. Thus the two entities are different, to the extent of this change.

The medium stick is more similar to the small stick than to the large stick, in that the extent or degree of change to make the medium stick like the short stick is less than the extent of change needed to make it like the long stick. The two extents of change could actually be compared to each other, and one found to be longer than the other.

(It may be that the perceptual systems detect similarity and difference on a logarithmic scale. For example, 3 would be as similar to 9 as to 1. The intensity of sound is often measured in decibels, a logarithmic scale. But the principles identified above still apply.)

Thus we have found an objective basis for stating that two existents are different, or for stating that two existents are similar in comparison to a third existent that they are different from. Whereas difference entails a comparison of at least two things, similarity entails a comparison among at least three things. 'Similarity' is 'less difference', by some objective measure.

The same point is made by an unnamed colleague (who we now know, from Binswanger 2020, is Harry Binswanger), and agreed with by Ayn Rand (1990, 138), as follows:

> Take the concept of "blue." You begin as a child with two blue objects of different shades perhaps (so their specific color measurements differ), and, say, one red object. And then you are able to see that the two blues belong together as opposed to the red; whereas if you just consider the two blues by themselves, you would only be aware of the differences between them. You wouldn't see them as similar until you contrasted them to the red.

Recall that the second of our three recurring themes is "similarity, difference, and range of measurement." Now we see why these three ideas go together. Similarity and difference exist with respect to ranges of measurement. For example, for a certain cognitive purpose we might consider a stick within the range of length of one foot and three feet a short stick, because they are of similar length compared to a stick twenty feet long.

Ayn Rand makes a direct connection between similarity and concept formation when she writes (1990, 13),

> The element of *similarity* is crucially involved in the
> formation of every concept; similarity, in this context, is
> the relationship between two or more existents which
> possess the same characteristics(s), but in different
> measure or degree.

Ayn Rand also states her agreement with an unnamed colleague (who we now know, from Binswanger 2020, is Allan Gotthelf) who says (1990, 140),

> similarity is the form in which we perceive certain
> quantitative differences within a range.

For example, all sticks have a similar shape compared to other objects. The characteristic shape of a stick is itself a range of measurement of shape—a range within which an object is thin enough to be graspable, long enough to extend the grasper's reach significantly, and not so long as to be unwieldy.

Indeed, a characteristic can be conceived of as a range of measurement. This perspective on a characteristic will be crucial to the theory of induction presented in Chapters 8 and 9.

5.5.2 Discovering Additional Commensurable Characteristics

Let us take a more difficult example. How do we know that hue is a commensurable characteristic of redness, blueness, etc.? How do we know that blue is commensurable with red, without knowing the science of light, wavelengths and frequencies? And although triangle and square are commensurable (as shapes), and blue and red are commensurable (as hues), why are blue and triangle not commensurable?

Two attributes are commensurable if they cannot both be attributes of the same entity at the same time ("in the same respect" would be redundant here)—that is, if one precludes the other. If you perceive one and then the other in the same entity, then the entity has changed.

A thing can be blue and square at the same time, but not (pure) blue and (pure) red, and not triangle and square, at the same time. How do we know these facts? In the case of blue and red, we observe many, many instances of red and blue appearing separately, and no instances of red and blue appearing in the same exact place. In the case of triangle and square, we know this fact by a certain kind of observation: the kind of observation we described in the previous section regarding sticks of differing lengths. A good name for this kind of observation is *comparison*. We grasp that an object cannot be triangle and square at the same time in the same respect, because we compare a triangular object with a square one and see that the triangle would have to change to square (or vice versa) in order for the two objects to look the same. The triangle would have to change from having three sides to having four sides.

In our previous example of sticks, the man could not have detected a difference between the two sticks by focusing on the hue of one and the length of the other. Why not? Because a certain hue does not preclude a certain length. A stick being blue (or any hue) does not preclude it being a foot long (or any length).

Isn't it interesting that scientists eventually found a mathematical unit by which to measure hues, and that scientists continually find units by which to measure characteristics we already knew to be commensurable? Here is the reason. Characteristics preclude one another when they are different quantities or measurements of the same thing. Weighing three pounds precludes weighing five pounds. Whatever the attribute being measured, having the measurement x precludes having the measurement y. The fact that we never see red and blue in the same place at the same time is evidence that different hues are different measurements of some underlying attribute, such as wavelength, amount of energy, etc.

However, we can see blue and bright at the same time in the same place; therefore, it is not surprising that blue and bright are measurements of two different attributes, hue and brightness. Moreover, we do see hues that resemble other hues. In the hue purple, we do see both a kind of blueness and a kind of redness. This fact suggests that blue and red, though in one respect commensurable because purple is in one sense neither blue nor red, are in another respect *not* commensurable, because purple is in another respect *both* blue and red. Not surprisingly, therefore, man eventually discovered that some hues are mixtures of non-commensurable, "primary" hues including blue and red. And today we know that we detect the different primary hues with different groups of nerves in our eyes.

In summary, to augment Ayn Rand's statement (1990, 11): "Length must exist in some quantity, but may exist in any quantity"—and may exist in only one quantity at a time in a given respect.

5.6   THE LAW OF NON-CONTRADICTION

The fact that some attributes preclude others is the basis for the Law of Non-Contradiction. This law tells you that when you know—by careful observation, comparison, and induction—that some attributes preclude others, don't forget it.

For example, when you know that red precludes blue in the same place at the same time, then—and only then—do you know that an object cannot be red and blue in the same place at the same time.

The Law of Non-Contradiction from Aristotle (2009, 1005b19–20) states,

> that the same attribute cannot at the same time belong
> and not belong to the same subject and in the same re-
> spect;

Do we ever perceive not belonging, literally? A thing cannot be blue and not blue at same time and in the same respect. Do we ever see "not blue"? No, we see red or green, which we *infer* is not blue, because we know by careful observation, comparison, and/or induction that if the thing is red (for instance), then it is precluded from being any other hue—including blue. We know that a red thing would have to change in order to be any other hue.

In a speech that she (Ayn Rand 1961, 117) describes as "the philosophy of Objectivism," Ayn Rand (1957, 1016) writes,

> Whatever you choose to consider, be it an object, an attribute or an action, the law of identity remains the same. A leaf cannot be a stone at the same time, it cannot be all red and all green at the same time, it cannot freeze and burn at the same time.

I add the following. You know the above facts about leaves, stones, red, green, etc., by experience, comparison, and induction. Then you form the more general principle that many attributes in the world preclude others. That general principle is the Law of Non-Contradiction. An entity cannot have two attributes that preclude each other. Or, to regard this principle from another perspective I noted earlier, an entity is not different from itself.

Let us illustrate the importance of the Law of Non-Contradiction by illustrating the bad result of allowing a contradiction. Take a simple example: considering an entity red. In so doing, we place the entity in a mental group of all red things; in regard to redness, the entity is interchangeable with the other entities in the group of red entities.

But suppose we also consider the entity to be not red. Then we have placed it in the group of all things that are not red; in regard to redness, the entity is interchangeable with the other entities in the non-red group.

Of course these facts cannot both be true, because then the entity would be different from itself. But the damage extends further.

Combining these two contradictory facts implies that, in regard to redness, our entity is interchangeable with every entity in existence; thus, in regard to redness, we are not distinguishing our entity from any other, and so we are not furthering our purpose of identification.

Because every entity is thought to be interchangeable with our entity in regard to redness, every entity, by transitivity, is thought to be interchangeable with *every other* entity in regard to redness. Thus we have obliterated the concept of redness; the concept no longer distinguishes any entity from any other; and further, the concept implies that every entity in existence is different from itself, and thus violates the Law of Identity.

When we relate the concept of redness to every other concept it depends on or on which it depends, those concepts too become obliterated. Because everything is ultimately related to everything else, the whole corpus of knowledge can eventually be destroyed. Thus the process of integration, reason's most crucial process, becomes a process for spreading a cognitive cancer.

Note how the Law of Non-Contradiction is not something known apart from or prior to experience. The law summarizes a great deal of experience. Only after identifying numerous instances of one characteristic precluding others do we reach the generalization that many characteristics preclude others. The Law of Non-Contradiction is a reformulation of that generalization.

5.7 ABSTRACTIONS FROM ABSTRACTIONS – WIDER AND NARROWER CONCEPTS

Chapter 3 of *IOE*, "Abstractions from Abstractions," begins with this paragraph (Ayn Rand 1990, 19):

> Starting from the base of conceptual development—
> from the concepts that identify perceptual concretes—
> the process of cognition moves in two interacting directions: toward more extensive and more intensive
> knowledge, toward wider integrations and more precise
> differentiations. Following the process and *in accordance with cognitive evidence*, earlier-formed concepts

are integrated into wider ones or subdivided into narrower ones.

For example, "tree" is a first-level concept, a concept that identifies perceptual concretes. A wider concept would be "plant," and a
narrower concept would be "oak."

To begin to understand the payoff of conceptualization over mere
perception of entities, consider the following simple example.

Looking at the ground, I perceive a mixture of rocks, twigs and
leaves. Then I exert mental effort to begin to employ my conceptual
faculty: I consider each of these objects as a unit, and I organize these
units, in my mind, into three conceptual groups: rocks, twigs, and
leaves. To aid in the conceptual process, I take physical action: I move
the objects into three corresponding piles before me.

Then I look at the pile of leaves. To my surprise, I notice differences among the leaves, differences that had hitherto escaped my notice. Some leaves are yellow, some are red with yellow around the
edges, some are a bit brittle, some are shriveled and very brittle, and
so on. When I look at the pile of rocks, I notice for the first time that
some rocks are smooth, some have sharp edges, some are gray and
some are yellow, and they vary in size. When I look at the twigs, I
notice differences among them too.

Only after having formed the concepts "rock," "twig," and "leaf"
do I perceive more subtle differences between one rock and another
rock, and so on. When I form more advanced concepts such as
"granite" and "slate," I thereby put my mind in a cognitive state of
being able to notice differences between one kind of granite and another kind.

As well as forming progressively narrower concepts, such as
"rock" (or "stone") to "granite," I can form broader concepts, thereby
making it possible for me to grasp similarities that I would not have
grasped by perception alone. For example, the twigs and the leaves—
which perceptually are very different—are parts of a tree, and are
more broadly organic compounds, meaning that they can be burned.

The same principles apply when we narrow and widen the concept "tree." Once I form the concept "tree" and focus my attention on trees only, I am in a better cognitive state to notice that some trees have leaves and some have needles. Once I have formed the concept "pine," I am in a better state to notice that the needles on some pine trees are green, and the needles on other pine trees are blue-green. Regarding widening, once I have formed the concepts "tree," "flower," and "grass," I am able to grasp similarities among trees, flowers, and grass as compared to other kinds of objects, and I am able to form the concept "plant" based on my observations that all such plants are stationary and need soil, water, and sunlight in order to grow.

In short, conceptualization opens the door to grasping a vast and subtle world of similarities and differences that we could never notice by perception alone. Each new concept is new knowledge and also a door to more new knowledge.

Now let us see how all of this conceptual knowledge is placed in a logical order that can be validated.

6 PROPOSITIONS

6.1 INTRODUCTION

A proposition is to a declarative sentence what a concept is to a word. For example, "The big red book fell off the table" is a sentence denoting a proposition.

Knowledge is stated not as isolated concepts but in concepts organized into propositions.

Imagine trying to read a book on American history, for example, in which there were no sentences, but rather just a series of words. Or imagine trying to write about the Civil War using only isolated concepts instead of propositions.

The questions answered by Ayn Rand for concepts should also be asked for propositions. To what precisely do propositions refer in reality? What is their role in cognition?

Ayn Rand (1990, 75) begins Chapter 8 ("Consciousness and Identity") of *IOE* with this passage:

> The organization of concepts into propositions, and the wider principles of language—as well as the further problems of epistemology—are outside the scope of this work, which is concerned only with the nature of concepts. But a few aspects of these issues must be indicated.
>
> Since concepts, in the field of cognition, perform a function similar to that of numbers in the field of mathematics, the function of a proposition is similar to that of an equation: it applies conceptual abstractions to a specific problem.

The present chapter attempts to build on Ayn Rand's theory of concepts in order to explain the meaning and cognitive function of propositions. I will explain how the specificity of propositions complements the "open-end" nature of concepts, in both senses of open-endedness described by Ayn Rand. (See Ayn Rand 1990, 17–18 for one sense of open-endedness, and 66–68 for a second sense.) Given a vocabulary of concepts, propositions allow more highly-differentiated and more intensively-integrated identifications than are possible merely by using each concept in isolation. One cognitive purpose thereby fulfilled by propositions is that this high degree of differentiation is achieved while preserving the unit-economy of concepts. The other purpose fulfilled by propositions is that, through an ordered sequence of propositions, one's knowledge can be put into highly specific, intensively integrated, logical orderings.

6.2   WHAT IS A PROPOSITION?

We all learned in grammar school that a proposition—or a declarative sentence, which symbolizes a proposition—is an expression of a complete thought. Aristotle (1941b, 42, 17a21) writes more specifically that a proposition "asserts or denies something of something." A proposition identifies, via the predicate, some attribute(s) of some existent(s) isolated via the subject.

Thus we can state a definition: A proposition is a sequence of concepts that consists of two parts—a subject and a predicate—which together express an identification by mentally isolating (via the subject) one or more existents, and identifying (via the predicate) one or more characteristics of those existents.

In short, the subject directs attention to the *existence* of some specific existent(s), and the predicate directs attention to some aspect(s) of the *identity* of the existent(s).

Let us take an example sentence: "The big red book fell off the table." The subject, "The big red book" directs attention to the existence of a certain existent—a certain book. The predicate, "fell off the table," directs attention to one aspect of that book's identity—namely, that the book fell off the table.

Before investigating in depth the cognitive function of propositions, it is simpler first to consider the means by which the subject and predicate perform *their* functions. The reason is that the subject and predicate are usually themselves sequences of words, and the means for understanding these simpler sequences have already been presented in *IOE*. After we address these simpler sequences, we will have more of a basis for understanding propositions.

6.3 PHRASES, INCLUDING SUBJECTS AND PREDICATES

6.3.1 Phrases Are Like Narrowed Concepts

In grammar, a phrase often is taken to mean a sequence of words without subject or predicate. However, I will use 'phrase' to denote any sequence of words (or concepts) less than a sentence (or proposition) but still integrated into a unit of thought. By this usage, subjects and predicates are two special kinds of phrases.

Though the subject of a sentence can be a single word, as in the sentence, "Man is rational," the subject is often a phrase—as in "An educated man knows philosophy." Likewise, a predicate can be one word, but is often a phrase.

In the sentence, "Man is rational," the subject "Man" directs our attention to all units subsumed under the concept "man." In other words, "Man" refers to all men.

In contrast, the subject "An educated man" is a narrower idea: it refers to a more delimited group of units; it refers only to a man who has the characteristic of being educated.

In general, a subject phrase is like a narrowed concept, as described by Ayn Rand (1990, 25–27), but without making use of a single word to denote it. For example, "drawer table" (modifying one of Ayn Rand's examples) is a phrase that means what the narrowed concept "desk" means, but without making use of that concept; "dining table" and "coffee table" (examples from Ayn Rand 1990, 23, 71) are phrases that are narrower than the concept "table," and for which there are no single concepts.

(This particular idea, that a phrase can be like a narrowed concept, is certainly not unique to me, nor do I cite Ayn Rand as the source of this idea. For one discussion of this idea, see Joseph 1916, 137. However, the larger thesis within which Joseph presents this idea is not one that I endorse.)

Another example from *IOE* (Ayn Rand 1990, 71) is "Beautiful blondes with blue eyes, …"—which is, of course, narrower than "blondes." The phrase "beautiful blondes" refers to only those units that are subsumed under the concept "blondes" and, of those units, only those units with a characteristic subsumed under the concept "beautiful." The phrase "beautiful blondes with blue eyes" refers to only those units that are subsumed under the phrase "beautiful blondes" and, of those units, only those units with a characteristic subsumed under the phrase "with blue eyes." Likewise, "red book" refers to only those units that are subsumed under the concept "book" and, of those units, only those units with a characteristic subsumed under the concept "red." Thus, to grasp the meaning of "red book," you can first think of "book" and then further specify, or overlay, the narrowing condition that the book be red.

In terms of Ayn Rand's theory of measurement-omission, adding the word "red" to "book" specifies an additional measurement, and thus the range of measurements specified by "red book" is narrower than the range of measurements specified by "book" alone. A book can be of any color; but a red book can be only the color red.

Now suppose we wanted to refer to a single concrete, but the concrete was not available for us to point to using a demonstrative pronoun. We would instead choose a sequence of words, and we would continue to add words to our sequence until there was only one concrete that was subsumed under the whole sequence. For example, we might say "the big red book on the table in the living room."

We start with the word "the" because we want at the end to refer to a specific existent (or group of existents) that we have in mind. Further, when we use the singular form of "book," we mean that when we are finished we intend there to be only one unit within the range of omitted measurements specified by the overlaying of concepts in the phrase. (The word "a" instead of "the" would mean "some or any one of the units" instead of the specific unit we have in mind.)

We have already overlaid "red" onto "book" to get the narrowed group of units represented by "red book." Now, let us overlay "big" onto "red book." We now have a smaller group of units subsumed by the overlaying of these three words. Thus "big red book" refers to only those units that are subsumed under the concept "book" and, of those units, only those units with the characteristics subsumed under both the concepts "big" and "red." The phrase "<u>the</u> big red book" indicates that there is only one such unit.

Now, what if in reality there is more than one such unit? Then the subject we have created is ambiguous; to remove the ambiguity, we must add more overlays until we have narrowed the range of measurement so that it specifies only the one unit we want to refer to. Let us add the prepositional phrase "on the table."

We will start by overlaying the word "on." This word refers to a specific kind of relational characteristic. The phrase "big red book on (something)" refers only to those units that are subsumed under the phrase "big red book" and, of those units, only those units with the characteristic of being on something. (The referents must be on *something*, because "on" in this usage is a relational characteristic.) Now let us overlay "table." Our new range of measurement is further restricted to big red books that are on a table. Now let's overlay the "the" that precedes "table." This word indicates that, in our context, there can be only one table we mean; therefore, our new range of measurement is further restricted to subsume only those big red books that are on the specific table we intend to refer to. But suppose it is not clear which table that is; then we must add the further overlay, "in the living room." The pattern of overlay for "in the living room" likewise continues one word at a time. After we have overlaid all the words in the full phrase, we see that there is only one particular existent we can be talking about, and we have succeeded in specifying the existent we originally had in mind.

Thus phrases enable us to take general, open-ended devices—concepts—and use them in combination to specify groups of existents of any useful size or classification, down to the size of a single existent. Without phrases, we would need more concepts than there are existents in reality, and we would thereby defeat the purpose—unit-economy—of concepts in the first place. Phrases enable us to apply abstractions—which refer to open-ended groups of existents—to identify smaller groups of existents, or a single existent.

We can make an analogy with analytic geometry: A phrase is like a set of coordinates in which each word in the phrase is a coordinate. The referents of the phrase are only those existents that match the full set of coordinates.

Thus far, we have examined subject phrases. What about predicate phrases? Consider the sentence, "The big red book fell out the window." The predicate phrase is "fell out the window."

The predicate "fell," by itself, denotes a certain characteristic of the subject. By overlaying the words "out the window," we narrow the range of measurement referred to by the concept "fell"; we specify the characteristic more narrowly.

Thus, as with phrases in the subject, a phrase in the predicate is like a narrowed concept.

In a later section, we will discuss some partial exceptions to the rule that a phrase is a narrowing.

6.3.2   The Integrating Role of Phrases

The preceding section focused on the differentiating role of phrases; let us now consider the integrating role.

Observe how, when dealing with phrases, as with single words, our main focus is not the words but rather the units referred to by the words. A few seconds after having uttered or heard the phrase "the big red book on the table in the living room," one might not be able to repeat it verbatim; but one distinguishes the unit in reality being referred to by the phrase, and one could reconstruct the phrase—or an equally accurate one—by focusing on the unit and then thinking of what phrase would isolate that unit. Indeed, even in the midst of constructing or hearing a phrase, one's mind is primarily focused on the units being referred to, not on the phrase itself.

Often, however, it is important to remember a phrase verbatim in order to focus on precisely the right group of units *isolated according to precisely the right set of characteristics*. In such cases, the phrase should be written out. The cognitive rules for what makes precisely the right phrase are analogous to the cognitive rules for what makes the right definition of a concept. The phrase should differentiate precisely the right units, *isolated according to their essential distinguishing characteristics in the given context*. For example, in the context of wanting to locate a book, it is better to use the phrase "the red book on the table" than "the book, somewhere in the house, with 356 pages."

Observe that these two phrases may both refer to the same object, including all the characteristics of that object; both phrases refer to an object that is a book, that is red, that is on the table, that is 356 pages long, and that has many other characteristics not mentioned explicitly in either phrase. But the two phrases imply two different cognitive *hierarchies* of characteristics. The first phrase implies that, in the given context, the fundamental characteristics (those characteristics, at the base of the cognitive hierarchy, that best imply the others) are that the object is a book, that it is red, and that it is on the table. These characteristics are indeed the fundamental ones in the given context: once the book is located, all of its other characteristics—such as author and title—can be observed.

In another context, "the red book on the table" would be a bad way to specify the given object, and a better way would be "my

autographed copy of *Atlas Shrugged*" as in "My autographed copy of
Atlas Shrugged is my most prized possession."

Later I will discuss how all phrases have certain characteristics of
definitions—which are themselves phrases.

The above example illustrates that a phrase, while being a narrowing of some concept—that is, while being a more precise differentiation than one of its constituent concepts—is not a step in the direction of pre-conceptual, concrete-bound mental functioning. A
phrase is like a narrowed *concept;* like a concept, a phrase is an integration. Indeed, a phrase represents more advanced—in the sense of
being more intensive—conceptual knowledge than its constituent
concepts do. Recall Ayn Rand's (1990, 19) opening paragraph of *IOE*,
Chapter 3, "Abstractions from Abstractions":

> Starting from the base of conceptual development—
> from the concepts that identify perceptual concretes—
> the process of cognition moves in two interacting direc-
> tions: toward more extensive and more intensive
> knowledge, toward wider integrations and more precise
> differentiations. Following this process and in accord-
> ance with cognitive evidence, earlier-formed concepts
> are integrated into wider ones or subdivided into nar-
> rower ones.

In relation to its constituent concepts, a phrase is a subdivision of
one of those constituent concepts into a narrower mental integration. In relation to its referents, a phrase is a more precise differentiation—and a more intensive and thorough integration—of its referents than is afforded by any of its constituent concepts individually.

Note the relationship between more intensive, thorough integration and more precise, narrow differentiation. Every time we added
a word (for example, "red") to our subject phrase, we specified another characteristic of our referent-units. In so doing, we made another integration of our referent-units with other units in reality (all
red things), thereby intensifying the overall integration performed by
the phrase; and, in so doing, we decreased the number of referent-

units that meet all of the specifications of the full subject phrase
(there being fewer red books than books).

One might ask, "If a phrase is always narrower than one of its
concepts, how do we refer to a wider group of units?" The answer is
to use one of four options: Remove words from the phrase (for example, use "book" instead of "red book"); or use a wider concept (for
example, use "object" instead of "book)"; or *coin* a wider concept; or
use a conjunction, such as "and" (which will be explained in the section on partial exceptions) or "or," plus another concept or phrase
(for example, use "orange or red book" instead of "red book").

6.3.3   A Class of Example Phrases: Definitions

Every definition is a phrase. For example, the definition of "man" is
"the rational animal."

Every definition has a genus and differentia. (The genus of the
definition of "man" is "animal.") The full definition is a differentiation within the genus; thus, the full definition is narrower than the
genus alone.

A definition's genus is either a word or itself a phrase. For example, in the definition of "pencil," the genus is "implement for writing." If the genus is a phrase, that phrase itself is a narrowing of some
part of the phrase. (In this example, "implement for writing" is a narrowing of the concept "implement.") The whole phrase is narrower
than some part; and if that part is itself a phrase and not a single concept, then that phrase too can be seen to be a narrowing of some part
of itself. We can continue this process of analysis until the part we
examine is a single concept in the original phrase. Thus we see that a
whole definition is narrower than some concept in the definition.

Every phrase—not only a definition—can be thought to have a
genus and differentia. The phrase as a whole is a differentiation
within the phrase's genus; thus the full phrase is narrower than the
phrase's genus alone.

Take our earlier example, "the big red book on the table in the
living room." We can think of "book" as the genus, and the rest of

the phrase as the differentia. Or, we can think of "the big red book" as the genus (with "on the table in the living room" as the differentia), and then think of "book" as the genus of that genus. Either way, we see that the full phrase is a differentiation within—that is, a narrowing of—the concept "book."

Consider the prepositional phrase "on the table." We can think of the concept "on" as the genus (because it refers to all relations in which one existent is on another), and the rest of the phrase as the differentia (because it narrows the original referent group so that it refers only to relations in which an existent is on the table.)

Thus we see another sense in which every phrase is both an integration and a differentiation. Some concept (designated by a single word) in the phrase is a genus. Without some single concept performing that function, there is no single connection of the phrase's referents to one's wider context of knowledge. In short, for the same reasons that a definition needs a genus, so does any phrase. Every phrase includes some one concept (a genus) that is wider than the full phrase, and that is narrowed by the full phrase.

Moreover, principles that apply to the objective formulating of definitions also apply to the objective formulating of phrases. For example, a phrase, to be objective, must not be too broad or narrow in its designation of units; and, as explained earlier, it must obey the rule of fundamentality. (For principles of formulating objective definitions, see Ayn Rand 1990, 40–54).

6.3.4 Further Understanding Through Partial Exceptions

Now consider some partial exceptions to the rule that phrases are narrowings.

Consider a non-restrictive phrase or clause that modifies a noun. For example: "Man, needing to sustain his life, must take physical action." The phrase "needing to sustain his life" describes, but does not narrow, the subject "man"; instead, the referent-group of the full subject is left unchanged. However, it is interesting to note that another name in grammar for a non-restrictive element is a *non-*

essential element, which is why such an element is set off by commas. Therefore, a non-restrictive element can be thought of as a separate phrase apart from the subject.

Keep in mind that "non-essential" in this context does not mean "unimportant." Nevertheless, setting a phrase off as non-restrictive does make the phrase less important, subordinating the phrase to the main part of the subject. (See Section 6.4.2 for the function of non-restrictive elements.)

The fact that non-restrictive elements have the name "non-essential" is further evidence that a subject phrase is generally a narrowing of at least some one concept in that phrase itself.

Here is another partial exception, which applies to predicate phrases. In the sentence "This car is new," consider the predicate phrase "is new." Now suppose we add a word to create the predicate "is almost new." The adverb "almost" has not *narrowed* the range of measurement denoted by the predicate "is new"; instead, "almost" has altered or *modified* that range of measurement.

According to a well-known grammar book (Warriner 1982, 9), "To *modify* means 'to describe or make more definite.'" But, as the above partial exception shows, sometimes "to *modify*" means literally to modify—that is, to change.

Other partial exceptions similar to the word "almost" are adverbs such as "nearly" and "not." For example: "This car is not new."

The modification of the concept "new" to arrive at the phrase "almost new" involves two steps: first a widening, and then a narrowing. To understand the meaning of "almost new," one must understand something about the range of measurement that includes "new" as one of its measurements. One must know that "new" is a measurement of age or degree of use. In effect, we widen our focus from "new" to "of some age or degree of use." This is the widening step. The next step is a narrowing: we re-narrow "of some age or degree of use" down to a measurement commensurable with and near to "new." Because "new" means "of age zero or used not at all," "almost new" therefore means "of age nearly zero or used only to a small degree." In other words, the concept "age" (or the phrase "degree of use") is implicit, and is indeed the *implicit genus*, in the phrase "almost new."

The case of the concept "not" is analogous to the case of "almost." The concept "not" means "characterized by a measurement that excludes some other commensurable measurement to be specified." The phrase "not new" is a modification (a widening followed by a narrowing) of "new." To understand the meaning of "not new," one again must know that "new" is a measurement of age or degree of use; one must also know some other measurement of age or degree of use—such as "old." (After all, "blue" is not an example of being "not new" in the sentence "This car is not new.") Again, the concept "age" or the phrase "degree of use" is the implicit genus of the phrase. The whole phrase with the implicit genus made explicit would be something like "an age not new."

Now consider an analogous example pertaining to subject nouns. Consider the prefix "non-" placed before a subject noun, as in the following proposition: "Non-students should sign in before attending the lecture." Observe that this statement is not an invitation for people to bring their pet monkeys to the lecture. The subject-phrase "non-student" contains an implicit concept, which is also the phrase's implicit genus: "people." "Non-students" means "*people who are non-students.*" Observe how the application of the prefix "non-" to "students" causes a two-step process: a widening followed by a narrowing. First, the concept "student" is widened to the implicit concept "people," and then "people" is re-narrowed to a new range of measurement commensurable with the measurement "student." In the case of "non-," that new range of measurement is every measurement *except* "student."

Now consider the word "and." This word, in one of its usages, builds groups of existents into a wider group. For example, the subject "Americans and Canadians" refers to a wider group than either "Americans" or "Canadians."

Nevertheless, this seeming exception helps to confirm the rule. When there is no special word (namely, "and") supplied, narrowing (or modifying) is the rule. In order for there to be widening, the phrase must include a special word whose only purpose is to denote the widening. Moreover, even a phrase using "and" entails a narrowing of an implicit genus.

Consider the statement, "John and lunch are already in the conference room." One would not normally make such a statement, and one would be confused hearing it. One might eventually realize that the speaker means, "Some of the things—John, lunch—that we need for the conference are already in the conference room." In other words, the sentence makes sense only if one grasps how John and lunch are commensurable. Once one sees the commensurability, one performs the indicated widening step, arriving at the implicit genus "some of the things we need for the conference"; then one must re-narrow that phrase by adding "John" and "lunch," which are the two narrowing measurements that constitute the differentia.

Consider Ayn Rand's (1990, 37) example, "Smith, Jones, and Brown are walking." The word "and" again indicates that one must first perform a widening integration by knowing some commensurable characteristic that becomes the implicit genus of the phrase, and then one must perform a re-narrowing step by specifying the measurements "Smith," "Jones," and "Brown." In this example, the implicit genus is "individual." With the implicit genus included, the full statement is: "The individuals Smith, Jones, and Brown are walking."

One would not normally say, "Smith, Jones, and Jones' dog are walking." The reason is that the commensurable characteristic, and thus the genus, is not obvious. When using "and," one must take care that the implicit genus is obvious. Otherwise, the genus must be stated explicitly.

Thus we see a common thread in all the partial exceptions that involve some widening: the genus of the phrase is *implicit*. The entire explicit part of the phrase is the differentia, which narrows the implicit genus. The fact that the genus is only implicit in these cases is the reason that these cases are (partial) exceptions. In most cases, clarity requires that the genus be stated explicitly.

6.3.5   The Mathematics of Narrowing and Widening

As we have seen, one can refer to a widened group of units (such as "Americans and Canadians" from "Americans" and "Canadians") by using concepts such as "and" and "or." But such constructions are the (partial) exception, not the rule. The main reason is that, in most contexts, such phrases would not be well-integrated; they would not have a clear genus. For example, in most contexts, "my hammer, screwdrivers, pliers, and wrench" would not be as well-integrated as "my tools."

Related to the issue of integration is the issue of efficiency, or unit-economy. A grammar built on narrowings is much more unit-economical than is a hypothetical grammar that might be built on widenings, as the following example shows.

Suppose there to be a simple environment which contains only one thousand different kinds of objects. Suppose these objects come in ten different shapes (sphere, cube, egg, doughnut, disc, cone, pyramid, wedge, bell, and dumbbell), ten different colors (red, purple, orange, yellow, green, blue, violet, brown, black, and white), and ten different materials (stone, marble, plastic, wood, clay, brass, steel, ivory, lead, and porcelain).

In English, any one of these kinds of objects can be identified by a phrase of only three words—for example, "green porcelain bell" or "blue steel cube." Each word is like a coordinate measurement; "green" is a coordinate measurement on the "color" axis, "porcelain" is a coordinate measurement on the "material" axis, and so on. Each word in the phrase divides the number of kinds of objects by ten; for example, there are a thousand kinds of objects, a hundred kinds of cubes, ten kinds of steel cubes, and one kind of blue steel cube. Most importantly, to specify any of the thousand different kinds of objects, only at most thirty-four concepts are needed: ten concepts for colors, ten for materials, ten for shapes, and—for good measure—the concepts "color," "material," "shape," and "object."

But what if we had a language that tried to go in the opposite direction, starting from narrow concepts and using combinations of words to form wider concepts? First off, we would have to have a thousand different concepts, one for each combination of material, shape, and color. We would have no coordinate system. Instead of having different concepts for different measurements along each of three coordinate axes, we would need a different concept for each location in the three-dimensional coordinate "space."

Moreover—supposing that we did indeed take the trouble to form a thousand different, cognitively confusing, narrow concepts—observe the difficulty we would face in combining them to form wider groups. Suppose we had a different word for each different-colored steel cube (such as blip, glip, plip, etc.), and we wanted to identify the group consisting of steel cubes of any color. We would have to string ten words together (e.g., blip glip plip etc.). And if we wanted to identify cubes of any color or material, we would have to string a hundred words together. Thus we see this contrast between using phrases—instead of new concepts—to narrow vs. to widen: Whereas narrowing permits iterative *division* of the group of referents being identified, widening requires repeated, tedious, non-integrated *addition* of more concepts than one can keep in one's mind at one time.

In our normal English usage, it is rare to widen common groups by using a widening conjunction. For example, one would say, "This movie is in color" instead of "This movie is in blue and green and red and yellow, etc."

On the other hand, one *would* say, "This movie is in black and white." And one would usually say "nuts and bolts" instead of "industrial fasteners," and one might say "brothers and sisters" instead of "siblings." In these cases, there are only two possible measurements for the quality in question, and conjoining only two concepts may not cause a mental overload. But most qualities, such as color, have many more than two possible measurements, making it over-loading and disintegrated to widen without coining a new concept.

Now that we understand phrases, we are ready to return to propositions.

6.4 THE COGNITIVE ROLE OF PROPOSITIONS

6.4.1   The Purpose of Propositions

Propositions make an identification more specific than is possible with single concepts or even with phrases. A proposition allows one to hold in one's mind a specific item of knowledge—to focus on a specific characteristic (or specific combination of characteristics) of a specific unit (or specific group of units).

Consider the concept "man." Having that concept as adults, we know many characteristics of the units referred to by that concept. We know that men are rational, that they have two arms, legs, eyes, and ears, that they see, hear, speak, etc. We also know there are other characteristics of men that are still to be learned. Now consider the sentence, "Man has a nose." By stating this proposition, we are directing our attention to one of the many facts we know—a fact that we may have just discovered—about man. We are specifying a bit of our knowledge more narrowly than we would by just calling the word "man" into consciousness.

As Peikoff writes in "The Analytic-Synthetic Dichotomy" (1990, 100),

> A similar type of analysis is applicable to *every* true
> statement. Every truth about a given existent(s) reduces,
> in basic pattern, to: "X is: one or more of the things
> which it is." The predicate in such a case states some
> characteristic(s) of the subject; …

Cognitively, such specificity is extremely valuable. By calling some specific fact about the referents of a concept or phrase into one's awareness, one is in a better position to observe or infer other facts that may depend upon the identified fact.

Most importantly, by using propositions to be more specific about what one knows, *one can put one's knowledge in order,* an order much more specific than is possible with isolated concepts alone. One can form an ordered series of propositions, each proposition representing a specific item of knowledge. In the realm of thinking, order means *logical* or *hierarchical* order. For example, one can say, "Man has eyes. *Therefore,* man can see."

Let us take a more complex example: "A body at rest or in uniform motion will remain at rest or continue in uniform motion unless acted upon by an external force." This is a statement of Newton's First Law of Motion.

This statement illustrates that a proposition, while narrower and more specific than individual concepts that make it up, can still be enormously broad. Yet this particular proposition is still much more specific than the concept "body," which includes many other characteristics. For example, a body obeys *all* of Newton's laws and has mass, size, weight, shape, color, etc.

Consider how such a broad proposition as Newton's First Law can be known. It was arrived at through a long and careful process of inductive and deductive reasoning. Many, many prior, more-specific propositions had to be stated. For example: "This ball, when pushed with this much force, rolls at this rate in the first second and at this rate during the next second, etc." Many intermediate inductions and deductions also had to be stated. Only after this long sequence of propositions could Newton arrive at his First Law. This sequence is a specific, hierarchical ordering of specific items of knowledge into a logical argument, culminating in the argument's concluding proposition: Newton's First Law. Such a specific ordering is not possible through sequences of lone concepts or phrases. Imagine if Newton could write in his *Principia* only isolated words instead of full sentences.

An explication of how propositions are sequenced to form logical inductive and deductive arguments is beyond the scope of this book. Such an explication would address, among other issues, maintaining context from one proposition to the next.

Here is another perspective on the cognitive value of putting one's knowledge in order through the use of propositions. The very act of using propositions to order one's knowledge creates derivative orderings that function as cognitive "shortcuts." For example, once one has proved that "a body at rest or in uniform motion will remain at rest or continue in uniform motion unless acted upon by an external force," one can remember this proposition without having to recall the long ordering of propositions that was needed for the proof. In effect, one has created a new "shortcut" or "hyperlinked" ordering, in which the predicate "will remain at rest or continue in uniform motion unless acted upon by an external force" is now earlier than before in the hierarchy of known facts about the subject "a body at rest or in uniform motion." Of course, this "hyperlinked" ordering makes it much easier to apply Newton's First Law to particular cases that arise. (Imagine instead having to re-prove Newton's First Law every time one wanted to apply it.) To solidify this proposition's important place in one's hierarchy of knowledge, the proposition can be given its own conceptual name: "Newton's First Law."

Because propositions are more specific than single words, it might take thousands of propositions, each identifying one more fact, to identify all the facts included in one concept. As Ayn Rand (1990, 48) writes,

> on the higher levels of abstraction, a concept stands for
> chains and paragraphs and pages of explicit proposi-
> tions ... .

Although a man knows only several thousand different words, he may have to read or write hundreds of thousands of sentences—in several books—to grasp or explain just one topic (such as the history of the founding of the United States of America), which is itself much narrower than the specific concept "history." The purpose of a book is to put a substantial body of conceptual knowledge into a particular order, an order that will allow one to validate each item of knowledge in turn and to acquire more knowledge.

Moreover, many concurrent orderings are possible, in accordance with cognitive need. Many of the same propositions in a history of the founding of America might go, in a different order, into a book on political philosophy.

The power of sequences of propositions to place items of knowledge into a specific order is essential not only for adding new knowledge to one's hierarchy, but also for making implicit knowledge explicit. Although words and sentences may seem indispensable for thinking, men must have had thoughts about entities before a vocabulary and grammatical language were invented. For example, some caveman must have thought that a certain cavewoman is pretty, or that climbing a mountain takes great effort. In the same way, a child can know implicitly—before being able to state a proposition—that man has the faculties of sight, hearing, etc. Therefore, the child can form the concept "man" without first having expressed his knowledge of each attribute of man in a series of explicit propositions. But once the child *can* express each thought in a proposition, he can scrutinize each thought more carefully than he could when the thought was only implicit. He can keep track of each thought in its proper, logical sequence, return to each thought when it can help him understand another fact, and so forth.

This relation between concepts and propositions highlights the very importance of philosophy. Although propositions are more specific than concepts in the particular facts they designate, we formed some important concepts before we knew how to form explicit propositions. And we may have formed many important concepts—such as values, rights, logic—without having based these concepts on a detailed, precise sequence of propositions. In philosophy, we use propositions to direct our attention back to the initial forming of these concepts. Then we use propositions to form these concepts again, to make sure they are valid, to help us see further implications of what we already know, and to specify and ultimately simplify our hierarchy of knowledge.

Now that we have explained the purpose of propositions, let us examine the mechanics by which propositions fulfill this purpose. To that end, we will examine the role of the axiomatic concepts of existence and identity in the forming of propositions.

6.4.2   Existence and Identity in Propositions

Recall my statement earlier: The subject directs attention to the *existence* of some specific existent(s), and the predicate directs attention to some aspect(s) of the *identity* of those existent(s). Let us examine this principle in more depth, first considering the subject and then the predicate.

How does the subject direct attention to the existence of some specific existent(s)? If we keep invoking more and more aspects of an existent's identity, eventually that existent will be the only one in existence that has that combination of attributes, and we will have thus uniquely identified that existent. That is what a subject does. Each concept of the subject invokes another aspect of the existent's identity. For example, "The big red book on the table in the living room" invokes the fact that the existent is big, is red, is a book, is on something, etc. The subject successfully performs its function when it has invoked enough of the existent's identity so that this existent cannot be confused with any other. Our subject is complete if the big red book on the table in the living room is the *only* big red book on the table in the living room.

Thus the subject invokes aspects of an existent's *identity* in order to direct attention to the existent's *existence*. And, of course, the existent's existence includes *all* of the existent's characteristics.

The predicate, on the other hand, relies on the existent's existence established by the subject, and directs attention to some aspect(s) of the existent's *identity*.

Just as a subject phrase narrowly specifies some existent(s), so a predicate phrase narrowly specifies some characteristic(s) of that existent. An example is the predicate "fell off the table."

It can be said that a subject and a predicate perform two different kinds of identification of an existent, or that they *identify* the existent in two different senses of the term 'identify'. The subject identifies an existent by naming enough characteristics to differentiate that existent from all others. The predicate identifies an existent in the sense that it names some specific characteristic(s) of that existent. Furthermore, it can be said that a predicate identifies a characteristic in the same sense that a subject identifies an existent.

Finally, a third kind of identification can be distinguished: an identification performed by a proposition, combining both subject and predicate.

To illustrate the difference between subject and predicate, consider the sentence, "The big red book on the table in the living room is old." And compare this sentence to the phrase, "the big, old red book on the table in the living room." The phrase names exactly the same attributes as does the original sentence. But the phrase does not focus our attention on any one of the attributes it names; our attention is spread equally among all the named attributes. Indeed, if this phrase is used as the subject of a sentence, what the phrase focuses on primarily is not the named *attributes* of the book, but rather the *existence* of the book—*through* its named attributes. Some aspects of the book's identity are invoked in order to focus on the book's *existence* including *all* its attributes. In contrast, our original sentence focuses on *one* attribute specified by the predicate: that the book is *old*.

Let us take a few more examples of propositions.

"Man is rational." The predicate identifies one characteristic of the existents identified by the subject. In this example, because the subject is only one word, the subject directs attention to a wide range of concretes, not just one concrete as in our prior example.

"Men born in America are eligible to be President." Here the subject is more than one word, and so is narrower than "man," but it is not so narrow as to specify only one concrete.

"The man is tall and thin." Here we see the word "and"—this time in the predicate—specifying a pair of attributes rather than a pair of entities as in one of our earlier examples with "and." In this predicate usage of "and," the phrase containing "and" specifies a set of characteristics that is more extensive than "tall" and "thin" separately. The implicit genus is something like "in possession of physical characteristics of being." (The precise genus depends on the context in which the proposition is placed. For instance, if the context is a discussion of the physical virtues of the man, then the genus is "in possession of physical *virtues* of being.") The full phrase, including the implicit genus, is therefore "in possession of physical characteristics of being tall and thin." Observe that one would not normally say something like "The man is tall and early"—except for comic effect. In such a proposition, the implicit genus of the phrase "tall and early" is obscure.

Now recall our prior example containing the non-restrictive phrase. "Man, needing to sustain his life, must take physical action." In stating this proposition, we are first calling attention to the existence of man, and then we are calling attention to the fact that one aspect of man's identity, that he must take physical action, is a consequence of another aspect of his identity, that he needs to sustain his life.

No matter how complex we make our examples, the pattern of identification is the same. The subject directs attention to existence (through aspects of identity); the predicate builds from existence, indicated by the subject, and directs attention to an aspect of identity.

6.4.3   Propositions' Specificity as Complement to Concepts' Open-Endedness

Let us now return to the idea that propositions are narrower and more specific than some individual concept they contain. We have seen how this idea holds in two ways:

- The proposition's subject, when it is a phrase (for example, "the big red book") and not just a single word, identifies a group of existents that is narrower than the group of existents identified by at least one of the individual concepts (for example, "book"). In other words, the subject phrase further limits the range of measurements specified by one of the individual concepts (the genus) in the subject.

- Second, the proposition's predicate (for example, "is old") identifies a set of the subject's characteristics (being old) that is narrower than the set of all of the subject's characteristics (is old, worn, red, written by Chaucer, etc.).

These two ways of narrowing correspond to and complement the two respects in which a concept is "open-ended," as described by Ayn Rand in *IOE*.

The first sense of open-endedness is that a concept refers to an open-ended group of units:

> For instance, the concept "man" includes all men who
> live at present, who have ever lived, or will ever live.
> (Ayn Rand 1990, 17–18).

The subject of a proposition narrows this open-ended group down to either a smaller open-ended group (for example, "A good man," "Big red books") or a definite group (for example, "The oldest man alive," "Those two big red books").

The second sense of open-endedness is that a concept includes an open-ended set of its units' *characteristics*. (Ayn Rand 1990, 66–68.) The predicate of a proposition narrows this open-ended set down to a smaller set of characteristics (usually one or a few; for example, "is old," "is old and gray").

The first way of narrowing enables us to specify referent-groups of any size and composition while preserving the unit-economy of concepts. The second way of narrowing enables us to focus more specifically on certain characteristics; therefore, by constructing a *sequence* of propositions, we can put our knowledge into a very specific, intensively integrated, logical order.

6.4.4 The Analytic-Synthetic Dichotomy vs. Logical Order of Knowledge

In relying on Ayn Rand's theory of concepts as open-ended, in the sense of a concept meaning its units including *all*—not merely *some*—of the units' characteristics, the theory of propositions presented here relies on Ayn Rand's rejection of the widely-held "analytic-synthetic distinction." This distinction was named by Kant, building on Plato's distinction between "essential" and "accidental" characteristics, and on other philosophers' distinction between "necessary" and "contingent" truths. (Ayn Rand rejected these distinctions too. In the Objectivist literature, these distinctions are referred to as dichotomies. I will adopt this terminology.) Kant writes (1994, B 10–11):

> In all judgments in which the relation of a subject to the predicate is thought (if I consider only affirmative judgments, since the application to negative ones is easy) this relation is possible in two different ways. Either the predicate B belongs to the subject A as something that is (covertly) contained in this concept A; or B lies entirely outside the concept A, though to be sure it stands in connection with it. In the first case I call the judgment *analytic*, in the second *synthetic*. Analytic judgments (affirmative ones) are thus those in which the connection of the predicate is thought through identity, but those in which this connection is thought without identity are to be called synthetic judgments. One could also call the former *judgments of clarification*, and the

latter *judgments of amplification*, since through the
predicate the former do not add anything to the concept of the subject, but only break it up by means of
analysis into its component concepts, which were already thought in it (though confusedly); while the latter, on the contrary, add to the concept of the subject a
predicate that was not thought in it at all, and could not
have been extracted from it through any analysis. E.g., if
I say: "All bodies are extended," then this is an analytic
judgment. For I do not need to go beyond the concept
that I combine with the body in order to find that extension is connected with it, but rather I need only to
analyze that concept, i.e., become conscious of the man-
ifold that I always think in it, in order to encounter this
predicate therein; it is therefore an analytic judgment.
On the contrary, if I say: "All bodies are heavy," then
the predicate is something entirely different from that
which I think in the mere concept of a body in general.
The addition of such a predicate thus yields a synthetic
judgment.

Thus philosophers who accept the analytic-synthetic dichotomy
do not view a concept's meaning as including all the attributes,
known and yet to be known, of the units subsumed by the concept.
Therefore, they do not view the meaning of a concept to be as encompassing as Ayn Rand explains it actually is, and certainly not encompassing enough to be wider than the propositions that use the
concept.

Many modern philosophers endorse the analytic-synthetic dichotomy. (See Peikoff 1990, 88–121, which reports on and rejects
this endorsement.) They claim that an "analytic truth," such as "Man
is rational," is a "tautology"—that because the predicate of such a
proposition reiterates a fact already implied by the nature of its subject, such a proposition states nothing. In discrediting this dichotomy, Peikoff explains that *all* propositions—not only those claimed
to be "analytic"—are in a sense "tautologies," because concepts are

open-ended and already include all the characteristics that can be predicated to them. But this fact of course does not imply that propositions state nothing. In the context of the topic of the present chapter, I offer this additional point: Advocates of the analytic-synthetic dichotomy misunderstand the role of a proposition. It is never the role of a proposition to state something wider than or beyond a concept (as in a so-called "synthetic" proposition), but rather to state something narrower, more specific than a concept, for the purposes I have explained in this chapter.

Consider this example passage:

> Unlike animals, man uses language. Unlike animals, man often significantly improves his environment, way of life, and life span from one generation to the next. What is the cause of these facts? Man is rational. By using his faculty of rationality, man can solve the problems currently facing society, and mankind can enjoy even greater happiness than we have today.

Clearly, the proposition "Man is rational" means more than nothing in this passage; imagine the passage with that proposition removed. But the cognitive value of the proposition "Man is rational" is not easy to see merely by observing that proposition in isolation; it must be seen as part of a logical *sequence* of propositions, as part of a hierarchy of knowledge. Each proposition in the passage above is an item of knowledge about man. The sequence of propositions is knowledge in a (very abbreviated) logical order. Many propositions about man must be composed before one reaches the conclusion that man is rational. Once that conclusion is reached, many more propositions about man can be composed—including the proposition, "Rationality is a good differentia for the definition of 'man'."

Recall the introduction of epistemology with which I opened this book:

> Epistemology addresses how to take the evidence of your senses and form concepts, statements, sequences of statements, and a corpus of knowledge that is true,

organized, readily applicable to new situations, and conducive to the discovery of new knowledge.

It is in the form of concepts and logical sequences of statements—propositions—that a mature adult holds "a corpus of knowledge that is true, organized, readily applicable to new situations, and conducive to the discovery of new knowledge."

6.4.5   A New Theory of Meaning

In the previous section, I wrote that philosophers who accept the analytic-synthetic dichotomy do not view a concept's meaning as including all the attributes of the units subsumed by the concept. In my judgment, not only does a concept (or phrase) not mean *less* than its subsumed existents including all their characteristics (known and yet to be known), but rather a concept means even *more* than its subsumed existents including all their characteristics. A concept means its subsumed existents including all their characteristics—known and yet to be known—*as understood according to a certain cognitive hierarchy of known characteristics.*

For example, the characteristics of being an animal and possessing a rational faculty are at the base of the hierarchy of characteristics for the concept "man." Being able to use language is a derivative characteristic for that concept.

When a new characteristic is discovered, it assumes a place in the hierarchy, according to the chain of reasoning—which can be expressed by a chain of propositions—by which the newly discovered characteristic is best understood. The hierarchy of known characteristics is identified in significant part by the definition of the concept. A definition must obey the rule of fundamentality; the definition explicitly names characteristics at the root of the hierarchy for that concept. Man is "the rational animal."

In other words, a concept means not merely the *existents* it refers to; a concept means the *units* it refers to. It is significant that Ayn Rand (1990, 40) uses the word "unit," not "existent," when she writes, "the meaning of a concept consists of its units." Ayn Rand also writes

(1990, 11), "units are things viewed by a consciousness in certain existing relationships." Nevertheless, I do not claim that Ayn Rand held the position I present here.

From my position, it is clear why we sometimes have two concepts to refer to the same existents. For example, the concepts "man" and "homo sapiens" refer to the same existents, including all the characteristics of those existents. Yet these are two different concepts. Though they refer to the same existents—men, including all the characteristics of men—they have slightly different meanings. Their genera differ. Basic in the hierarchy of characteristics for "man" is the distinction between men and other animals. The distinction between men and other hominids is a more derivative distinction. In contrast, for "homo sapiens," the hierarchical order of characteristics is different: The distinction between men and other hominids is basic, and the distinction between men and animals is derivative. For both concepts, all the same distinctions are made eventually, but they are made in a different hierarchical order, thereby enabling each concept to serve a different cognitive purpose.

On the basis of my position, which rejects the analytic-synthetic dichotomy, all the alleged problems that perplex modern philosophers regarding the meaning of concepts, phrases, and propositions fall away. Consider the familiar puzzling example of the phrases "the morning star" (Phosphorus) and "the evening star" (Hesperus). Both of these phrases refer to the same entity, Venus, including all of the characteristics of Venus, but have slightly different meanings. The morning star has the fundamental distinguishing characteristic of being visible in the morning sky. Using that characteristic, and through other evidence, one can infer the characteristic of being visible in the evening sky. For the evening star, the order of characteristics is reversed. Observe that each phrase implies the same full set of characteristics, but in a different *order* of inference. Thus we might have the following sequence of propositions:

"The evening star is the star visible in the evening sky. By observing the evening star continually over its path in the sky from evening until morning, I discovered that this star is the same star that is visible in the morning sky, and which I have known as the morning star. Therefore, the evening star is the morning star. That is, Hesperus is Phosphorus."

Notice the sequence of propositions to build knowledge of the evening star in a hierarchical order. The hierarchy of knowledge for the morning star is the reverse.

What, then, is the cognitive value of the proposition, "The morning star is the evening star"? This proposition in effect creates a shortcut ordering of one's knowledge of Venus. The shortcut goes straight from the characteristic of rising in the morning to the characteristic of rising in the evening. In other words, the fact that the morning star is the evening star is already included in the meaning of the subject "the morning star"; but the predicate serves to promote that fact in the hierarchy of all the facts included in the meaning of the subject "the morning star."

6.4.6 Why a Definition Does Not Mean the Concept that it Defines

One important application of my theory of meaning is the conclusion that a definition does not equal the meaning of a concept. An example is that the defining phrase "the rational animal" is not the same as the concept "man." For one analysis of the difference between a definition and the meaning of a concept, see Peikoff 1990, 94–106. My own analysis below (taken from Pisaturo 2015, 133–135) has some significant departures from Peikoff's.

It is true that the phrase "rational animal" refers to all men (including women) and only to men. It is true that all rational animals are organized to stand upright and move gracefully on two legs, have faces that express their powerful emotions that can be consistent with their rationality, have hands to shape the world in accordance with their rationality, have the capacity to integrate rational values with sexual desire, and are all members of a single species that has a distinctive physical appearance and other distinctive physical characteristics. That is, the phrase "rational animal," once informed with the above knowledge, can identify all the attributes identified by the word "man." But the words "rational" and "animal," taken separately, do not so identify all these attributes.

As Ayn Rand (1990, 66–67) has identified, a concept is (metaphorically) a kind of "file folder" that includes open-endedly many attributes of the referents of the concept. In my judgment, a phrase—such as "rational animal"—can also be such a file folder. However, in accordance with my theory of meaning presented in the previous section, the content of such a file folder, of either a concept or a phrase, is not a mere list of characteristics. The characteristics within a conceptual file-folder are arranged in a hierarchy. Such a hierarchy is the basis for, among other things, the rule of fundamentality, which state the following: The most fundamental characteristics of a concept, such as the characteristics "rational" and "animal" of the concept "man," belong in a concept's definition. Other characteristics, such as that man can speak language, are derivative of the more fundamental characteristics.

And here we arrive at the crux of the issue. Although the phrase "the rational animal" means more than its constituent parts "rational" and "animal"—that is, although the phrase "the rational animal" encompasses all the characteristics encompassed by the concept "man"—the phrase nevertheless encompasses all of these characteristics in a different hierarchy, a different order of importance than the order entailed by the concept "man." The phrase "the rational animal," if substituted for the concept "man," further emphasizes the characteristics identified by each word—in particular, the word "animal"—taken separately, in an order of importance relevant to each word taken separately. That is, the phrase "the rational animal" elevates and emphasizes all characteristics of all animals (such as that animals locomote and have a certain kind of cell structure in contrast to plants), and it de-emphasizes characteristics beyond rationality, and even derived from rationality, that are specific to and important to men (such as the characteristics of standing upright, having expressive faces, and having the capacity to integrate reason and emotion). Even on a perceptual level, the phrase "the rational animal" does not as readily summon to mind the figure of a man as does the word "man."

From another perspective, the phrase "rational animal" emphasizes the distinction between men and other animals, and it de-emphasizes the distinction between men and all other kinds of entities. For instance, I do not have to think of animals to grasp the irreplaceable value of a man compared to the value of a piece of property. You do not begin teaching a child to value human life by explaining that a human being is more valuable than a dog. You say something like, "We can get a new car, but we cannot get a new Johnny." Therefore, the phrase "rational animal" does not do justice as a stand-in for the concept "man."

Similarly and even more starkly, the phrase "female spouse of a male spouse" does not do justice to the concept "wife." Beyond being awkward and difficult to hold in one's mind, this phrase overly emphasizes strictly biological features of being female and male (such as having specifically male or female reproductive organs), along with legal and social characteristics of being a spouse, and de-emphasizes the distinctive kind of regard that a rational married woman *qua* woman has for her rational husband *qua* man (and vice versa).

From another perspective, the phrase "female spouse of a male spouse" overemphasizes a distinction from "female spouse of a female spouse" and "male spouse of a male spouse," and it underemphasizes the difference between a husband and a wife in a marriage. This problem of emphasis is much worse in the case of "female spouse of a male spouse" than it is in the case of "rational animal." The reason is that "rational animal" is a good definition of "man," but "female spouse of a male spouse" is a bad definition of "wife." Indeed, if the meaning of marriage were broadened to include homosexual couples—as has now occurred by declaration of some governments—then there would be no good definition of "wife" or of "husband" or "marriage" as we have traditionally understood these concepts, because "heterosexual" would have to be included among the distinguishing characteristics stated in any definition.

Even the phrase "woman spouse of a man" de-emphasizes essential characteristics of being a wife, characteristics that are not contained in the meaning of the words "woman," "spouse," and "man" considered separately.

6.4.7   Truth and Knowledge

I subscribe to the correspondence theory of truth. A true proposition corresponds to reality. A false proposition contradicts reality. In the famous words of Aristotle (*Metaphysics* Book IV Chapter 7, 1011b25),

> To say of what is that it is not, or of what is not that it is,
> is false, while to say of what is that it is, and of what is
> not that it is not, is true; so that he who says of anything
> that it is, or that it is not, will say either what is true or
> what is false.

To assess the truth of a proposition, we proceed as follows. We mentally isolate the existent(s) identified by the subject. Then we assess whether the existent has characteristics identified by the predicate. If so, then the proposition is true. If not, then the proposition is false.

Sometimes, however, there may be no existent identified by the subject, as in the proposition "The horse on the moon is white." In that case, the proposition is neither true nor false, but rather has a false premise, namely that the horse on the moon exists. A premise of every valid proposition is that the subject identifies an actual existent.

Ayn Rand (1990, 48) writes, "Truth is the product of the recognition (i.e., identification) of the facts of reality." Furthermore, truth is expressed in the form of propositions.

This concept of truth is similar to the concept of knowledge. Each of these concepts has similar referents, but the conceptual units formed from these referents differ in hierarchy and emphasis. Truth differentiates primarily from falsehood. Knowledge differentiates primarily from other forms of consciousness (such as fleeting sensations and feelings of pleasure, pain, and emotions), and also between various items of knowledge within an integrated corpus or system of knowledge.

As a corpus of knowledge must be arranged in a logical ordering of propositions, so the truth or falsehood of a proposition generally can be assessed only by considering—either implicitly or explicitly—an entire sequence of propositions.

Prompted by the concept of truth, we can formulate a more mature definition of knowledge as follows. Knowledge is a persisting, recallable awareness of an aspect of reality, expressible in a sequence of propositions.

6.4.8   Objects of Belief

One problem that perplexes many contemporary philosophers is how to construe complex propositions of the form "John believes that X," where X is itself a proposition, such as "Mary is a student." The problem arises from considering X an 'object of belief', raising questions about the metaphysical status of such an 'object'. (See, for example, McGrath and Frank 2018.)

I do not think this problem rises to the level of a philosophical problem. The problem is an elementary misunderstanding of the grammar of the case.

In "John believes Mary," "believes" is a transitive verb with "Mary" as its direct object. In "John believes *that* Mary is a student," "believes" is an *intransitive* verb with no direct object.

In "John believes that X," there is no 'object' of belief. The word "that" causes "believes" in the sentence to be an intransitive verb. The X is not an object of belief but rather an adverbial specification of the belief. That is, X is an 'adverbial object', like "mile" in "to run a mile," with "run" as an intransitive verb (as opposed to the transitive verb "run" in "to run a store"); or like "night" in "to stay the night," or like "backstroke" in "to swim the backstroke."

The subordinate clause "that X," following "believes," provides a specification of the belief. "John believes that X" does not mean that John believes a belief, but rather that John *has* a belief, and the ensuing clause provides specifics—namely, X—about that belief.

6.4.9   Notation

Some modern and contemporary philosophers propose a special notation, such as the predicate calculus, to depict all propositions. The foregoing theory demonstrates that statements written in English can be understood precisely without translating them into another notation.

Nevertheless, it can be useful to introduce specialized notation for specialized kinds of propositions. For example, mathematical equations are propositions that are best written in mathematical symbols instead of in English. But even mathematical papers are best written mostly in a traditional language such as English.

6.5   SUMMARY OF PROPOSITIONS

At the start of this chapter, I set out to identify the precise respect in which a proposition is narrower and more specific than some individual concept it contains, and to identify the cognitive purpose a proposition fulfills. To summarize my conclusion: A proposition can be narrower and more specific than some individual concept (the subject noun) it contains in precisely the two respects in which Ayn Rand identified a concept to be open-ended. The cognitive purposes fulfilled by propositions are a high degree of differentiation while preserving the unit-economy of concepts, and the ability to put one's knowledge into highly specific, intensively integrated, logical orders.

7 MATHEMATICS

This chapter is a lightly edited version of Pisaturo and Marcus 1994. If readers find parts of this chapter clearer than the rest of the book, it is probably because Glenn Marcus co-wrote it.

This chapter provides a philosophic development of the fundamental concepts, principles, and methods of mathematics. Because this chapter does not deal with advanced mathematics, you, the reader, will not learn the mathematics needed to build bridges or rockets. If, however, you ever do study the mathematics of rocket science, this chapter may help you to understand it, and any mathematics, much better. You will see mathematics as a system of principles and methods—principles induced from factual observation and methods devised to measure aspects of reality.

7.1 COUNTING

Let us develop the foundation of mathematics from the very beginning, assuming we know nothing about mathematics. We will start with a scenario that cavemen, who knew no mathematics, might have faced. We make no claim that this scenario is historically accurate. As with our development of a hierarchy of knowledge throughout this book, we are not seeking to replicate a chronology of knowledge. Instead, we are trying to build a logical hierarchy, starting with observed facts and building a logical sequence of further identifications.

Suppose we sent each of our children to a different location to fish, and each child returned with a pile of fish. To which location should we send all of our children tomorrow? All the fish are virtually the same size and almost identical in every perceivable way, but the piles are not the same size. Which pile of fish is the largest?

Figure 1 shows the result of the children's expedition. Looking at the groups of fish, we can easily perceive similarities and differences in the size of some groups. Clearly, we perceive that both group A and group B are larger than group C. Nevertheless, we cannot easily perceive a difference between the sizes of groups A and B. What are we to do?

Figure 1

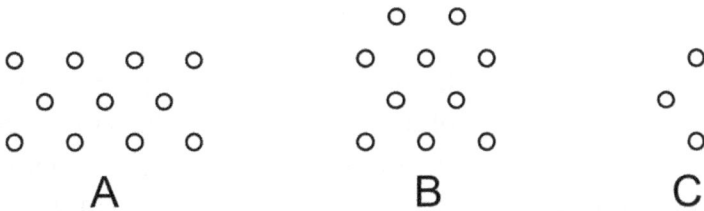

Before we figure out what to do, let us examine in more detail precisely what we mean by the size of a group. What exactly do we mean when we say that one group is larger than another? Do we mean it is larger the way a suitcase is larger than a purse? Do we mean it takes up more space? Is the larger and smaller we are perceiving the volume? Is it the area? Let us look at the groups in Figure 2(a).

Figure 2(a)

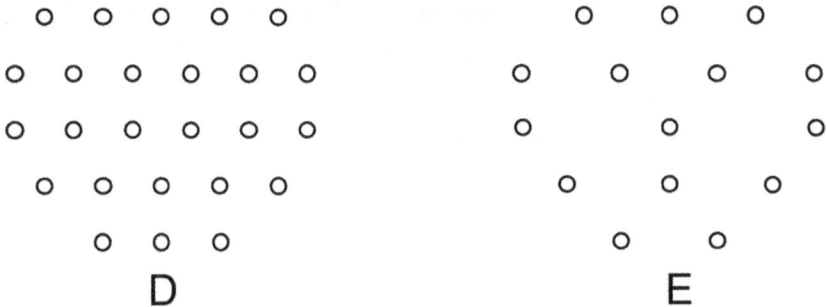

Group D takes up the same amount of space as does group E, yet we would say group D is larger than group E.

Let us also examine the groups in Figure 2(b). Here group F takes up more space than does group G, yet we would say group G is larger than group F. These examples show that the spatial extent of the group is not what we mean by its size.

Figure 2(b)

F   G

To what, then, are we referring when we say group A is larger than group B? We are referring, of course, to *quantity*. When we say group A is larger than group B, we mean that there are more objects in group A than in group B. But what exactly does *that* mean? What exactly *is* quantity?

"There are more objects in group A than in group B" means the following: There is more repetition of the same thing or same kind of thing in group A than in group B. A group's quantity is the degree of repetition, or degree of "another-ness," in the group.

Quantity is the degree of repetition of like existents in a group or region.

Now that we know we are to compare the *quantities* of groups, we can return to our original groups of fish shown in Figure 1. Recall that we could not tell the difference in the quantities of groups A and B. But what if the children had placed the fish of groups A and B in the arrangements shown in Figure 3(a)?

Figure 3

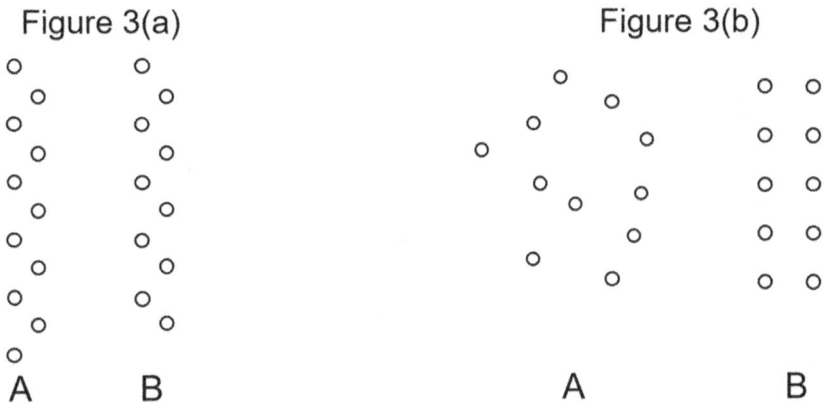

Figure 3(a)   Figure 3(b)

A   B   A   B

Now we can say it seems that group A has more fish than does group B, but we are still not completely sure. As a third possibility, what if the children had placed the fish in the shapes shown in Figure 3(b)? Then we could not tell at all which of the groups is larger. The reason we cannot compare the quantities of the groups is that the shapes of the groups are so different.

We have now learned something important: differing shapes or arrangements do not allow us to perceive the differences in the quantities of the groups. This is true even with the groups in Figure 4. Without counting in some form, we cannot tell the difference in quantity even when the groups are so small. But as we saw in Figure 3(a), if the shapes are more similar, then we do start to see a difference in the quantities of the groups. Let us exploit this idea of "similar shapes," taking a similar approach to our pursuit, in Section 5.5.1, of an objective basis of similarity and difference.

Figure 4

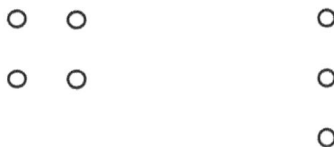

So far in our analysis, we have been at the perceptual level, observing objects *passively*, i.e., observing them as they happen to be arranged in reality. What could we *do* to help us tell the difference between the quantities of groups A and B? Using the "similar-shape" idea, we can take our first active step that will lead us to the process of counting. We will take the "similar-shape" idea to the extreme. We actively *arrange* the fish in the groups so that the groups have identical shapes. As shown in Figure 5, we have now *lined up* the groups of fish. Now we can compare the quantities of the groups precisely. We now easily perceive that group A has more fish than does group B.

Figure 5

By placing the fish in this arrangement, we have *faced off* the fish in the groups. We now observe a fish-to-fish correspondence between the groups. We observe that every fish in group B has a "mate" in group A, but that a fish in group A is left over.

Our "facing-off" process is definitely an advance over mere perception. (Indeed, the only way to distinguish the quantity of the groups in Figure 4 without physically rearranging them into similar shapes is mentally to face them off, as shown in Figure 6.) Using this process, we now know to which location to send all our children tomorrow to increase our yield of fish.

Figure 6

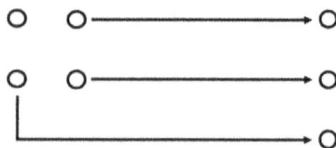

The key to the advantage of the facing-off process is that it faces off the equal parts of the groups, leaving the remaining part of the larger group not faced off. This arrangement allows us to perceive clearly a difference in the quantities of the groups. Indeed, the concepts "more," "larger," and "greater" mean "equal plus some extra." (Recall our discussion of an objective basis of similarity and difference in Section 5.5.1.) The larger group is the group with some extra repetitions, some extra "anothers."

This process of facing off equal parts and of leaving an unequal part remaining is not restricted merely to comparing quantities. We also use this process to compare amounts, as in volume or weight. For example, suppose we have two glasses, one tall and narrow and the other short and wide, each filled with water. Which glass has more water? With these different shapes, we cannot tell easily. How much of the greater width of the second glass makes up for the greater height of the first glass? We don't know, because there is an "extra" amount on each side. To solve the problem, we must use glasses with identical shapes. Then we would observe that some of the water in one glass matched exactly all of the water in the other glass, and that there was some water left over in the first glass. This glass, we would then know, has more water than the other glass does.

Let us now return to the development of the facing-off process. We have stated that once we face off the fish, we know with certainty which group has more fish. But what if we put the fish back into their respective piles and then do the facing-off process all over again? Will we get the same result? What the caveman probably did was to try the process several times, getting the same result. Would he get the same result every time?

We can begin to answer this question by examining when our facing-off process might not yield consistent results. For example, what if we tried to face off two groups of raindrops? During the facing-off process, some raindrops from the same group might join. Some might evaporate. Joining of objects might also occur if we were facing off portions of applesauce. The problem with objects joining is that the degree of repetition changes: a pair of repetitions becomes a sole repetition. What used to face off against another pair now faces off against a lone repetition in the other group. Another situation that could result in a change in result would be if we were to face off crumb cakes. A single crumb cake might crumble and become many crumb pieces.

Therefore, one condition we require for the facing-off process to yield consistent results is that the degree of repetition—that is, the quantity—of the groups remain unchanged. For the quantity of each group to remain unchanged, we require that each fish in each group retain its identity as a single distinct fish during the process. That is, each fish does not join another fish as applesauce piles might, or break apart into many fish as crumb cakes might. We further require that each fish not transform in such a way that it would no longer be considered a fish. (Also, we require that no fish disappear, and no fish appear out of nothing. In addition, in our example, we require that no one remove a fish from or add a fish to either group.)

We have now discovered the condition that we require for our facing-off process to yield the same result each time we use it. It does not matter if the fish change color or skin texture. We only care that each fish retain its identity as a separate, distinct fish during the process. If each fish does, then there is nothing to affect the outcome of the process. Thus, if we observe that the fish do retain their distinctness as individual fish, and if we do the facing-off process the same way, we must get the same result. We have now made our first *induction*; we have gone from specific cases to a more general conclusion! (We will have more to say about the method of induction soon.)

But what if we don't do the process the same way the next time? What if we vary the *order* in which we line up the fish? Might that change the result? Let us take an example, examining the fish in Figure 7(a). What if we now rearrange the fish in group B. Suppose we now face off fish Y from group B with the first fish from group A, as shown in Figure 7(b).

Figure 7

Figure 7(a)

A ○ ○ ○ ○ ○ ○
B ○ ○ ○ ○ ○ ○
  W X Y Z

Figure 7(b)

A ○ ○ ○ ○   ○
B ○   ○ ○ X
  Y   W Z

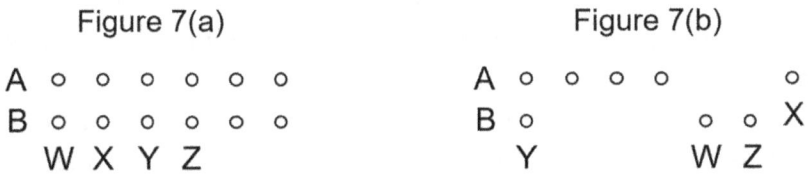

Will this change in the order of the fish affect our facing-off process? Note that the facing-off process will not be identical. In fact, we will face off at least fish Y and W with different fish in group A, but possibly all the fish in group B will face off with different fish in group A. Nevertheless, we can distinguish the results of the process only if we can distinguish among the fish in group B. If these fish are interchangeable, then so are each of the results. (Mathematicians often use the word "exchangeable" instead of "interchangeable.") If the fish are interchangeable, then the differences in facing-off are, in our context, irrelevant.

Happily, we have already isolated the conditions that will make the fish in group B (and group A) interchangeable in our context. The only attribute of each fish we need for it to do its job in the facing-off process is that it remain a distinct, separate fish during the process. If the fish do so, then the fish are interchangeable. If the fish are interchangeable, then at any step of the facing-off process, whichever fish we choose from groups A and B, the process remains the same. The order does not affect the result. Therefore, the facing-off process must always give the same result, no matter whether we use the same order or a different order. We may call this conclusion "facing off always gives the same result." Note that this conclusion is our second induction.

Not only will the facing-off process work on the piles of fish our children just brought back, but it will also work on any new piles of fish they bring back next week. It will work on *any* piles of fish. This is our third induction.

Let us now re-examine the facing-off process from an epistemological perspective. Our first step was to consider each fish in a group to be a *unit* in the group. Note that we are using the word "unit" in its philosophical meaning identified by Ayn Rand. The mathematical term "unit," as in "unit of measure," is a different concept. As we shall see later, the two concepts are closely related.

The unit-perspective is what enabled us to be active in the arrangement of the fish in the groups. In forming concepts, the unit-perspective allows us to do more with units than simply to regard them in the order and arrangement in which reality presents them to us; it allows us to perform an active (volitional) rearrangement (a classification) of them into groups according to their similarities and differences. (See Figure 8(a).) In devising our facing-off process (see Figure 8(b)), the unit-perspective allowed us to perform an active (volitional) rearrangement of the units *within* each group. In both cases, the unit-perspective is seen to be the first cognitive step distinctive to human, volitional-conceptual consciousness.

Figure 8

Figure 8(a)   Figure 8(b)

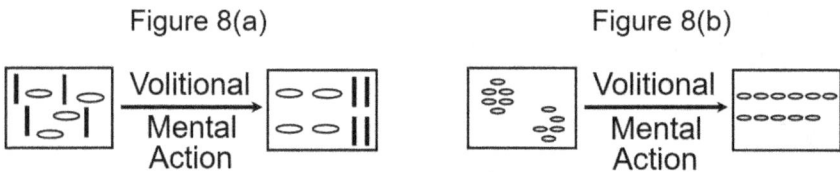

Next, let us examine how we arrived at our "facing-off-always-gives-the-same-result" conclusion. What allowed us to pass inductively from a specific case to a general conclusion?

For all of our inductions above, we identified a certain condition that must be met: Each fish must retain its unity; that is, it must retain its identity as a distinct, separate member of its group of fish. This condition is all that we need for the facing-off process to yield a consistent result.

We can now give a name to our process of facing off units of groups; we can call our process *counting*. Our process of counting is not exactly what we call counting today. It is counting before the advent of numbers.

Observe that counting precedes numbers conceptually. Men needed some primitive form of counting to arrive at specific numbers, let alone the concept "number." Observe also that, counter to more than two thousand years of tradition in mathematics, mathematics is not strictly a deductive science. Mathematics, like all sciences, is a mixture of induction and deduction, and some inductions have to precede any deductions.

We will now continue our development of counting. Thus far we have been facing off fish vs. fish. What if the objects we faced off were not fish, but spears or apples? Would this make any difference in our facing-off process?

First, we could face off two groups of spears. We observe that the facing-off process does work in this case. Under what conditions, we now ask, will it work for any kind of unit? The answer is that we require the same condition as we did for fish. Each unit must remain a distinct, separate unit during the process. If each unit does so, then the facing-off process will yield consistent results.

Now we know, by this latest induction, that we can use our process to face off two groups of any kind of units. But what if we want to face off a group that contains one kind of unit with a group with a different kind of unit? Let us take an example, turning our attention to group A in Figure 9.

Figure 9

A ○ ○ ○ ○ ○

This group is especially important to us because it has just enough apples for each of our children. How do we know this? We observe that whenever the children play with the apples, each child has an apple, and there are no apples left over. How did the children get the apples? Well, we took an apple from the group of apples and gave it to a child, and continued until there were no more apples, and no more apple-less children. Therefore, each child has an apple and each apple belongs to a child. This reminds us of the facing-off process. We realize that what we are doing is facing off apples and children.

Facing off apples and children is an important step in our development of mathematics. There is something the same about the group of apples and the group of children: it is the quantity of the groups. When we faced off the children and the apples, we omitted the differences in the kind of units we considered. This omission leads us to our next induction. We can perform our facing-off process between groups even when one group has a different kind of unit than does the other group. All we require for the facing-off process to work is that the entities remain units in their group. With this induction, we now can compare apples to children, apples to spears, spears to fish, etc. We need not restrict ourselves to comparisons of groups with the same kind of units. An example of using this conclusion is a sheep herder counting out a pebble for each sheep that left to graze in the morning. When the herd returned, he would know that he still had the same quantity of sheep by matching his pebbles to his sheep.

To summarize, it does not matter what kinds of units we face off; it matters only that they are units. Our facing-off process deals with "units *qua* units," and places the units in a unit-to-unit correspondence.

Now, we may ask, do we need to restrict our process to groups of a particular quantity or range of quantity? Note that every counting step is the same as every other one. As the count increases, the only factor that can come into effect to change the process is that at some point we run out of units to count. Therefore, by induction, the process can continue so long as there are units to count.

Taking an example will illustrate how we know we can continue as long as we have units to count. Suppose we need to count two large groups of apples. (See Figure 10(a).) We have already counted out some apples in each group. We can remove this quantity of apples from each group, as in Figure 10(b). We observe that removing these apples has absolutely no effect on the process of counting; we could have continued counting even if we had not removed the counted apples.

Figure 10

Figure 10(a)

Apples

Figure 10(b)

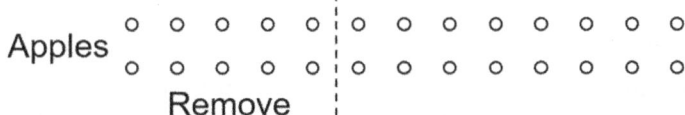

Apples

Remove

By considering the following example, we can enhance our ability to count. We want to fish on our canoe and make sure that we bring back a fish for each child. We could take our group of children with us and face off each new fish with a child until we get a match. But taking our children is dangerous, or at least troublesome. We instead could first face off a group of pebbles with our group of children until we get a match. We then could take our group of pebbles with us instead of our group of children. We would face off the group of pebbles with the group of fish until we get a match. Can we then know that the group of children will face off exactly with the group of fish? The answer is yes. Let us *prove* it.

In this situation, as shown in Figure 11, we are considering three groups (children, pebbles and fish) rather than just two groups.

Figure 11

Children
Pebbles
Fish

First, we face off the groups of children and pebbles and get an exact face-off. We now reason that these *groups* are interchangeable in our context. For observe: we can replace each child with its faced-off pebble. If we do so, we will have replaced the group of children with the group of pebbles. We can now substitute the group of pebbles for the group of children. Anything that matches the group of pebbles must also match the group of children. Next, we face off the group of pebbles with the group of fish, and find that they match exactly. Now we also know that the group of children matches the group of fish, *without having physically to face off the groups of children and fish.*

We now know that if the group of children matches the group of pebbles, and the group of pebbles matches the group of fish, then the group of children matches the group of fish—but only for this particular case. Now let us generalize. What allowed us to show that the group of children matches the group of fish in this case was the interchangeability of the groups of children and pebbles. What allowed the interchangeability of the groups was that the same condition as before was present: that each unit in each group retained its unity during the process. Now we can make an induction, we can pass from the particular to the general. If all the entities in any two groups remain as distinct, separate entities during the process, and if the two groups face off exactly, then the groups are interchangeable or identical in our context. Thus whenever one of these groups faces off exactly with another group, then the other group will also. Therefore, if we face off any two groups A and B and they match exactly, and then we face off groups B and C and they also match exactly, then we know that groups A and C match exactly, without having to face them off. This result is true, not just for these groups of children, pebbles and fish, but for all entities, given that the condition of retained unity is present.

Now we can say the following: If *a* faces off exactly with *b*, and *b* faces off exactly with *c*, then *a* faces off exactly with *c*. The small letters stand for any groups A, B and C. This inductively-proven principle is the mathematical principle of *transitivity*.

Let us now turn our attention back to group A in Figure 9, remembering that this group of apples faced off exactly with our group of children. The particular quantity-attribute of this group of apples is important to us because we might need to find just enough fish, pebbles, or even bearskins for our children. It is time to give a group with this common quantity-attribute a name. We can call it a "flock." A "flock" is a group whose quantity matches the quantity of our group of children. Any time a group's units face off exactly with the units of our group of children, we will call it a "flock." "Flock" is our first *number*.

We can now state a working definition of a primitive number. A number is a group whose quantity matches the quantity of some standard group.

Note that in early usage, numbers were nouns. Note, for example, Euclid's (2008, 194, Book VII, Definition 2) definition of number: "a number is a multitude composed of units." Each number had "group" as its genus. Examples of primitive numbers were hand, pair, brace and dozen. A dozen was a group of a certain size. As we note later, numbers today are adjectives. For example, when we say "seven rocks," "seven" modifies the group of rocks.

Returning to the example of going fishing, let us further enhance our ability to count. A clever idea is to realize that instead of facing off our children with pebbles, we can face off our children with our fingers. Luckily, we see that the count of our children is the same as the count of our fingers on a hand. We can now call our first number "hand" rather than "flock." This number is much more convenient, because hands are always readily available for counting. Also, everybody in the tribe has different quantities of children but the same "hand-many" fingers on each hand. Communication using the number "hand" is much clearer.

We can exploit our number "hand." We can use it and our fingers to count quantities other than "hand." For example, we would call a group with a single object "lone-finger" or simply "one." As another example, we might want to keep track of the number of spears we need. We could call this quantity "spear-quantity," but the number "spear" has all the disadvantages of "flock." Why not face off the spears with our fingers? Doing so, we might realize that "spear" is "hand-without-thumb." Using our hand, we can now give names to other counts up to the count of "hand." With these numbers, we now have a primitive *collection* of numbers.

We can, if we need, develop some more numbers. What if we need to count more than "hand"? Clearly, we can count with both hands. The number of arrows we might need, "arrow-many," might be "hand-and-thumb"; the first name for ten might well have been "both-hands"; and the first name for nine probably would be "both-hands-without-a-thumb." As a result, we now have a collection of numbers up to ten.

Although these numbers are members of a collection, they are still not fully related to each other. To develop further our use of numbers, we can take an example of counting with our current collection of numbers. Suppose we want to count, using our fingers, the group of fish shown in Figure 12(a). Right now all we can do is choose a group of fingers, face them off with the group of fish, and see if they match. If they do, then we know that we have the same number of fish as fingers. If they don't match exactly, we need to pick another group of fingers and try the process again. We continue this process until we have an exact match. Counting right now is simply a process of "guess and try." If we try "hand-many" fingers, we don't have enough fingers. If we try "both-hands-many," we have too many fingers. Eventually, we use "hand-and-pair" fingers and get an exact match. (See Figure 12(b).) We have a "hand-and-pair" group of fish.

Figure 12

Figure 12(a)   Figure 12(b)

○ ○ ○ ○ ○ ○ ○   ○ ○ ○ ○ ○ ○ ○

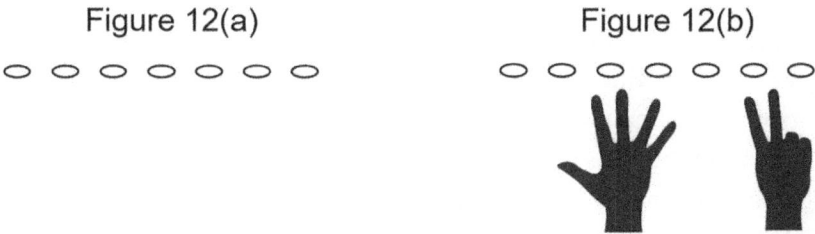

Though using our fingers is an advance, we can improve our counting process over "guess and try." With guess and try, we guess at a matching group of fingers ahead of time. Why bother guessing ahead of time? Why not face off a finger and a unit of whatever we are counting, a finger and a unit at a time, until we use up all the units? Then we look at the group of fingers, recognize it by its shape, and remember its number-name. Using the group of fish in Figure 12(a), we would match off a fish and a finger at a time, until we faced off all our fish. We would then look at our group of fingers and see that we had a "hand-and-pair" group of fish.

After using this method for a time, we will start to recognize the shapes of the groups of fingers, which we could not as readily do if we faced off the fish with pebbles. We can recognize the shapes of the groups of fingers because our hands provide unit-economy. A group of eight pebbles is too large for us perceptually to distinguish it from a seven- or nine-group of pebbles. But a group of eight fingers breaks up into a hand and a three-group of fingers. We can easily distinguish a hand-and-trio of fingers from a hand-and-pair of fingers and from a both-hands-without-a-thumb group. We can call this new method of counting "recognizing the finger-formation." Note however, that the numbers are still not fully related to each other. They are not quite yet a system of numbers.

We can improve our counting method still further. As we face off the units, we can assign a number count after each face-off, stopping only when we have no more units left. We can count the group of fish in Figure 12(a) using this method. First, we face off a finger with a fish in the group. Looking at our faced-off finger, we now say, "If this were the total group, we'd have a one-group." We then take the next fish and face it off with the next finger. Looking at our group of so-far-faced-off fingers, we recognize it, and say, "If this were the total group, we'd have a pair-group." We keep going until we run out of units. Finally we say, "We have a 'hand-and-pair' group of fish." Let us call this new method of counting "keeping a running result."

We now have almost arrived at the modern process of counting. But we are still physically using our fingers to count. Observe that our latest method of counting illustrates an interesting fact. We have now placed our finger-groups, and thus our numbers, in a clear *order or sequence*. We started with a group of quantity one, and continued with each new group with a repetition more than the preceding group. By group-interchangeability (which we have already proved by induction), we see that this sequence of quantities—and thus our sequence of numbers—will always be the same. We also see that we can ensure that there are no gaps in our sequence of numbers: After we count each additional unit, we simply make sure we have defined a number to denote the quantity counted so far.

We can now memorize this sequence of quantities, which will remain unchanged, a sequence we can use every time we count. (See Figure 13.)

Figure 13: The sequence of numbers, based on the sequence of quantities obtained by repeated addition of a unit at a time.

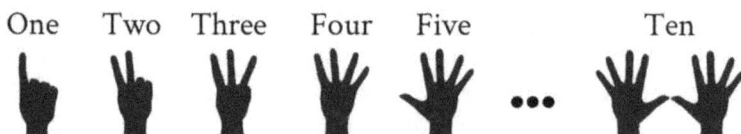

One   Two   Three   Four   Five   Ten

Let us start again with a single fish. Rather than using our fingers to face off with the fish, we say "one." That number denotes a group consisting of a lone finger. When we count the next fish, we say "two," which denotes a pair of fingers, and so on. Every time we do a face-off, we will say the next number in our sequence of numbers.

We have just performed *modern-day counting*. Although we are still "keeping a running result," we need not physically use our fingers; instead, we use the memorized sequence of numbers, and we can rest assured that quantities of our fingers are denoted by these numbers. The use of our fingers (or another standard-sized group) is still implicit. We are still ultimately facing off the units in the group of fish against the units in a standard group, such as the group of fingers on our hands. Therefore, if we want to reduce modern-day counting down to the perceptual level, we can reduce it back to comparing a group of units to the group of fingers on our hands. The memorized sequence of numbers stands for the sequence of quantities, such as our standard finger formations. The number 7, for example, stands for the finger formation "hand and pair."

What happens if the group is larger than a ten-group? (Note that we wrote "ten," not "10." "10" is millennia away.) We can make up a new number to denote each new-sized group, remembering that our process will work for a group of any quantity.

Let us say something about the nature of numbers. Notice that when we used numbers in our analysis of counting, we used an unusual syntax, such as "a seven-group of fish." We did this to show that numbers in their modern usage are *adjectives* describing groups, or, more philosophically, they specify the measurement of the quantity-attribute of groups of units.

In a popular modern-day erroneous notion of numbers, a number is taken to be a distinct entity. ("Object" is the usual technical mathematical term used.) This notion exhibits the error of reification. A number, whether in the old "noun form" or the more modern "adjective form," refers to a group, not to some individual object apart from any group. (If this point is understood, then the problem of infinity, which arises from the attempt to reify infinitely-many objects, does not arise. A large number has an actual referent only if there is a group with that many units in it.)

Let us summarize our development of mathematics thus far. We have developed the modern process of counting, and we have developed a system of numbers we can use to count any sized group. If we were to continue to develop the process of counting, we would observe that relating the quantities of different groups using counting can still take a long time. Are there more efficient methods to relate the quantities of different groups? The answer is, of course, yes. The simplest new methods are addition and subtraction. Addition tells us the result of combining groups of certain quantities. Subtraction tells us the result of removing a certain quantity of a group from a certain-sized group. Rather than continuing to make advances with counting, however, we shall turn now to a parallel development in mathematics: the application of counting to general measurement.

7.2   MEASUREMENT

In this chapter so far, we have traced the logical development of counting, the most basic method of mathematics. When we count units in a group, we are measuring the quantity of the group. Now we ask the following question: What about measuring the size of something that is not a group, but a single entity? For instance, what if we want to measure the size of a pile of applesauce, the length of a spear, or the weight of a rock?

7.2.1   Measurement Without Counting

As we know from Ayn Rand's theory of concepts, we use measurement implicitly to form every concept. Consider the concept "rock." If the weight of a hard, dense, non-organic, natural object is less than a certain amount, the object is not a rock, but a pebble, and if the weight is more than a certain amount, the object is a boulder.

Without employing counting, we can say only some general things about the relative weights of rocks. We can say that this rock is lighter than that one, or this rock is much heavier than that one. We can also rank the weights of rocks (although we cannot assign a number to each ranking), and we can place every new rock we encounter into this ranking. Ranking the weights of rocks can be of value. For example, we might give rocks to our youngest child to use to grind meal, and so we would want to know which rocks are too heavy for him to lift. If we know that our child can just barely lift a specific rock, we know that any new rock placed above it in the ranking will be too heavy for him to lift.

Observe the method underlying the example above. We began with a group of rocks, which had been categorized as rocks by the kind of measurement implicit in concept-formation. We considered each rock to be a unit subsumed under the concept "rock." Then we chose one specific rock, the one our child could just manage to lift. We thus made this unit our *standard of measure* for this situation. Every rock heavier than this standard rock is too heavy for our child to lift. This particular rock is now a *unit that serves as a standard*. It is the unit, among all the units subsumed under the concept "rock," that serves as our standard for measuring weight.

This kind of measurement, what we may call "pre-scientific" or "pre-mathematical" measurement, is quite limited. More than sufficient for forming concepts, for forming abstractions from abstractions, and for qualitative descriptions (such as "bigger" and "smaller"), it is not in the realm of quantitative measurement—that is, measurement of degree of repetition. All that this method tells us is that a certain rock is heavier, lighter, or possibly equal in weight to our standard.

The ability to count leads to one immediate improvement in measurement: the ability to assign ordinal numbers (that is, "order" numbers, such as first, second, etc.) to the ranking of measurements. But this use of our counting process is not a powerful way to measure. To bring the process of measurement into the realm of the mathematical, we need to be inventive in the employment of our newly-developed, inductively-validated process of counting.

7.2.2   Measurement With Counting: An Example

Suppose you must take a seven-day trip through the desert. You want to take enough water with you, but you don't want to take too much because water is heavy. You have nine small pouches of different sizes. But you cannot take all the pouches with you because your family needs to use most of them in your absence. Some pouches can hold about enough water for a day, others hold more and others less. You also have a large skin that can hold much more water. Does the skin hold enough water for the seven-day trip? More generally, how many days can you travel before you would run out of water from the skin?

The first solution that primitive man might have thought of, after thousands of years of counting, is the following. Fill the skin with water and empty all the pouches. Then pour water from the skin into the first pouch until the pouch is full. Then pour water from the skin into each remaining pouch in turn until the skin is empty. Then count how many pouches we have filled in order to empty the skin.

This is a major advance. We have used counting to measure the size of something that was not a group of units, but rather a single entity. We did this by dividing the entity *into* a group of units. Then we counted those units, and we concluded that the size of the entity was equal to the size of the group of the units. Suppose the water from our skin filled six of our nine pouches; now we can say that the skin holds as much water as six pouches.

But have we answered our initial question of how many days the water in the skin will last us? Is the answer six days, an answer we would get by facing off each pouch with a day? No, because, as we stated, the size of each pouch is different; some have more than enough water for a day, and some have less. In fact, our counting process will not always yield the same result. Suppose we try our process again, but this time we place our pouches in a different order. We might now fill only five pouches, because some of the larger pouches, which last time were the ones not filled, are this time the ones filled. On our next try we might fill seven pouches. What's wrong with our process?

What's wrong is that our units are not interchangeable. In our previous examples of counting, for each unit to be interchangeable required merely that it remain a separate, distinct unit of its group. In this example, however, each unit must also be *the same size* as each other unit. Therefore, let us amend our solution as follows. Again we fill the skin with water, and empty all the pouches. Then again we pour water from the skin into the first pouch until the pouch is full. But then, instead of moving on to the second pouch, we stay with the first one. We pour the water in the first pouch into a bucket until the first pouch is empty again; but we keep track of the count of "one unit" (one full pouch) by saying the number "one" or by drawing one tally or by placing a pebble by itself on the ground. Then we pour water from the skin into the first pouch again until the pouch is full. Then we empty the pouch again, and record the count of "two." We continue this process until the skin is empty. Our final count ("five," for instance) of "full pouches" holds as much water as the full skin.

This amended solution is another major advance. As long as we use the same pouch each time, our result will always be the same. This result identifies a precise relation between the size of the skin and the size of the pouch. However long a pouch will last us, a skin will last us five of those intervals of time. Moreover, we can now re-late the capacities of any new skins we obtain. For example, suppose one skin holds five pouches, and two other skins hold three pouches each. We now know not only that the first skin is the biggest, but that it is not as big as the other two skins combined.

But we can make our solution better still. Why did we pick our first pouch as the one to use in our measuring process? Was it the best pouch to use? Suppose our first pouch holds more than enough water for a day, but not enough water for two days. Five such pouches would hold enough water for how many days? What about six pouches, or seven? We can figure out answers to these questions, but we can also avoid this complexity. Let us choose a different pouch to serve as our standard. Let us choose the pouch that has just enough water to last us one day. Then a skin of seven pouches would last us seven days. Thus we have devised a solution to our initial question.

The number of days that the water in a skin will last is equal to the number of one-day pouches it holds.

7.2.3   A More Advanced Example With Philosophical Explanation

Let us take one more example of measurement by counting—one requiring a slightly more advanced solution—and explain our steps more philosophically as we take them.

Suppose again you are taking your seven-day trip through the desert. In addition to taking enough water, you want to take enough meat for you to eat. You have some large slabs of meat that you know can last you several days, but you don't know precisely how many days. When you eat at home, you usually cut a chunk of meat out of one of the slabs you have stored. Each chunk you cut is enough to feed you for a day. You usually cut only a chunk at a time, because the meat stays fresher when it is kept in slabs. Which slabs have enough meat for the seven-day trip? More generally, how many days can you travel before you would run out of meat from each slab?

This problem is a little more difficult to solve than was the problem of measuring the amount of water in a skin. The difficulty is that, although we could physically break up the water into units, we are not allowed to break up the slabs of meat into chunks. Where, then, do we find our units to count?

Fortunately, the solution is similar to the solution to the water question, though it may have taken thousands of years more to discover. (Also, the solution requires a balance scale.) The key to the solution was alluded to by Ayn Rand when she wrote (1990, 7),

> Measurement is the identification of a relationship—a quantitative relationship established by means of a standard that serves as a unit.

Notice that Ayn Rand wrote "a standard that serves as a unit," rather than "a unit that serves as a standard." Is there a difference between these two phrasings, or are they interchangeable? Ayn Rand once said in conversation (1990, p. 188) that she "did not intend any different meaning." Nevertheless, the process described in our next paragraph identifies a crucial difference.

First, we choose a chunk of meat that we know is just the right amount for one day. This chunk is our "unit that serves as a standard," that is, a specific unit subsumed under the concept "chunk" that serves as our standard for weight. (See Figure 14(a).) Then comes the key step: We choose this *standard to serve as a unit* in a newly-conceptualized, open-ended group of objects—a group of objects all of which weigh exactly as much as our standard chunk. We actually construct physically a group of objects (such as iron bars) all equal in weight to our standard chunk. (See Figure 14b.) The standard chunk serves as a unit, but a unit in our *new* group, a group whose units are all *uniform* in weight. We shall call this unit a *uniform unit*, or a *unit of measure*. Whereas the units subsumed under the concept "chunk" may be within a range of weight, our units of measure have no range in weight. All the units weigh precisely the same amount (although they may vary in other measurements, such as color, composition, etc.).

Figure 14

Figure 14(a)

Figure 14(b)

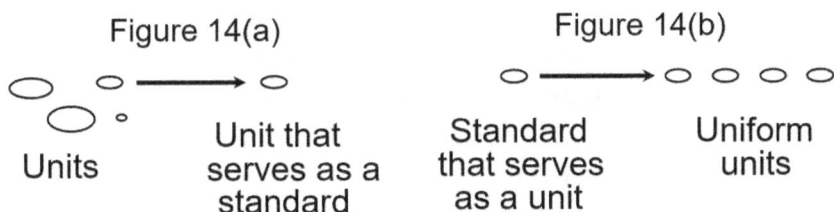

Units | Unit that serves as a standard

Standard that serves as a unit | Uniform units

Using our new group of uniform units (and using a balance scale), we measure the weight of each slab by counting how many of our standard units taken as a group are equal in weight to that slab. As the example in Figure 15 illustrates, we now can say that this slab weighs as much as seven one-day bars. We now can relate the weights of all our slabs by relating their counts, just as we related the sizes of groups of fish or apples by counting.

Figure 15

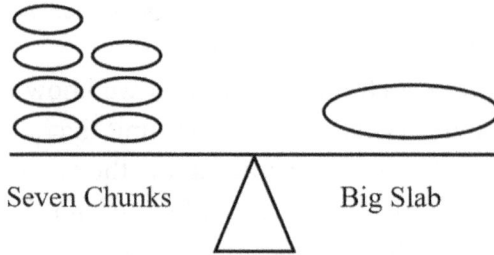

Seven Chunks   Big Slab

To reemphasize our key point: Whereas choosing a unit to serve as a standard makes possible qualitative measurement, choosing a standard to serve as a unit makes possible quantitative measurement via counting.

Notice that our standard of weight for measuring slabs was not one of the slabs, but rather a chunk, which is much smaller. This relation is exactly what we see in numerous historical examples. For instance, in measuring the height of a horse, the standard of length was a "hand," not a whole horse (not even a whole man). This way, the counts differ enough for different-sized horses, resulting in more precision.

Notice also that, in principle, the method we used to measure the amount of water in a skin was the same as the method we used to measure the weights of slabs. In the case of the skin, we constructed a group of uniform units of water by pouring a standard amount of water repeatedly into the same pouch. And, as our standard chunks were much smaller than the slabs we measured, our pouch-units of water were much smaller than the skin.

Thus we have succeeded in using our method of counting to obtain a precise measurement of a single entity. By combining the ideas of counting and the uniform unit in this manner, we have now transformed the art of measurement into the science of measurement—the science called mathematics. It is a *science* because it is based on a system of inductively-derived principles that can be applied systematically and consistently to a broad range of specific cases to deduce specific conclusions. It is the science of *measurement* because its methods can be applied to the measurement of any attribute for which a uniform unit can be devised.

7.2.4   Unit and Unit of Measure

What we are calling the "unit of measure" is a concept used routinely by scientists. In fact, the primary meaning of the word "unit" in common usage is "unit of measure."

What is new is the philosophical meaning of "unit" from Ayn Rand. Her philosophical concept is broader and more fundamental than the mathematical concept of unit (of measure). A unit of measure is simply her philosophical unit used in a specific way. In our discussion in the preceding section, we have tried to explain in more detail the link between the two concepts.

In considering the concept of "unit of measure," notice again the active, volitional nature of the unit-perspective. To form concepts, we actively rearrange units to classify them into groups. To count, we rearrange units *within* groups. Now, to measure, we *create* units— entire *groups* of them. We literally manufacture uniform weights to place on a balance scale; we engrave twelve rulings on a wooden ruler, with each ruling marking off a segment of wood an inch long; we construct hourglasses and clocks to mark uniform intervals of time. Analysis of the unit-perspective shows an important way in which all conceptualization, and the formulation of mathematics in particular, is a volitional process. It also shows that mathematics is based on reality, because units—whether chosen or created—are real. In using mathematics, man chooses units that bring reality within his grasp.

The uniform unit is the key to the unit-economical power of mathematical measurement. If you have 25 pouches of water of different sizes, to recall how much water you have in total requires that you recall the size of each pouch. But if each pouch is the same size, you need recall only two mental units: the number 25 and the size of your standard pouch.

7.3   THE LOGICAL STRUCTURE OF MATHEMATICS

We have developed and validated the basic methods of the science of mathematics. Let us now identify more explicitly the hierarchy of ideas in our new science. What are the basic concepts of mathematics? To answer this question, we can look back at the concepts we relied on in our development of the foundation of mathematics. Where did we start? We had the need to measure quantity, which is an attribute we perceive of groups of units. We then further employed our unit-perspective to invent a method to measure quantity; that method is the process of counting. We then invented numbers to denote specific counts.

Thus, the basic concepts of mathematics include the concepts of "quantity" and "unit," and the conceptual process of counting units (arranging units in unit-to-unit correspondence). The concept of "number" is based on these three concepts.

Now we shall identify the axioms of mathematics—the principles upon which all of mathematics rests. We will do this by examining the principles we relied on in our development of the science.

Every time we applied the logical principle of induction in counting, we relied on the premise that each unit in the group we were considering was interchangeable in our context with any other unit in that group. That premise was the only premise we used. A familiar colloquial expression of this condition is: "You cannot add apples and oranges." (You *can* add them, but only if you're considering them as pieces of fruit, in which context they *are* interchangeable.) The condition required to make each unit interchangeable was simply that each unit retain its unity—that it retain its identity as a separate, distinct unit in the group.

But what about general measurement? What condition do we need here? Again, the units must be interchangeable in the context being considered. In the context of general measurement, that condition is: each unit must be of uniform size; that is, each unit must be uniform in magnitude for the attribute being measured. In other words, "You cannot count oranges of different sizes to know how much juice they will make."

The premise of the interchangeable unit is what we may call the axiomatic condition of mathematics; when the condition is true, mathematics applies.

In most applications of counting, in which we are measuring amounts and not quantities of discrete objects, interchangeability will require the condition of the uniform unit, or, in familiar mathematical terminology, the "unit of measure."

Let us now translate the condition of the interchangeable unit into an axiom:

$$1 = 1$$

Observe that the concepts of quantity and unit are contained in this axiom. The concepts of counting and number are also contained in it: the symbol used for a unit is the number "1," denoting a *counted* unit.

This axiom of mathematics is *not* a restatement of the axiom of identity, "A is A." "A is A" means a thing is what it is. The statement "1 = 1" is not merely an attempt to restate "A is A" in the form "a thing equals itself." Rather, "1 = 1" means that each thing in the group equals each *other* thing in the group; each "one" equals each *other* "one." Furthermore, "1 = 1" does not mean that the *number* "one" equals itself. This axiom is not, most fundamentally, a statement about numbers; it is, most fundamentally, a statement about *units*. The axiom states that every group of one unit within a larger group of units equals every other group of one unit within that group of units.

Whereas the philosophic axiom "A is A" is true of all things, of "being *qua* being," "1 = 1" is not true of all things; it is much more restrictive. It states in mathematical terms the condition under which mathematics applies. If 1 = 1, that is, if our units are identical in the context being considered, then we can use mathematics. If our units are not equal or might not be equal (as with raindrops or applesauce over a period of time, different-sized oranges, etc.), then we cannot use mathematics.

That the axiom "1 = 1" is implicit in all mathematics can be seen by trying to devise a mathematical statement that does not assume it. Furthermore, because this axiom was the only premise beyond philosophy that we needed to develop mathematics, we believe that it is the only basic axiom of mathematics.

7.4   HISTORICAL CONTEXT

The fact identified by the axiom "1 = 1" was understood by the ancient Greeks. Klein (1968, 45) writes:

> The fundamental phenomenon which we should never lose sight of in determining the meaning of *arithmos* [the ancient Greek concept of "counting-number"] is counting, or more exactly, the *counting-off,* of some number of things. These things, however different they may be, are taken as uniform when counted; they are, for example, either *apples* or apples and pears which are counted as *fruit;* or apples, pears, and plates which are counted as "*objects.*" *Insofar* as these things underlie the counting process they are understood as *of the same kind.*

Plato (1994–2009, *The Republic*) writes about numbers, for which "each unit is equal, invariable, indivisible." (526a.) Plato states further, however, that such numbers are "numbers which can only be realized in thought." Thus, for Plato, the units constituting such numbers are equal in *every way* (equality thus being considered an intrinsic property of "pure" units), not merely equal in a given context (equality being an objective property of things).

In contrast to Plato's intrinsicism, Aristotle (1941, *Metaphysics*, Book X, Ch. 6, 1057a3,) writes that "number is a plurality measurable by one." Implicit in this statement is that all the units in the plurality are equal *in measure* (to the unit of measure), but not necessarily equal in every other way also.

The fact that "1 = 1" is an underlying premise for all mathematical statements was identified explicitly by Mill (1919, 170, III. xxiv.5). Mill, however, implicitly accepting another intrinsicist view (as opposed to an objective view), claims that "1 = 1" means that the units of mathematics are equal *to every degree of precision*; he therefore concludes that the premise "1 = 1" usually is not literally true in reality. Thus, instead of regarding "1 =1" as an axiom, Mill regards it as a faulty premise. Instead of using the axiom "1 = 1" to establish the certainty of mathematics, Mill concludes that this alleged faulty premise reveals mathematics to be as uncertain as other sciences such as physics (which he, as an Empiricist, also holds to be uncertain). In short, Mill finds fault with intrinsicism and consequently embraces what he thinks is the alternative: skepticism.

7.5   APPLICATIONS

Let us now look at some applications of our development of mathematics, including arithmetic, the number system, fractions, algebra, and geometry.

7.5.1   Arithmetic

Arithmetic is a system of methods for inferring the quantity of a group formed by combining or separating groups whose quantities are known. The four methods, or operations, of arithmetic are addition, subtraction, multiplication, and division. We shall briefly discuss addition and multiplication.

Suppose you have a group of four units and another group of five units. How many units would be in the group formed by combining these two groups?

You could answer this question by combining the groups and then counting the units. As long as each unit retained its unity after the combining, you would have a group of nine units. Addition tells you that whatever answer you get one time will be the answer you get *every* time. Therefore, now you know that whenever you add four units and five units of anything, you will end up with nine units. How can you prove this principle? By induction, of course. When you count, the only thing that matters about the units you count is that they are units interchangeable with each other. Therefore, you can substitute another kind of interchangeable unit for each unit you counted the first time, and you will get the same result as the first time.

Addition also tells you that the order of addition does not affect the result. For example, $4 + 5 = 5 + 4$; also, if you add three groups, the order is still irrelevant. The irrelevance of the order is a direct inference from the interchangeability of each unit.

Suppose you want to combine not merely two or three groups of units, but several groups. Suppose you want to combine five separate groups into one. You could perform the operation of addition four times. But if each of the five groups has the same number of units, you can use the operation of multiplication to calculate the combining in a single step.

The operation of multiplication is an application of the concept of the uniform unit. Multiplication works only if the groups being combined are of the same quantity, that is, if the groups themselves are uniform units of a larger, "second-order" group.

7.5.2   The Number System

Our modern method of counting is quite powerful. Nevertheless, if we need to count large-sized groups, we face the problem of "too many numbers," violating unit-economy. To handle this situation, men began to divide big groups into "subgroups" or "bundles," and then proceeded to count the subgroups.

For example, quinary grouping is grouping by fives. Today, some South American tribes count thusly: one, two, three, four, hand, hand and one, etc. Duodecimal grouping has twelve units in the subgroup; examples include twelve months in a year, twelve inches in a foot, twelve ounces in an ancient pound, twelve pence in a shilling, twelve hours on the clock, and the word "dozen." (See Eves, 1990,

12.) As we know, our modern number system uses groups of ten. The obvious reason is that ten is the number of fingers on both hands.

Note that bundling is an implicit use of the uniform unit. No one would bundle the first subgroup into five, the next into seven, and the next into three. All the subgroups always contain the same quantity of units. That way, each bundle is interchangeable and equal. One bundle equals any other one bundle.

The use of bundles did not stop with only one level of bundling. For example, the English system of linear measure has the following hierarchy of bundles: 12 inches is 1 foot (the first level of bundling), 3 feet is one yard (the second level of bundling), 5 1/2 yards is 1 rod (third level), and 320 rods is 1 mile (fourth level).

This system of bundles, though much better than no system at all, is complicated because the bundles of bundles contain different quantities than do the bundles of basic units. We would have a simpler system if each level of bundling bundled the same number of sub-bundles as did every other level. That way, the arithmetical rules we learned at one level would apply to any level. For example, we would not have 9 inches + 9 inches = 1 1/2 feet, while 9 feet + 9 feet = 6 yards.

This idea of standard-proportioned levels of bundling is the idea of a *base*. For example, ten tens is one hundred, ten hundreds is one thousand and so on. The metric system uses the base of ten consistently.

7.5.3   Fractions

In the previous section, we were concerned with handling large quantities with our number system. What if we want to *subdivide* a unit, such as a pizza pie? We might, for example, divide the pie into eight unequal slices, and then take three slices. Because the slices are unequal in size, we cannot say how much of the pie we have. We cannot compare the slices (except using nonmathematical comparisons such as bigger, smaller, equal), or add or subtract them. The reason is that to compare them mathematically, we need the slices to be of *uniform* size. That condition will allow us to use mathematics with pieces of a whole, that is, with fractions. Thus, we see how the uniform unit is implicit in the concept of fractions. Fractions are not merely parts of a whole; they are a count of *uniform-sized* parts of a whole.

Now let us look at two different pizza pies of equal size: the first pie is cut into three equal slices, and the second into four. How much of a pie is the sum of one slice from each? To make arithmetic possible with fractions of different sizes, men developed the method of finding a common denominator. In our example, the common denominator is twelve. This means that, conceptually, we cut each of the three slices from the first pie into four equal slices and each of the four slices from the second pie into three equal slices. Now all the conceptual slices are the same size, equal to one twelfth of a pie. A slice from the first pie equals four one-twelfth-sized slices, and a slice from the second pie equals three. Taken together, the two slices equal seven twelfths of a pie. When we take two fractions and convert them both to a common denominator, we are, conceptually, converting them to counts of units of the same size. Again, this development relied implicitly on the concept of the uniform unit.

We have already seen that with large numbers we want each higher-level bundle to contain the same number of lower-level bundles. The same kind of efficiency is important with fractions. The decimal system achieves this kind of efficiency.

7.5.4   Algebra

We will now give a brief overview of algebra. Numbers are a system of first-level abstractions. For example, the number "five" is a measurement describing *any* group of units of a certain quantity. The units must be some kind of existents, but they may be any existents, as long as they are interchangeable units in the context being considered. Arithmetic identifies relationships among these first-level abstractions—for example, $4 + 5 = 9$. In algebra, we let variables substitute in equations for numbers. Variables are abstractions from abstractions, because they are abstractions from numbers. Variables stand for some number, but they may stand for any number. Algebraic equations make wider generalizations than do arithmetic equations. For example, "$v \times t = d$" means that any velocity v maintained for any interval of time t results in a total distance traveled of d. Algebra then prescribes methods for using these more general equations to deduce specific conclusions. For instance, if we know in any specific case the values for any two of the variables v, t, and d, we can use algebra to calculate the value of the third variable.

7.5.5   Geometry

Where does geometry fit in the hierarchy of mathematics? The concepts of quantity, counting, and number (and, therefore, the axiom of mathematics, "$1 = 1$") are not implicit in many geometric statements. Consider these examples: "Straight paths that do not share a plane will not cross." "A circle can fit inside another circle of greater diameter." Moreover, geometric statements rely on *other* basic concepts, such as "physical extension," "direction," and "shape."

Is geometry, then, a counterexample to our entire theory of mathematics? No. Our conclusion is that geometry is not a branch of mathematics! In fact, geometry should be a branch of physics. Geometry deals with only one kind of uniform unit: units of physical extension, that is, length. On the other hand, mathematics deals with general principles about units that are uniform in *any* attribute—weight, length, time, function, etc.

Because geometry attempts to *measure* physical extension ("geometry"), it makes sense to apply mathematics to geometry—for example, to determine the area of a circle—but that does not make geometry a branch of mathematics. Mathematics is also applied to electricity and magnetism, but that does not make those branches of physics branches of mathematics either. Mathematics, as a science of method, must be applied to *some* content, but it can be applied to *any* content where there are units to count.

How, then, did geometry and mathematics get placed together in modern studies? The Pythagoreans believed that numbers were physical entities composed of elemental objects arranged in perfect geometric shapes. All areas of study that exhibited the "perfection" of numbers were claimed to be fields of mathematics. These four fields were music, geometry, astronomy, and number theory. Indeed, algebra was excluded from mathematics because of the discovery of irrational numbers, which were considered to be imperfect. This demarcation of mathematics persisted until the Renaissance. (Clawson 1994, 109–111, 119.)

There is no essential characteristic common to both mathematics and geometry that distinguishes these two fields from all other sciences; this fact is implied unintentionally by one textbook's definition of mathematics: "the study of quantity and space." But there is something that modern mathematicians *think* is shared by these two fields. They think that these two fields deal with "pure" abstractions—such as number, point, and line—which are unconnected to the world we perceive. In keeping with that metaphysical premise is this epistemological corollary: mathematics and geometry use neither facts of reality nor induction; they use only deduction from arbitrary (or "intuitive") postulates. Indeed, one of the habits that modern educators impart in the teaching of both mathematics and geometry is the use of this kind of contextless deduction.

Of course, the premise that mathematics deals with abstractions divorced from reality is true of no field of knowledge.

7.6   THE INFINITE IN MATHEMATICS

"Infinite" means "without end or limit." In contrast, open-ended means "with end or limit omitted, not specified, not significant, not relevant; with no extra end or limit imposed *onto* reality over and above those that already exist *in* reality"—that is, not "unlimited" but rather "unlimit*ing*."

For example, the concept "man" imposes no limits, beyond those that already exist in reality, upon how many units in reality can be men—nor does it remove any limits that *do* exist in reality. The concept "big" imposes no extra limits onto how big the biggest thing can be; whatever limits there are, they are already in reality.

Likewise, the concept "number" imposes no extra limits onto how large the largest quantity is or can be or on how many numbers there are or can be—nor does it remove any limits that already exist in reality.

The issue of infinity is not merely a matter of Aristotle's distinction between potentiality and actuality. The forming of the concepts "man" or "number" does not establish the potential for infinitely-many men or infinitely-large quantities any more than it establishes the actuality for these things. The issue is the primacy of existence vs. the primacy of consciousness. The open-ended feature of concepts is in keeping with the primacy of existence. Being open-ended—that is, unlimiting—a concept is designed to conform to reality, neither augmenting nor removing limits that exist in reality. The conventional notion of infinity is based on the primacy of consciousness: just because one's notion of number does not specify a limit, it is assumed that reality follows suit and is itself unlimited.

7.7 BASIC DEFINITIONS

The number "1" is the most basic number. It means "a uniform unit considered by itself." The number "1" can be used to express, in mathematical terms, the basic axiom of mathematics: $1 = 1$.

But what are the other numbers? A common question is: Are the natural numbers (1, 2, 3, etc.) the only "true" numbers? For example, is a fraction a number, or is it a composite of two numbers in a certain relation? And what about negative, irrational, and complex numbers? And what about mathematical expressions in general? If "7" is a number, is "4 + 3" also a number? What about a number like

"25," which means 2 tens and 5 ones? Is "25" not one number but a combination of four numbers (2, 10, 5, and 1)?

Answering these questions will deepen our understanding of the cognitive function of mathematics, and of numbers in particular.

Recall the following from Section 7.2.4:

> The uniform unit is the key to the unit-economical power of mathematical measurement. If you have 25 pouches of water of different sizes, to recall how much water you have in total requires that you recall the size of each pouch. But if each pouch is the same size, you need recall only two mental units: the number 25 and the size of your standard pouch.

But further, for the mental unit "25" to be as useful as possible cognitively, its relation to the mental unit "1," and to mental units such as "24" and "26," should be clearly grasped.

Now we are ready to define the concept "number."

A number is a measurement of quantity, expressed as a count of uniform units reduced to a single mental unit, that brings the measurement within the clearest possible conceptual grasp in relation to the number 1 (a lone unit) and other numbers. (Recall that quantity is the degree of repetition of units in a group.) A more concise definition would remove the clause after the comma.

Therefore, "25" is a number; although it is composed of other numbers, it is still a single mental unit and the relation of "25" to "1," "24," and "26" is quite clear. In contrast, a row of 25 hash marks is not a number because it cannot be held as a single mental unit nor is its relation to a single hash mark or to a row of 24 hash marks clear. Also, an expression like "4 + 3" is not a number because it must be reduced to "7" to clarify its relation to "6," "7," and "8," for instance.

Although there is some optionality, I think it is preferable to consider negative numbers and irrational numbers to be numbers. Regarding fractions, I would also consider simple fractions (such as ½), decimal fractions (such as 1.5), and "mixed numbers" (such as 3½) to be numbers. My reason is that each of these numbers is a single mental unit that provides a clear grasp of its respective measurement in relation to a single unit and to other numbers.

For example, if one pole is 1 foot long, another 2 feet long, and another 1.5 feet long, it is possible to see instantly that 1.5, though a fractional number, is a single measurement that falls between the other two measurements in a clear and precise way. The fact that 1.5 is a fraction, whereas 1 and 2 are whole numbers, is less significant cognitively than the fact that they are all clearly ordered numerical measurements that can be dealt with using the same mathematical tools. The same argument holds for a number like $1.414 \rightarrow \sqrt{2}$, as introduced in Section A.1.3 of the Appendix. On the other hand, I would generally consider the same measurement expressed as $\sqrt{2}$ a mathematical expression, not a number: Although $\sqrt{2}$ can be held as a single mental unit, it must be reduced to a number like $1.414 \rightarrow \sqrt{2}$ to be clearly related to 1 and other numbers. Likewise, I would generally not consider "improper fractions" (such as 9/4) to be numbers, because to grasp such quantities fully, one must reduce them to mixed numbers (such as 2¼). Nevertheless, the distinction between a number and a mathematical expression made up of numbers can vary with context.

A borderline case is complex numbers (see Section A.1.5 of the Appendix), which can be viewed as a pair of numbers, because they are a count of two different (though related) kinds of units and can be considered as two measurements; but because they can also be considered as a single measurement using two kinds of units that are so precisely related—indeed, one kind of unit ($i1$) is defined in terms of the other—I think it is also valid to consider a complex number a single number.

In light of the central role of the uniform unit, here is my proposed definition for mathematics: *Mathematics is the science of measurement through the numeration of uniform units.* (Numeration is the assignment of a number to a quantity of uniform units.) One could state, more concisely, that mathematics is the science of numerical measurement, because the concept of the uniform unit is implicit in the concept "number"; nevertheless, the concept of the uniform unit is so important and so little known that I prefer to include it explicitly in the definition of mathematics.

7.8   PROBABILITY AND STATISTICS

Probability and statistics, like geometry, are not part of mathematics. They are part of epistemology, enabling precise measurements of certainty, possibility, and probability.

For probability and statistics, what are the right uniform units to count? The "classicist" school, which I support, counts "equally likely possibilities." The "frequentist" school counts outcomes of large groups of repeated actions. (The "subjectivist" school does not count anything; their method is as mathematical—and as valid—as guessing weights or distances by feeling.) Which, if either, of these two schools is right? The answer does not come from mathematics. But now we are on the subject of a different chapter—the next one in this book. The important issue for mathematics is to see that properly delimiting the subject of mathematics clarifies its essence: the uniform unit.

The important issue for epistemology will be to discover how considering probability and statistics part of epistemology can advance all three of these fields.

Probability theory will be essential to the theory of induction presented in Chapters 8 and 9.

7.9   SUMMARY AND CONCLUSION

In this chapter, we have taken the fundamental concepts and principles implicit in mathematics and made them explicit. We first saw that mathematics begins with the process of counting units to measure quantity, which is the degree of repetition of units in a group; this process depends on the unit-perspective, identified by Ayn Rand. We validated and generalized the process of counting through a series of inductions. We then developed a system of numbers as a means to improve the counting process. The essential concept that makes mathematical measurement possible is the concept of the "uniform unit," or the unit of measure. The uniform unit is the means by which we applied the process of counting to measurement in general. The basic axiom of mathematics is "1 = 1". This axiom is the expression of the interchangeable or uniform unit. We used the uniform unit to explain several developments in mathematics, such as arithmetic, the number system, fractions, and algebra.

Whereas mathematical statements are usually thought to be statements about numbers, we show that all mathematical statements—from the axiom of mathematics to the most complex equation—are, most fundamentally, statements about units chosen for grasping reality. "Three plus four equals seven" is not a statement about abstract number-objects in a non-real "world"; it states that three *units* plus four *units* equals seven of that kind of *units*. Whether one is studying simple arithmetic or trying to devise the most advanced new mathematical technique, remembering that fact will keep one's mathematical concepts anchored to reality.

Because it deals with units in reality, not abstractions divorced from reality, mathematics uses the logical method of induction as well as deduction.

* * *

When considering units in mathematics, the only attribute we care about is that the units retain their unity in the context being considered. This attribute—the retaining of unity—is taken as a conditional, an "if-then." *If* the units being considered retain their unity, *then* mathematics holds. If I count some number of apples, then mathematics tells me that there are that number of apples—*so long as the apples remain apples.*

But outside of mathematics, we must know more than such a conditional. Sure, if a rock remains a rock, then it will continue to act like a rock, by definition. Sure, if the laws of motion continue to hold in the future, then they will predict future motion. But how do we know that the rock will remain a rock? How do we know that laws of motion, which have held in the past, will continue to hold in the future? How reliably can the past and present tell us about the future?

It is questions such as these that we will answer in the next two chapters, with a richer form of induction.

8   CAUSALITY AND INDUCTION

We have seen that any instance of a state of consciousness is an interaction between existence and our faculty of consciousness (our
self), with existence acting on our self to bring about a state of consciousness. Existence and our faculty of consciousness are the cause,
and our state of consciousness is the effect.

A corollary to this fact is that all knowable action is through *interaction*. Suppose there were some existent that acted but never interacted with anything else. Then we would never know about it or ever
be affected by it in any way. If any such existent does exist, it is *ineffectual*, and therefore irrelevant to our lives.

As we shall see, it is this connection between action and interaction that makes identifying the causal interaction between existence
and consciousness such an important cognitive basis for establishing
a more general knowledge of causality as underlying all action.

But we have established more than just that there are causal interactions between external existence and consciousness. We have
established that there is a *constancy* or *regularity* to causal interactions between external existence and consciousness, and a constancy
or regularity to the interactions among parts of external existence.
Indeed, this constancy led us to validate the conclusion that *we perceive entities.*

Now we must validate the plausible assumptions that our perception of entities will continue in the future (Section 8.2), and that entities interact causally with one another and will continue to do so
(Section 8.3). To perform these validations, we will introduce and
employ probabilistic reasoning and a method of induction that goes

163

from a large number of observed instances to a conclusion about future instances.

Some readers may think that these validations do no more than prove the obvious. Nevertheless, aside from defending reason and knowledge from the legion of skeptics since Hume and Kant, and aside from providing philosophical grounding and mathematical precision to certain methods that most laymen use implicitly and fallibly, these validations reveal a powerful method of induction with wide applications. To that end, beginning in Section 8.4, we will further develop and use the same method of induction to offer a philosophic validation of scientific causal laws such as the laws of motion.

(For readers interested in how my theory of induction compares to other contemporary theories in the philosophy of science, Norton 2018 provides a thorough survey and interesting analysis of the leading theories—replete with many fascinating, in-depth examples from the history of science.)

Let us begin then with an introduction to the probabilistic reasoning underlying this method of induction.

8.1 PROBABILISTIC REASONING UNDERLYING INDUCTION

8.1.1 The Meaning of Probability

Let us begin with the proper meaning of probability. Probability is epistemological—a statement about cognition.

The statement, "There is a one in 18 probability that the next roll of a pair of dice will be 11" means that out of 18 outcomes that exhaust all the possible outcomes and which are equally likely in my current context of knowledge, in one of those outcomes the roll of the dice will equal 11.

This statement does not mean that the roll of dice definitely will be 11 or definitely will not be 11. The statement does not mean that, in 18 rolls, 11 will come up once. Nor does it state that, in 18 million rolls, 11 will definitely come up approximately one million times. Nor does it state that, as the dice are rolled more and more times, the proportion of times that the dice will come up 11 will approach 1 in 18. (Nevertheless, it can be inferred that, as the dice are rolled more and more times, the proportion of times that the dice will come up 11 will more and more *probably* approach 1 in 18.) The statement simply means that on the next roll of the dice, out of 18 possibilities that, in my context of knowledge, are exhaustive, mutually exclusive, and equally likely, one and only one of those possibilities is that the dice will come up 11.

Recalling the idea of the uniform unit (or unit of measure), introduced in the previous chapter, the uniform units in this case are the 18 equally likely outcomes.

The steps required for this reasoning are as follows: First, identify a set of outcomes that are mutually exclusive, exhaustive, and equally likely in your context of knowledge (based on the fact that you have no rational basis for choosing any among them to be any more or less likely than any other). Then, tally up how many of those outcomes imply the more-generally-stated outcome whose probability you are trying to assess.

For example, in the case of a pair of dice about which you know only that each die has six faces from 1 through 6, you can identify 36 equally likely, exhaustive, and mutually exclusive (that is, disjoint) outcomes: 1-1, 1-2, 1-3, ..., 6-4, 6-5, 6-6. Out of those 36 outcomes, two—5-6 and 6-5—entail the outcome 11. Therefore, the probability of an 11 is 2 out of 36, or 1 out of 18. (Of course, the 36 outcomes can be combined into 18 equally likely, exhaustive, and disjoint paired outcomes: 5-6 or 6-5, and 17 other pairs. Accordingly, the probability of an 11 is still 1 out of 18.) Equivalently, the probability of rolling a non-11 is 17/18.

For most inductions in science or engineering, a probability of 17/18 is not nearly high enough for us to be reasonably assured of the outcome we are depending on. For example, such a probability is not high enough for the safety of an airplane's flight. The industry standard for the airlines has historically been on the order of "six nines": .999999. Establishing such a high probability requires that we find at least one million equally likely outcomes. Moreover, establishing such a high probability for a flight of an airplane requires an astronomically higher probability for the truth of the laws of physics underlying the construction of the airplane. How, then, do we find so many equally likely outcomes?

Sometimes, a single instance of a single experiment can have astronomically-many possible outcomes. We already saw how the roll of a pair of dice has 36 equally likely outcomes. Well, a roll of a set of 16 dice has $6^{16} = 2.8$ trillion equally likely outcomes.

In other cases, a high number of equally likely outcomes requires a high number of instances of a given experiment. In such cases, we need an argument by which the many instances lead to many equally likely outcomes. The present chapter presents my argument and an introduction to obtaining astronomically many instances. The subsequent chapter explains in more depth how to obtain astronomically many instances, and identifies further methods for making our inductions more powerful and robust.

8.1.2   The $n/(n+1)$ Method

My argument, first presented in Pisaturo 2009 and then expanded in Pisaturo [2011] 2016—and building on arguments by Jeffreys (1932), Hill (1968, 1988), and Coolen (1998) regarding a method now known as nonparametric predictive inference (Coolen 2011)—exploits Ayn Rand's identification of characteristics as ranges of measurement (1990, 6–11). Let us take an example.

The hue red is a range of measurements of frequency of light; in particular, the hue red is on the low end of frequencies for visible light. Suppose that I have randomly selected a large number—call the number n—of pebbles from a bunch of pebbles. Suppose that I have observed all n pebbles to be red in hue. Suppose that I know nothing about these pebbles relevant to hue except what I have just observed. (The bunch of pebbles might all have been inside a mysterious black bag I have just stumbled upon, or they might have been on the floor of a deep well I have just discovered in a region I know little about.) Those n pebbles are the many instances. What is the probability that the next selected pebble will also be red?

As we are about to see, the answer to my question is embedded in the phrase "randomly selected" in my supposition for this example. This phrase means that my order of selection of pebbles is not known to predict or to be predicted by any hue. That is, in our context of knowledge, the order of selection is not a causal factor of hue, nor is hue or something causing hue known to be a causal factor of order of selection.

Now comes the probabilistic argument leading to equally likely outcomes. The next measurement of hue is equally likely to be the lowest, second lowest, third lowest, ..., third highest, second highest, and highest. That is, we have $n+1$ equally likely outcomes. Of these possible outcomes, only if the new measurement of hue turns out to be the highest is it possible that the hue is not red. Therefore, the probability that the frequency of visible light reflected by the next pebble will be the highest among all the pebbles sampled is $1/(n+1)$, or less than $1/(n+1)$ because of the possibility of ties. Therefore, the probability that the next pebble examined will be red is greater than or equal to $n/(n+1)$. The "greater than" condition applies not only because of the possibility of ties, but—more importantly—because it is possible that a new highest frequency of visible light will still be within the range of red.

If the hue of all the pebbles being considered were not red but instead green—a hue that is somewhere in the middle of the spectrum of visible light—then the final probability would be greater than or equal to $(n-1)/(n+1)$. That is because a non-green hue could be either of greater or lesser frequency than green.

This simple argument and simple conclusion are extremely powerful—especially when combined with Bayes' Theorem, a fundamental theorem of probability theory. Let us apply these ideas to my earlier discussion about the four characteristics of entities.

8.2   Using Induction to Validate the Future Persistence of Entities

The first of the four characteristics of entities is as follows: An entity acts on our senses such that both our sight and touch sense distinctive action and distinct boundaries (implying a distinct shape) of the entity. We can call this characteristic 'distinctiveness'.

For the purpose of the present analysis, we can combine this first characteristic with the third characteristic, which is as follows: An entity acts on our senses in a persistent way. We can call this characteristic 'persistence'.

Let us take sight. Suppose we have observed a stick for the duration of an hour. We can divide that duration into 3,600 seconds. In each of those seconds, as we moved around the stick or moved the stick, the visual appearance of the shape of the stick obeyed the laws of optics in such a way that was consistent with the stick retaining its rigid shape within some measurement—say, epsilon—in all dimensions. What is the probability that the stick will retain its rigid shape, within the measurement epsilon, in the next second? By the same reasoning used in the above case of the red pebbles, the probability is greater than or equal to 3,600/3,601.

It is important to note that we are not establishing a probability for the existence of causality. We already know with absolute certainty that existents are exerting causal forces on our consciousness. The probability pertains to the regularity and predictability of the sum of all the causal factors and their effects in the future.

These examples rely on advanced knowledge: knowledge of the color spectrum and of laws of optics. Are we begging the question or using circular reasoning? As in our earlier example of the engineer discovering oil (Section 3.2), the answer is no. We had to assume the future persistence of entities based on automatic integrations of our perceptual faculty, an automatic faculty similar to the faculty possessed by animals. Starting from these plausible assumptions, and following a long chain of scientific experimentation and inference, man was able to reach advanced knowledge in the form of advanced formulas relating mathematical measurements not only of past phenomena, but also of expected future phenomena. However, the knowledge that these past phenomena were of persisting entities, which will persist in the future, was not fully validated until we could validate the initial assumptions. We are validating those initial assumptions now. Although we needed those assumptions to precede our advanced scientific formulas *chronologically*, we are no longer relying on those assumptions *logically*.

Similarly, a scientist might use plausible assumption in order to formulate a hypothesis; but once he proves the hypothesis, the hypothesis is proved.

Part of our validation of the plausible assumption of the future existence of entities is to show the great degree of consistency between our sensory evidence for entities and our advanced scientific and mathematical formulas. We are showing that our automatic perceptual integrations, which gave us awareness of entities, were not capricious or idiosyncratic. These integrations are consistent with scientific laws we later identified.

We can perform the same analysis for other visual characteristics such as brightness and visually perceived texture (such as the rough texture of the bark on the outside of the stick), and for tactile characteristics such as shape, texture, hardness, flexibility, and heaviness.

But what is the probability that our stick will retain its rigid shape, within measurement epsilon, for the duration of the next half hour? Our past observations, of sight and touch, were over the course of two half hours, and now we have to consider a third half hour. By our method, and with only the evidence presented so far, all we can say is that such probability is greater than or equal to 2/3.

For most purposes, this probability is not informative enough. Indeed, suppose we are buying a walking stick or cane. We might observe the cane for only a few seconds, and we want the stick to retain its rigid shape for a year or more. The previous method, without enhancement, is useless for our purpose.

But there are things we can do to increase the number and/or duration of instances. We have observed other canes for long periods of time. We learn about materials; in particular, we learn about wood. Then we have an extremely large number of instances of pieces of wood in the approximate shape of a cane. More generally, we observe and learn about solids, and we then have an astronomically large number of instances of solids retaining their rigid shape. Then we learn about chemical bonds, and we have an even more astronomically large number of instances of chemical bonds persisting. Each deeper level of knowledge, integrating more observations, increases the number of instances to bring to bear in formulating the probability that the stick will retain its perceptual characteristics. (See the subchapter "9.1 Greater Enumeration Through Integration" for more examples of this kind.) Thus our number of instances n becomes astronomical, and $n/(n+1)$ becomes extremely close to 1, validating our knowledge that the first and third characteristics of entities will continue into the future.

Now let us consider the second characteristic of entities: An entity acts on our senses such that our sight and touch of the entity are consistent with each other. We can call this characteristic 'consistency across sense modalities'.

We can readily measure this consistency. For one thing, we can measure characteristics by our visual perception of them and by our tactile perception of them. For instance, we can visually compare the length of a stick to the length of our hand, and we can tactilely make the same comparison. Then we can compare the two comparisons and measure the difference between the two comparisons. For example, by visual measurement, we might measure that the stick is equal to two hand lengths, give or take 1 millimeter. We might draw the same conclusion by measuring the stick by touch. Therefore, the visual and tactile measurements would agree to within 2 millimeters of accuracy. We can make these comparisons n times. Suppose each of the n times yields an agreement of measurement within 2 millimeters. Then we can conclude that the probability that the next comparison will yield the greatest difference—more than 2 millimeters—is less than or equal to $1/(n+1)$.

We can also measure the synchronicity of these two sensory modes. We can feel the stick with our hand, we can see the stick in contact with our hand, and we can measure the difference in time between when these two forms of awareness of contact begin and end. The probability that the next instance will be less synchronous than the n previous instances is less than or equal to $1/(n+1)$.

Of course, each of us personally has a lifetime of instances of very precise synchrony.

We are also aware of apparent exceptions. As mentioned earlier, if we are sitting in the outfield bleachers at a baseball game, our awareness of the ball flying off the bat precedes our hearing the sound. Similarly, we see distant lightning before we hear the thunder. We can treat these observations in at least three different ways—two primitive, and one more advanced and fruitful.

One primitive way is to include the baseball and lightning instances just like instances of nearby events. Then we might have a range of synchronicity from zero to ten seconds. Then we could conclude that the next instance will have a synchronicity of ten seconds or less with probability of greater than or equal to $n/(n+1)$.

A second primitive way is to note that p of the n instances had a synchronicity of within a fifth of a second. Then we could conclude that the probability of the next instance having a synchronicity of within a fifth of a second is greater than or equal to $p/(n+1)$.

Of course a far better way is to notice the mathematical correlation between synchronicity, of sight and sound, and one's distance from the action. Then one can conclude that the probability of deviation by epsilon—that is, a very small duration—from a mathematical formula for synchronicity is less than or equal to $1/(n+1)$. (I will capitalize on this idea further in Section 9.1.3, "Integration Through Lawful Quantification of Differences.") Then it is straightforward to amass a very large number n of instances, making $n/(n+1)$ extremely close to 1 for our second characteristic continuing into the future.

Thus we have validated the conclusion that the first three characteristics of entities will continue into the future.

In this section, we have considered the example of a stick; of course, our reasoning applies to all entities that we observe. One entity in particular is especially important for the further discovery of causal forces. That entity is one's own body. In the next section, we will begin to see the importance of knowing that one's own body is an entity.

8.3   CAUSAL INTERACTION OF ENTITIES

8.3.1   Proving Causal Interaction of Entities

Now let us consider the fourth characteristic of entities: In addition to acting on our senses in a distinctive and persistent way, an entity acts in a distinctive and persistent way in relation to other entities.

Recall some of our examples: Just as the wind knocks us over, so the wind can knock over the chair. Just as a mother lifts her child (and the child feels the force of his mother), so the mother lifts the chair. Just as I fall when I step over the ledge, so a rock falls when I drop it from a ledge. Just as a horse carries me in the saddle, so the horse carries a saddle.

Take the example of the horse and the saddle. Both the horse and the saddle exert causal forces on me: I know this because I perceive the horse and the saddle. The question then is whether the horse and the saddle exert causal forces on each other. We can answer this question with an even simpler and more widely known kind of probabilistic argument than the one we have been using.

The successful use of this argument hinges on my knowledge that the horse and saddle exert causal forces on me. To the question of whether the horse exerts causal forces on the saddle, there are only two possible answers: yes or no. Because I know that the horse exerts causal forces on me, it is reasonable to assign, in the absence of any further information, a non-zero, non-infinitesimal probability to the answer "yes." Indeed, it is reasonable to assign a probability of more than a half, but any non-zero, non-infinitesimal probability would be enough to prove our conclusion. Let us do the math using a probability of a half, still a conservative assumption given that we want to prove the answer of "yes."

We will use the well-known "product rule" from probability theory. (For a good primer on the product rule and on Bayes' Theorem, which follows from it, see Drake 1967, 13–27). I will use the notation of Jaynes (2003, 88): "X = prior information; H = some hypothesis to be tested; D = the data." By this notation, $P(H|X)$ is what is commonly known as the prior probability of hypothesis H given the prior information X, before observing the data D; and $P(H|DX)$ is what is commonly known as the posterior probability, after observing the data D.

In the present case,
- The hypothesis H is that the horse exerts causal forces on the saddle.
- The prior information X is that the horse and saddle exert causal forces on me.
- The data D is only one item, as follows: Precisely when the horse begins, the saddle goes with him and stays with the horse all the way through the time when the horse stops a minute later. This behavior of the saddle is similar to my behavior when the horse carries me.

The product rule states,

$$P(H|DX)P(D|X) = P(HD|X) = P(H|X)P(D|HX).$$

In English, this equation means the following:

(The probability of the hypothesis H given the data D and the prior information X) times (the probability of the data D given the prior information X)

equals

(the probability of the hypothesis H and the data D given the prior information X)

equals

(the probability of the hypothesis H given the prior information X) times (the probability of the data D given the hypothesis H and the prior information X).

From this product rule, Bayes' Theorem follows directly by dividing both sides by $P(D|X)$:

$$P(H|DX) = [P(H|X)P(D|HX)]/P(D|X).$$

Let us evaluate all the factors in this equation.

$P(H|X) = 1/2$, by our conservative assignment.

$P(D|HX) = 1$. That is, if the hypothesis is true, then the saddle will indeed go with the horse.

Evaluating $P(D|X)$ is a little more complex. We have to break down $D|X$, the data given the prior information, into two parts:

- $D|HX$, the data given the prior information and given the hypothesis H is true;
- $D|{\sim}HX$, the data given the prior information and given the hypothesis H is not true. (The symbol "~" means "not.")

To calculate the probabilities related to $D|HX$ and $D|{\sim}HX$, we again have to use the product rule, accounting for the probabilities of H and ${\sim}H$. Thus,

$$P(D|X) = P(D|HX)P(H|X) + P(D|{\sim}HX)P({\sim}H|X)$$

$$= 1(1/2) + \varepsilon(1/2)$$

$$= 1/2 + \varepsilon(1/2),$$

where ε is a very small number greater than zero. Let us explain these two terms, $1/2$ and $\varepsilon(1/2)$, in turn.

If the horse exerts a causal force on the saddle, in accordance with hypothesis H (which has probability $1/2$), then the saddle will go with the horse with probability 1. Thus,

$$P(D|HX)P(H|X) = 1(1/2) = 1/2.$$

But if, in accordance with ~*H*, the horse does not exert a causal force on the saddle, then there are many possible places that the saddle could go. Suppose the horse travels a straight path of 2,000 feet in a minute. If we consider that straight path the radius of a circle, then the circumference of that circle is more than 12,000 feet. When the horse carries me, my geographic location varies by much less than one foot compared to the geographic location of the horse. If we conservatively consider possible locations of the saddle to fall in one-foot increments, then there are 12,000 equally likely places on the circumference where the saddle could end up. But the saddle could also, with at least equal likelihood—end up within the circle. Because the area of the circle is πr^2, or more than 12 million square feet, there are more than 12 million possible final locations of the saddle, if we consider a conservative resolution of one foot in each coordinate. But that calculation accounts only for the final position after a full minute. What about all the seconds in between? And what about vertical position as well? And what about the possibility of the saddle remaining at rest, or ending up outside the circle? Thus we see that there are many millions of possible outcomes for the saddle's position, each outcome as least as likely—if there is no causality at work—as the outcome that the saddle remains on the horse.

Therefore, if the horse does not exert a causal force on the saddle, then there is only a tiny chance ε—where ε is much less than 1/12,000,000—that the saddle will move precisely with the horse (that is, as precisely as the horse's ongoing action on my senses). Thus,

$$P(D|{\sim}HX)P({\sim}H|X) = \varepsilon(1/2).$$

Therefore, we have evaluated $P(D|X)$ as follows:

$$P(D|X) = 1/2 + \varepsilon(1/2).$$

Therefore,

$$P(H|DX) = (1/2)/[(1/2) + \varepsilon(1/2)]$$

$$= 1/(1 + \varepsilon),$$

which is just a little less than 1. In other words, after only one observation of the saddle going with the horse, we are virtually certain that hypothesis H is true: that the horse exerts causal forces on the saddle, just as the horse and saddle exert causal forces on me. Of course, with more such observations—and we have many more such observations—we are even more certain of this conclusion. The key to our certainty of this conclusion is our certainty that existence causes our consciousness of it, so that the prior probability $P(H|X)$ is significantly greater than zero. Even if $P(H|X)$ were small, on the order of ε, it would not take many observations to reach the same conclusion with virtual certainty.

For clarity, let us directly connect our use of Bayes' Theorem, in the example above, to our earlier explanation of the meaning of probability in terms of equally likely possibilities.

In our example, we identified two equally likely possibilities: H, that the horse exerted causal forces on the saddle to the same degree of regularity as did the horse on our senses; and what we can call H_C, the contrary of H.

Then we divided H_C into 12 million (or more) sub-possibilities: all the possible spatial relations between the horse and the saddle, given H_C.

Then our experiment eliminated all but one of the 12 million (or more) sub-possibilities for H_C. The one remaining sub-possibility for H_C is one 12-millionth (or less) in magnitude compared to the possibility of H. That is, after the experiment, H is virtually certain.

Readers new to probability theory might think it odd that a hypothesis can start with a prior probability of only one half and become virtually certain after only one observation. But consider the following simple example. Suppose you forget to take your brand-new copy of *Cyrano* with you when you leave a coffee shop. You phone your friend who works at the coffee shop and ask him to leave the book for you on the bookshelf in the corner. Then you send your friend a text message to put a sticky note on the book with the number "459,385,072" written on it, so that you know the copy of *Cyrano* you see on the bookshelf is your copy. You arrive at the coffee shop without knowing whether your friend (or anyone else) has received your text message, and you figure that there is about a 50-50 chance that he did receive your text. You see your copy of *Cyrano* on the bookshelf, and—sure enough—it has a sticky note with "459,385,072" written on it. You rightly conclude that it is virtually certain that your friend (or someone) received your text. Indeed, even if you had started out thinking there is only a one-in-a-million chance that your text had been received, your seeing the note with "459,385,072" written on it would rightly lead you to conclude that your text had been received. Your conclusion is based on an implicit version of Bayes' Theorem, in the form of the following thought: "If my friend received the text, then it follows that he wrote the number; but if he did not receive the text, then it is extremely unlikely that he would write this particular number."

The same kind of reasoning goes into well-known procedures for verifying an individual's identity. If an individual logs on to a computer using John's strong 12-digit password on the first try, then it is very probable—though not certain—that the individual is John.

Thus we have proved—that is, we have proved with probability extremely close to 1—that the horse exerts causal forces on the saddle.

But we can strengthen and broaden our conclusion. For one thing, we can observe the horse and the saddle for more than just one minute. We can observe them for an hour, or a day, or a year, thereby providing the evidence to conclude that—with high probability—the horse will continue to exert causal forces on the saddle in the next minute or hour.

Then we can observe the action of the horse relative to entities other than the saddle: The horse carries a man, pulls a wagon, makes imprints on the ground, eats food, and so on. We can then conclude that the horse exerts causal force on these n entities for large n.

We can then identify a characteristic, "degree of causal interaction," to be measured by the degree of conjunction of action between entities. For all n observed entities, the degree of causal action with the horse was the same. Then we can conclude that, with probability greater than or equal to $n/(n+1)$, the horse will exert—to at least the same degree of causal interaction—causal force on the next entity it comes in contact with.

What about an object that is too heavy for the horse to carry or pull? Are such cases governed by causality? Of course the answer is yes. For a discussion of such cases, see Section 9.1.3, Integration Through Lawful Quantification of Differences.

We can perform a similar study of the saddle being acted on by n other entities. Then we can conclude that the next entity will also act causally on the saddle.

Then we can perform a study of n different entities interacting with one another. Then we can conclude that every new entity that we perceive (and that therefore acts causally on our senses) will obey causal laws with every other entity that we perceive.

Regarding the above Bayesian argument, one might object that I skip steps. I went from knowing that the horse acts causally on my senses to concluding that the horse acts causally on the saddle, without the intermediate step of proving that the horse acts causally on me *qua* physical entity.

But this intermediate step is not needed. Once I know that the horse causes my consciousness of it, it is reasonable—even conservative—to assign a prior probability of 1/2 or more that the horse will exert causal forces on other things, such as the saddle. And again, so long as this prior probability is more than infinitesimal, the proof goes through.

In the proofs above, note the division of labor among the various methods and items of evidence:
- Knowing that my body is a physical entity, acting in a certain kind of way in relation to the horse and the saddle, tells me what kind of actions to look for from the saddle and the horse in relation to each other.

- We used the product rule to prove the existence of causality in a given case, and also in n given cases.
- We used n cases plus the $n/(n+1)$ rule to prove the existence of causality in the next case.

Thus we have proved—by establishing a probability extremely close to 1—that entities act on each other with the same causality and causal regularity that they exercise in acting on our own consciousness, and will continue to do so.

8.3.2   Mathematical Units Revisited

Our proof above relied on our knowledge of existence causing our consciousness of it. There is other knowledge that we relied on. We relied on our knowledge that entities, including the horse and the saddle, have some amount of physical extension, occupying some physical location. We did not have to know that these entities would continue to occupy physical location in the future, only that they had done so up until now. We also had observed no tendency for the entities in question to occupy one location over another.

It was this combination of knowledge that enabled us mentally to divide the physical space in a certain region into equally-sized parts—or units—and to assign equal probabilities for each part to the eventual location of the saddle.

This process of mentally constructing equally-sized units is the bridge from Ayn Rand's idea of units of a concept to the mathematical idea of a "unit of measure," making mathematical measurement possible. (Recall Sections 7.2.3 and 7.2.4.)

8.3.3   Exclusivity

There is another corpus of perceptual evidence, perhaps even more basic and ubiquitous than the evidence we have just considered, that entities act causally on each other. Only one entity occupies a given place at a given time. We can call this characteristic 'exclusivity'. If one entity moves into a place previously occupied by a second entity, then the second entity moves out of that place. For instance, if I put my hand where a book had been—that is, if I push the book—the book moves away. That result occurs when oneself is one of the entities involved, and when both entities are not oneself. From this ubiquitous evidence, we can reprise the Bayesian and $n/(n+1)$ probabilistic arguments above, proving that entities act causally on each other, and that this behavior will continue for a long time into the future.

Returning briefly to our example of the horse and the saddle, even when an object is too heavy for the horse to carry, we still see a causal interaction between the horse and this heavy object. Among other things we see and feel, the horse and the heavy object never occupy the same place.

8.3.4 Further Proof of Causal Interactions of Entities

In Section 4.6.2, we noted evidence that our perception of entities is the result of a causal chain, from one entity to another, culminating in our perception. For example, the bat hits the ball, and they each hit the air, which hits our ears, etc. Therefore, the very fact that we see, hear, and feel the horse (and saddle) is evidence that the horse (and saddle) acts on other entities along with acting on our consciousness. We can use the same probabilistic arguments above to induce, with probability virtually equal to 1, that the horse interacts causally with other entities (such as the air, our ears, and our eyes), simply from the evidence that we perceive the horse.

If, in the future, we continue to perceive the horse, the saddle, and all the other entities in our perceptual field—and we also perceive the entities as possessing the characteristic of exclusivity of spatial location—then we have many instances n of entities continuing to interact causally. Therefore, the probability that the horse and the saddle are continuing to interact causally is greater than $n/(n+1)$. That is, the probability that the horse and saddle will cease to interact causally, while we continue to perceive them along with the rest of the world, is minuscule.

As long as I continue to perceive entities, then I know that entities are continuing to act causally on me and on one another.

8.3.5   The Causal Efficacy of the Self

It is important to give special attention to one particular conclusion I have just established. The self acts causally on other entities. To reprise one example above, when I—an entity—push a book (or push a ball, to use a common example), I make it move.

This particular conclusion is extremely important, of course, because the ability for man to take action to affect the future is the final purpose of knowledge.

Once we are aware of the self as a causal entity, we can better understand the role that the self plays in perception. We see something better when we direct and focus our eyes on it. We feel something better when we grasp it or run our hand over it, instead of just letting the thing touch our hand. Indeed, when we *initiate* a process of gaining sensory information instead of gaining it passively, we gain more information and are aware of a longer causal chain. We reach for the stick, and the stick makes our hand feel it. We then grasp the stick, and the stick gives us further tactile information about itself.

8.3.6   Validating Causality and Specific Causal Relations

So far in our inquiry into induction, we have focused on proving the ubiquity of causality itself in the past, present, and future. Our method of induction, however, also works to validate specific causal relations, such as laws of motion, laws of gravitation and electromagnetism, and much narrower relations such as the amount of fuel it takes to heat a certain house, or what I can use a stick for. In the remainder of the book, we will shift our emphasis from the validation of causality itself to the validation of specific causal relations.

8.4   SHAPE, RIGIDITY, EXCLUSIVITY, AND CONTINUITY

We perceive entities to have a specific shape and a certain degree of
rigidity, and we perceive that only one entity occupies a given place
at a given time (exclusivity). We have proved inductively that these
entities act causally on each other. We have also proved inductively
that such entities can be expected to retain these characteristics in the
foreseeable future.

These inductively-proven principles—the causal interaction of
entities, the retention of shape and rigidity, and exclusivity—are very
powerful when considered in combination.

For example, a stick that I have just seen for the first time is on
the ground. I bend down, grasp the stick, and lift and hold it in my
hand. I see and also can feel that the stick is three feet long. I also feel
and can see that the stick is rigid and that it will maintain its shape as
I move it, even if I exert substantial force against it.

To this knowledge, add my inductive knowledge that no object
can occupy a space that the stick is occupying. I can then conclude
the following: By extending the stick in front of me, I can make it
reach a book that is two feet in front of me. Based on my inductive
knowledge of my ability to push the book with my hand, I can deduce
that if I push hard enough with the stick against the book, the book
will move.

Similarly, I can deduce that if I push the stick against the ground,
the stick will help hold me erect, as my legs do. I can use the stick as
a walking stick or cane.

That is, just by perceiving the stick, and armed with inductive
knowledge about other entities, I can infer some actions that the stick
can take. (On this idea, for an account with some similarities to mine,
but with important differences, see Salmieri 2013, 66–68.)

I can draw similar inferences from perceptual characteristics of
other entities. From perceiving a ball, I can infer that its shape is invariant under rotation, and that therefore it has the potential to roll.
From perceiving a wheel, I can infer that its shape is invariant under

rotation in one specific direction, and that therefore it has the potential to roll in a specific direction only. From perceiving a wagon with wheels on axles, I can infer that the wagon has the potential to roll on its wheels. From perceiving a wagon with one wheel missing and its axle submerged in mud, I can infer that the wagon will not roll.

For more complex entities, such as an automobile, I can make inferences based on a combination of perception of characteristics and more advanced knowledge of characteristics. For example, knowing that an automobile runs on gasoline allows me to infer that an automobile with an empty gas tank will not run.

Another important causal aspect of entities is continuity, also known from induction on many observed instances. For example, for an object to travel from one location to another, it must traverse a continuous path between locations. For a seed to become a mature plant, it must traverse a continuous sequence of growth.

Also known by induction from many observations, some of these continuous sequences are reversible, and some are not. A man can walk from the kitchen to the living room, and back again. But the man cannot turn back into an infant.

One of the most important ways that we know that phenomena such as mirages, dreams, and hallucinations are not perceptions of entities is that the sensory-like projections of such phenomena do not conform to the known characteristics of continuity. For example, we might dream of or hallucinate a deceased elderly relative as a young person alive again. These phenomena are still instances of consciousness; a dream or hallucination is still a form of consciousness of something. But, no matter how vivid the dream or hallucination, our conceptual faculty can inform us later—through consideration of continuity and other causal inductions—that the something was not the something it appeared to be. That is, our conceptual faculty can override the automatic associations made by other aspects of our mental faculties.

8.5   RANGES OF MEASUREMENT

Returning to the second of our three recurring themes, the discussion in the previous section leads naturally to a further discussion of Ayn Rand's seminal identification that characteristics are ranges of measurement (1990, 6–11, 138).

Consider the three-foot-long stick in the examples just above. By the same inference that allows me to conclude that I can use the stick to push a book that is two feet away, I can also conclude that I can use a stick that is anywhere from two and a half feet to four feet long for the same purpose. With a four-foot stick, I can hold it somewhere in the middle instead of at the end; but a much longer stick would become too heavy for me to hold.

Similarly, I can use a stick within a certain range of measurement of length and width as a walking stick. From the perceptual qualities of the stick, I know that I can hold it and reach the ground, and that if I push on the stick, it will resist both my push and the ground, thereby supporting me.

Similarly, I can see and infer that a ball or a wheel within a certain tolerance of roundness will roll effectively, but that exceeding that tolerance will cause a different effect.

In other words, these objects must have their geometric measurements within some range in order to maintain other properties that they possess—such as rolling, pushing, supporting. More generally, geometric characteristics within certain ranges of measurement cause other characteristics within corresponding ranges of measurement. A three-foot stick can reach up to three feet. Roundness of a wheel is a characteristic with a range of measurement that causes a corresponding range of measurement of rolling, causing a corresponding range of measurement of amount of horse power needed to pull a wagon, causing a corresponding range of measurement of distance I can travel in a given duration of time. Ranges of measurement propagate, in various forms, from cause to effect to further effect. (For a brief discussion of this idea—of ranges of measurement propagating from cause to effect—in the writings of Aristotle, see Salmieri 2012 50–51.)

Of course, in addition to relating ranges of measurement, I can devise mathematical formulas relating precise measurements (within narrow ranges of errors in measurement). If the radius (r) of my wagon wheels is one foot, then 50 rotations per minute tells me that I am traveling at 100π feet per minute (because the circumference of a circle is $2\pi r$), give or take a small amount for spinning or sliding, and that I will travel about three and a half miles in an hour. But even if my measurements are a little off, each effect along the chain is similar, for my purposes, to the effect if the measurement were exact. In most applications, reaching my destination in an hour is similar to reaching my destination in 59 minutes, compared to reaching my destination in three hours. When I need more exact effects, such as when a rocket has to enter a certain exact orbit of the moon, then I must plan for my measurements and my actions to be within much smaller ranges of measurement. But usually I still have some range, albeit small, of acceptability.

When I observe an entity change, I observe that the change occurs gradually across a range of measurement. For example, when an object passes from one location to another, I observe it to traverse every location in between. When an object (larger than an atom) accelerates or decelerates from one velocity to another, I observe it to go through every velocity in between. When an object increases or decreases from one temperature to another, I observe it to go through every temperature in between. When an object increases or decreases in size, I observe it to traverse every size in between. From all these observations, I have further information that important cause-and-effect relationships—in particular, certain effects on my consciousness caused by the objects I perceive—change gradually across a range of measurement.

Similar measurements of a cause, including similar measurements of a cause's duration, generally—with infrequent exceptions discussed in this section and in Section 9.2.2—cause similar measurements of an effect.

Here is one moral of this discussion of ranges of measurement. Although our sensory systems function automatically to recognize similarities and differences according to ranges of measurement—such as recognizing a five-foot and six-foot stick as similar compared to a two-foot stick—we have explained conceptually why this automatic functioning is fortuitous. We have established an objective, conceptual basis for identifying these similarities and differences according to ranges of measurement. To continue our example, we have explained that, under most circumstances, a stick of any length between five feet and six feet should be placed in the group of similar objects compared to the two-foot stick—because most of the effects caused by the five-foot and six-foot sticks, in addition to the effects that are our perception of the sticks, will be similar.

Indeed, being objective rather than intrinsic—see Peikoff (1991, 142) for this distinction made by Ayn Rand—our conceptual method also identifies when to override or augment perceptions of similarity and difference. For example, suppose I have a machine that cuts wooden sticks into one-foot sticks, cutting any $(n+r)$-foot stick—where n is an integer and r is a fraction between zero and 1—into n one-foot sticks plus an r-foot remaining piece of scrap. Then, in one respect, a five-foot stick, a six-foot stick, and a two-foot-stick would be similar in comparison to a five-and-a-half-foot stick. That respect would be the amount of scrap left over from cutting.

Here is another moral of this discussion of ranges of measurement. Characteristics of entities are integrated. Change the shape or size of an entity, and you change its other characteristics accordingly. For example, when we shorten a stick, we reduce the range over which we can reach other entities with it; we reduce its weight, and we increase the ease with which we can wave it around. When we learn about the shape of the particles—such as the molecules—that constitute an entity, we learn how those shapes relate to other characteristics of an entity, such as the other kinds of molecules with which it can readily combine. Similarly, when one characteristic—such as an entity's hue—changes, it means that related characteristics have changed as well. For instance, when a piece of iron turns red, it is because the iron is very hot, and the iron also is then more malleable. Characteristics are not atomistic facts, but rather are integrated aspects of a whole that is an entity.

Understanding that our perceptual apparatus makes automatic associations according to ranges of measurement explains optical illusions. The stick in water looks crooked or like two sticks because the visual information we receive is not—in one respect—within the range of measurement for straight singular objects, but is within the range of measurement for crooked objects or pairs of objects. We need our conceptual faculty to override this automatic perceptual association. Initial evidence of a problem might be that what we see seems inconsistent with what we feel with our hands: the stick feels like one straight stick. Then, conceptually, we apply different ranges of measurement to what we see. We factor in our awareness that the stick is in water. We then apply our knowledge that light refracts at the surface of the water. When we factor in the measurement of this refraction along with our sight of the stick, then the overall measurement of the stick falls within the range of measurement of being one straight stick.

Another aspect of this optical illusion is that our visual information seems to contradict our tactile information. The visual information seems to indicate a change in direction or continuity of the stick, whereas the tactile information does not. We need our conceptual faculty to discover that the visual change in direction or continuity is a result of a change in medium, not a change in direction or continuity of the stick.

A question often argued about is of the following form: When an individual mistakes a straight stick, half submerged in water, for a crooked stick or two sticks, is the mistake a perceptual mistake or a conceptual mistake? From the foregoing, it is clear that my answer is "Both." The perceptual mistake is a mistake of automatic *commission*, and the conceptual mistake is—if the individual fails to override the automatic perceptual mistake—a mistake of *omission*.

In the present context, I deliberately use the word "mistake" instead of "error," to express my meaning as clearly as possible. The automatic integrating processes of our perceptual system causes us to *mis-take* the stick in water for two distinct sticks, unless we override this automatic integration with our conceptual knowledge.

It is also useful to note that a mistake of perception is a *perceptual* mistake, not a *conceptual* mistake. A perceptual mistake, not involving conception, is not a conceptual mistake. Nevertheless, a perceptual mistake is a mistake.

The present discussion illustrates why I take the world as we sense it as a whole—not as we perceive it to be composed of certain distinct entities—to be the veridical base of our philosophically validated corpus of knowledge. We can be mistaken in our automatic perception of entities, but not in our consciousness of the world.

8.6   SENSE, MEASUREMENT, AND CONCEPTUALIZATION

We can use a thermometer, or our hand, to measure the temperature of a pot of water. If we use a thermometer, then we use our eyes to measure the measurement taken by the thermometer. In either case, the measurement—the causal interaction between the water and the instrument of measurement—tells us how the water will interact causally with other entities. For instance, if the water is very hot, then it will cook an egg.

This brief example, combined with the foregoing parts of this book, leads to some integrating ideas regarding the senses, measurement, and conceptualization.

The senses are our most basic instruments for the measurement of reality, and obey causal laws of nature as precisely as do any other instruments of measurement. Concepts are a means of condensing and organizing the sensory measurements of reality into ranges of measurement, according to causal relationships among those ranges.

Propositions are a means of sequencing the steps taken to form this conceptual organization. Logic is a means of validating each proposition and the sequencing of propositions. The basic elements of logic are deduction and induction.

8.7   KEY QUESTIONS, ANSWERS, AND ISSUES

8.7.1   Skeptical Questions

Is it circular reasoning to argue that causality will continue in the future?

Many philosophers since Hume object to inductive generalization from the past or present into the future. They may grant that we know induction has worked in the past, but ask, "How do we know it will work in the future?" They argue that any claim that induction will work in the future assumes the claim, and so is circular. Hume (1902, 16 [Section 30]) writes,

> We have said that all arguments concerning existence are founded on the relation of cause and effect; that our knowledge of that relation is derived entirely from experience; and that all our experimental conclusions proceed upon the supposition that the future will be conformable to the past. To endeavour, therefore, the proof of this last supposition by probable arguments, or arguments regarding existence, must be evidently going in a circle, and taking that for granted, which is the very point in question.

Although the polemics in this book are very limited, I do have to distinguish my theory from sensualism and its concomitant nominalism. I reject the following idea expressed by Hume (1902, 29 [Section 49]):

> It seems a proposition, which will not admit of much dispute, that all our ideas are nothing but copies of our impressions, or, in other words, that it is impossible for

us to think of any thing, which we have not anteced-
ently felt, either by our external or internal senses.

Contrary to Hume and other sensualist-nominalists, a concept is
not a copy of "impressions" or a copy of existents, but rather a way
of mentally separating and organizing existents. In observing existence and consciousness, I am able to separate mentally these two existents along with the relation between them, that relation being a
causal relation.

There is another, ironic point to make on this matter. These sen-
sualist-nominalist philosophers, who claim they cannot observe causality, imply that they *can* observe time, in the form of past and future, as if time were some entity. However, there is no such *thing* as
time; there is no metaphysical clock on a metaphysical wall that says
what time it is. Because time is not a thing, not an entity that acts on
us or anything else, there is no such *cause* as time. As Aristotle (1984,
374, *Physics* Book IV, Part 12, 220b30) writes, "Time is a measure of
motion and of being moved ... ." That is, time is a measurement of
motion (and/or change) of entities. Hume (2019, Book 1, Part 2, Section III, Paragraph 11) himself recognizes this fact when he writes,

the idea of duration is always deriv'd from a succession
of changeable objects, and can never be convey'd to the
mind by any thing stedfast and unchangeable.

The current time is just another perspective on the current state
of all the entities that exist. If at some future time all the entities in
the universe returned to the same exact state as they had once been
before, then the universe at those two times would be exactly the
same, and each of those two states would be completely indistinguishable from each other. In general, two identical states can be
considered interchangeable (or "exchangeable"), and therefore as re-
orderable observations, because time is not a distinguishable characteristic in itself. Time is observable only through other characteristics.

Moreover, time is a relative characteristic. It is a measure of a certain amount of motion or change. *Qua* time, the change from

Monday to Tuesday is exactly the same as the change from Tuesday to Wednesday. There is no basis for distinguishing a future change in time from a past one, except through any differences in changes of entities.

The current time *per se* is not a causal factor, because time is not an entity. It is only entities—not attributes divorced from entities—that constitute reality. It is only entities that have causal efficacy on our consciousness and on other entities. It is the universe's entities (including conscious entities), in their current states, that will cause the next actions of those entities, irrespective of how many states have transpired so far and what those prior states were. (For one account of Aristotle's conception that it is entities that cause actions, see Gotthelf 1987, 208–211.)

In other words, causal chains do not hopscotch or leapfrog across time. They are unbroken across time. If an action of an entity a century ago is significant to what will happen in the next instant, it is because that action of that entity has had a lasting effect on some entity *throughout* the past century. Therefore, whereas our *evidence* for the future is our knowledge of the past through the present, the entire *cause* of the future is contained in the present.

Thus, the causal progression of the states of entities from time t to time $t+1$ is independent of the absolute value of t, if the absolute value of t could even be known. And that is why past causal progressions are evidence for future ones.

Therefore, the onus of proof is on him who would claim that a future change in time will be different in effect from a past one. To assert or even hypothesize that some absolute measure of time has causal significance is to make an arbitrary claim. (For my treatment of the arbitrary, see Section 9.7.)

Thus I have presented an argument, not made a supposition, that the future is conformable to the past. I was able to make such an argument because my power of conceptualization was not restricted by sensualism-nominalism.

* * *

The following example is included only to address the so-called "new riddle of induction," an argument familiar to academic philosophers. This argument makes the error of ascribing causal efficacy to times in the future. (See Goodman 1946 for an early statement of this argument.)

Suppose we have run an experiment n times and have measured the results each time. Suppose we have a mathematical formula that matches the results closely. Suppose we then add a factor to the formula, and this factor is concocted arbitrarily to depend on the present time, so that the factor takes effect only in the future. For example, suppose the factor is equal to 1 up to the present, and two times the number of days after the present date hereafter. For this modified formula, can we use our $n/(n+1)$ rule?

Of course not. The reason is obvious. We have good reason to believe that the results of the first n runs would more closely fit the modified formula than subsequent runs would, because we modified the formula specifically to make it wrong for future instances. We know that the formula is wrong for future instances because a specific time *per se* is not a causal factor.

The same kind of disqualification applies to any arbitrary grouping of concretes, such as "things that are red or things that were blue when I had my fingers crossed when I first saw them." Such groupings are perverse, contrary to the nature and purpose of conceptualization and of all cognition. Recall this statement from the previous section: "Concepts are a means of condensing and organizing the sensory measurements of reality into ranges of measurement, according to causal relationships among those ranges." (The actual, unstated range of measurement in this case is the entire range from red through blue.)

"A Thing in Itself"

In contrast to the Humean strain of skepticism is the Kantian strain of skepticism. What Kant himself thought, as evidenced by his full body of work, has long been a matter of scholarly debate. But contemporary Kantian skeptics draw on statements such as this one by Kant (B xxvi):

> we can have cognition of no object as a thing in itself,
> but only insofar as it is an object of sensible intuition,
> i.e. as an appearance;

Whereas Humean skeptics complain that we cannot observe causality, Kantian skeptics lament that we cannot have observation *without* causality—that is, we cannot have observation without a causal relationship between reality and our means of awareness, a relationship that depends on the identity of both. To Humean skeptics, consciousness fails because it does not show us causality; to Kantian skeptics, consciousness fails because it comes from causality.

Kantian skeptics claim that therefore we cannot know anything as "a thing in itself," as Kant put it, or "the world as it really is" (Blumenau 2001), as Kant is sometimes translated or paraphrased.

But an integral aspect of a thing is how it exerts causal forces on other things. Such other things include consciousness and also include things besides consciousness.

If a "thing in itself" is construed as a thing divorced from its effects on consciousness, then the same line of reasoning should construe a "thing in itself" as a thing divorced from its effects on all other things. The notion of a "thing in itself" is not merely a lament against the causal interaction between existence and consciousness, but rather a lament against all causal interaction.

The weight, mass, electrical charge, and gravitational attraction of any entity are attributes pertaining to how the entity interacts with other entities. Motion and location of an entity are in relation to other entities. Hue pertains to the frequency of light that an entity emits. Even the structure and shape of an entity pertain to the causal relationships among the entity's parts. The skeptic's notion of a "thing in itself" excludes all these attributes, leaving *no* attributes.

Recalling the opening of this chapter, suppose that an entity has some attributes that bear no relation to how the entity acts on other entities. If such attributes exist, why do we need to know them? We don't. They are ineffectual.

The very attributes we do need to know are the attributes by which entities have an effect on us, either directly or through their effects on other entities that have an effect on us. And those attributes are real. The fact that an attribute contributes to an entity's causal efficacy does not diminish the attribute's reality. What an entity *is* includes what the entity *does*, and what an entity *does* includes what the entity *does to other things*.

If a baseball hits a brick wall and a glass window, the wall and the window are affected differently, but both are affected by the baseball "as it really is." Similarly, if the baseball were to hit me, I would feel the baseball as it really is.

Moreover, effects are as real as their causes. (See Peikoff 1991, 44–46 for elaboration of this point.) The smooth surface we see and feel is as real as the array of atoms and electrical charges that causes the smooth surface.

8.7.2   Time as the Unit for Equal Likelihood

To see the power and breadth of our method of induction, using our probabilistic reasoning and our understanding of characteristics as ranges of measurement, consider another example.

Survival is a characteristic. Survival of a species can be thought to persist so long as a measurement of danger to the species remains below a certain threshold value. If the species has survived for a million years, then the measurement of danger has been below that threshold for each of those years. In the absence of any knowledge that the degree of risk at any given time is different from the degree of risk at any other time, the probability that the measurement of danger in the coming year will be the highest on record is less than or equal to $1/1,000,001$. Therefore, the probability of extinction in the coming year is less than or equal to $1/1,000,001$.

What is the evidence that each uniform interval of time should be equally risky, as this time-based danger-function argument assumes?

Instead of each unit of time being equally risky, why isn't it each *square* unit of time, or any other power of time, that is equally risky? Goodman 1994, for example, raises this objection to a similar argument by Gott (1993; 1994), called the delta *t* argument, which considers each unit of time equally risky.

The evidence is, again, that time is not an entity, but simply a measure of motion, and any measure of absolute time would be irrelevant. Moreover, there is no discernible significant trend in the amount or kind of motion on the Earth, or in its surroundings, *per unit of time*. (This condition is no more than that the laws of motion continue to apply to things we call clocks in the same way as they apply to other things.) Therefore, in the absence of any specific evidence of a particularly dangerous set of circumstances, the chance that there will be a calamitous motion is constant per unit of time. That is, each unit of time is an equally likely instance of danger.

Of course, our evidence regarding the expected survival of a species often goes beyond merely knowing the number of years the species has survived so far. We often can identify specific risks, such as the possibility of an asteroid hitting earth, the possibility of the species being overrun by a known predator, or the possibility of a mad scientist destroying the human race. In the presence of such knowledge, we can assess each risk separately. But the method of assessing each risk ultimately should reduce, in my judgment, to the method presented in this chapter and the next. And for some known risks, time is not the unit for equal likelihood, as the next section explains.

8.7.3   When Time is Not the Unit for Equal Likelihood

Suppose we have a new kind of machine that has not failed in its 1,000 days of operation. Suppose the machine has produced 50,000 widgets in that time. Suppose the output of the machine was only 10 widgets per day at the start of the 1,000 days, but the output was increased gradually until it reached its current output of 1,000 widgets per day. What is the probability that the machine will fail on the next day?

If we assume a danger function based on time, then we have 1,000 past successes and one new trial; and the probability of failure on the new trial is less than or equal to 1/1,001. But if we assume a danger function based on the number of widgets produced, then we have 50 past successes of the production of 1,000 widgets and one new trial of the production of 1,000 widgets; and the probability of failure on the new trial is less than or equal to 1/51.

How would we choose between these two danger functions? We would have to identify an objective, uniform measure of a successful trial. To do so, we would have to ask, "What factors would cause the machine to fail?" For example, would the factors be related to possible faulty raw materials used in the production of each widget? Or would the factors be such things as possible leaks or corrosion from the air, whose likelihood is independent of how many widgets are produced each day? Our choice would have to be based on previous inductions, based on numerous observations, identifying past causes of failure. Again, in the absence of such previous inductions or knowledge of daily output, the right choice would be units of time.

The above example points the way to a kind of circumstance under which a non-unitary power of time t would indeed be appropriate, just as a non-unitary power of t is called for in some physical formulas. Just as distance traveled in free fall is an accumulation of motion at an accelerating speed, thereby calling for a t^2 term for distance traveled, so there might be a t^2 term for a danger, such as corrosion, that builds and accumulates over time.

8.7.4   Trends, Periodicity, and Errors in Measurement

Sometimes there are trends, cycles, and other patterns over time in a sequence of data, due to cumulative and cyclical causal factors. We might measure the temperature of a lake over the course of sixty days and notice that the temperature is trending higher. In such a case, it clearly would be erroneous to conclude that there is less than or equal to a 1/61 chance that the temperature the next day will be the highest recorded.

Knowing that temperature changes with season, it would be more reasonable to compare tomorrow's temperature to the temperature on the same date in prior years. But there might also be trends in temperature over the course of years.

In such a case, we would want to bring to bear our other knowledge of what factors might affect temperature, thereby integrating our sixty measurements with a much larger group of measurements. See Chapter 9 for such methods of integration.

There are also well-established statistical and Bayesian methods to detect and account for trends and periodicity in data. See, for example, Jaynes 2003, 520–530, 534–549.

There are also errors in measurement. Although the $n/(n+1)$ method accounts for such errors automatically, the methods referenced above in Jaynes also can account for them.

8.7.5   Will the sun rise tomorrow?

The famous mathematician Laplace (1812, xii-xiii; [1825] 1995, 10–11) posed and answered a famous question in probability theory. From the context of a primitive man who knows nothing about the sun except that it had risen every day for the past n days, what is the probability that the sun will rise the next day (or in the next 24 hours). According to Laplace's "Rule of Succession," the answer is $(n+1)/(n+2)$.

So for example, if the man had seen the sun rise one time, then Laplace's rule would say that the probability that the sun would rise in the next 24 hours is equal to 2/3.

The answer from my probabilistic argument, used in this chapter, is different: greater than or equal to $n/(n+1)$. If the man had seen the sun rise one time, then my rule would say that the probability the sun would rise in the next 24 hours is greater than or equal to 1/2.

This difference between Laplace's rule and my rule may seem minor, but the inequality makes the difference major. In the next section, I will reconcile this difference between Laplace's rule and mine.

Of course, modern man knows much more about the sun than that it has risen n times. We can bring to bear on this question all of our knowledge of physics. In Chapter 9, I will explain how all of this knowledge improves our answer.

8.7.6   What if we know that a situation will come to an end?

To show that the possibility of an accumulating or timed danger does not undercut our inductive method, consider this extreme example: Suppose we are certain that someday the current process—whether the functioning of a machine, or the applicability of the laws of motion, or causality itself—would come to an end. How would that supposition affect our probability?

It turns out that the only change would be that our inequality would become an equality. For example, if our primitive man had seen the sun rise n times, and if he also happened to know that the sun eventually would not rise, then his rational probability that the sun would rise in the next 24 hours would be $n/(n+1)$ instead of our previously-derived probability of *greater than or equal to* $n/(n+1)$; and his rational probability that the sun would rise for at least the next n twenty-four hour periods would be $1/2$ instead of *greater than or equal to* $1/2$. Let us examine the argument for this result.

Gott (1993, 315) states, as a particular application of the principle of insufficient reason,

> Assuming that whatever we are measuring can be observed only in the interval between times t_{begin} and t_{end}, if there is nothing special about t_{now} we expect t_{now} to be located randomly in this interval.

If you are transported to an in-progress football game at a random time, then the game is as likely to be in the first half of play as in the second half of play; more generally, the game clock is as likely to show any given time left as any other. If you start eavesdropping on a conversation in-process, then the conversation is as likely to be in its first half as in its second half. And if we are in the midst of the reign of Newton's laws of motion, and we make the fantastical assumption that these laws will be overturned someday because of some as-yet undetected causal factor, then we should conclude that we are as likely to be in the first half of that reign as in the second half.

Translating Gott's statement above to mathematical notation, we have

$$p[(t_p/t_t)|t_pX] = U(0,1),$$

where t_p = an extant phenomenon's past longevity, t_t = the phenomenon's eventual total longevity, $U(0,1)$ is by definition the uniform probability density function from zero to one—that is, $U(0,1)$ specifies an equal probability density for each value between 0 and 1—and with one other crucial assumption: X = a certain notion of ignorance expressed by Gott's statement above. (The graph of $U(0,1)$ is just a horizontal line, with a height of 1, from zero to one.)

From this premise, a few mathematical steps can lead us to a formula for $p(t_t|t_pX)$, the probability density function for total longevity given a known past longevity. The first mathematical step will be to find a cumulative probability distribution function for t_t, and then we will differentiate that cumulative probability distribution function to yield a probability density function for t_t.

First, let us substitute the variable u for the formula t_p/t_t, so that $p(u|t_pX) = U(0,1)$. Therefore, $t_t = t_p/u$, a monotonically decreasing function of u for which the inverse function is $u = t_p/t_t$. We can use $P(t_t <= t)$, where t is any value $>= t_p$, to denote the cumulative probability distribution function of t_t. Therefore,

$$P(t_t <= t) = P(t_pu^{-1} <= t) = P(u >= t_pt^{-1})$$

$$= \int_{t_pt^{-1}}^{1} 1dx$$

where x is a dummy variable inside the integral. Evaluating this integral, we find our cumulative probability distribution function of t_t,

$$P(t_t <= t) = 1 - t_p t^{-1}.$$

Differentiating this function, we get the probability density function of t_t,

$$p(t_t \mid t_p X) = t_p t_t^{-2} \text{ for all } t_t > t_p.$$

This formula is known as Gott's "delta t formula."

It can also be shown that Gott's delta t formula is exactly equivalent to successive applications of Laplace's rule of succession. That is, every moment that a phenomenon persists, we update the probability that the phenomenon will persist in the next moment based on the number of moments n that the phenomenon has persisted so far. For a phenomenon to end after a total of exactly $N+1$ moments, the phenomenon must persist for exactly N intervals of time and then end in the $(N+1)$st interval. For those interested in the math, in the first equation below, the $(N+1)$st interval of time is represented by $1/((t_t/\Delta t)+2)$, and the first N intervals of time are represented by the N factors under the product sign. The numerators and denominators of these N factors mostly cancel each other, leaving only the numerator of the first factor over the denominator of the last factor.

$$p(t_t|t_p)dt_t = \lim_{\Delta t \to 0} \frac{1}{(t_t/\Delta t) + 2} \cdot \prod_{n=0}^{N-1} \frac{(t_p/\Delta t) + 1 + n}{(t_p/\Delta t) + 2 + n}$$

where $N = \dfrac{t_t - t_p}{\Delta t}$.

$$p(t_t|t_p)dt_t = \frac{1}{t_t} \cdot \frac{t_p}{t_t} dt_t = \frac{t_p}{t_t^2} dt_t$$

$$p(t_t|t_p) = \frac{t_p}{t_t^2}$$

Because Laplace and Gott produce the same result in the limit as Δt approaches zero, they succeed or fail together in producing a result that is valid.

Jaynes (2003, 152–160) explains that Laplace's rule of succession implicitly assumes, incorrectly and unknown to Laplace, one extra success and one failure. That is, if our primitive man has seen the sun rise n times, Laplace's rule of succession implicitly assumes—invalidly—that the sun has risen $n+1$ times and failed to rise one time. With this assumption, wrongly legitimating the possibility that the sun will fail to rise, the probability that the sun will rise tomorrow is calculated by Laplace's rule to be $(n+1)/(n+2)$.

(Even given this assumption of one extra success and one failure, Laplace's rule of succession is not validated by Jaynes, but merely made more plausible.)

Pisaturo 2016 covers Laplace's rule of succession (see also Jaynes 2003, 152–160, 553–588) and Gott's delta t formula in more depth, and explains how these formulas are in error in wide application. The delta t formula is correct only when we know that a certain phenomenon has an (unknown) expiration date or time, as in the case of a football game. (There are two unknown events: a start and end. As far as we know, it is equally likely that the start is farther in the past than the end is in the future, or vice versa.) In effect, the unknown but definite expiration is roughly equivalent to the one failure implicitly assumed by Laplace.

Given that Newton's laws have held for n years, and making the fantastical assumption that there is an as-yet undetected causal force that is scheduled (like a ticking bomb) to overturn Newton's laws, we can accept the rules of Laplace and Gott; then the probability that Newton's laws will be overturned within the next year is $1/(n+1)$, still an extremely minuscule probability given that Newton's laws have held for billions of years.

Of course, because we have no reason to think that there is such an undetected causal force, the probability that Newton's laws will be overturned in the next year is *less than* $1/(n+1)$. How much less? Gott's formula, rightly understood, provides no lower bound on how much less. That is, Gott's formula offers no argument against the conclusion that the probability is exactly zero.

8.7.7   Same Cause, Same Effect?

Can a cause always be expressed in one statement? Yes. The widest cause would be "any combination of entities and circumstances." The narrowest cause would be some one entity and circumstance. Any intermediate degree of breadth can be identified by some concept. Thus we may state the following principle: The same effect (that is, the same conceptual class of interchangeable units of effects) always has the same cause (that is, the same conceptual class of interchangeable units of causes), if the cause is stated at a certain appropriate level of generality.

8.7.8   Necessity

The concept of necessity, discussed often in epistemology (see, for example, Aristotle, *Metaphysics* Book V Chapter 5, 1015a20–1015b16) arises from man's ability to form conceptual groupings of causal relations.

For example, the clouds overhead, combined with the air temperature and other causal factors, caused rain yesterday. But rain is not a *necessary* result of clouds. That is, when I conceptually group together all the occasions of the existence of clouds, those clouds do not always cause rain; sometimes, the other *necessary* causal factors are not present.

A common application of this concept of necessity arises in conjunction with human purpose. "For me to write well about epistemology, it is *necessary* for me to think hard."

We can apply this concept of necessity to a fundamental conclusion of this book: In order to be conscious, it is necessary that there exist something apart from consciousness to be conscious of.

In an account of a single event of my consciousness of existence, the concept of necessity is redundant with the concept of causality. Existence caused my consciousness to be conscious of it; such a causal relation, being singular, is necessary because there is no other instance being considered.

Sometimes the concept of necessity is used to distinguish actions of human volition from actions of inanimate matter. An individual has the power to choose one action or the other, whereas inanimate matter has no such choice. For inanimate matter, there are no necessary causal factors aside from the physical factors. For a man, there is another necessary causal factor: choice. If the factor of choice is excluded, then the remaining causal factors—the physical factors—do not constitute necessity.

The concept of necessity is also used in contrast to the notion that inanimate entities might have acted differently, not because of any cause, but without being caused to do so. But so long as existence causes our consciousness of it, there are elements or factors of causality and therefore of necessity. As I have written, existence *makes* us aware of it. There is necessity in such making. The only question is whether there may be additional, non-necessary factors that might alter the way in which existence acts on our consciousness of it.

For example, might there be some non-necessary factors that would cause a rock to feel less heavy in our hand? I cannot rule out such a conjecture except by the evidence-based probabilistic arguments I have used. As I have noted throughout this book, entities act on our senses regularly and consistently; that is how we are able to perceive entities in the first place. Therefore, the probability that an entity will act contrary to this evident necessity in the reasonable future is minuscule.

Some might argue that there is evidence for such non-regular-acting entities at the quantum level, which is outside the range of measurement in which we observe regular consistent action, and that such entities on the quantum level act only according to laws of probability. Those claims are beyond my expertise to judge. I would just caution that probability, rightly understood, pertains to cognition, not directly to existence. Weather seemed to act probabilistically, in an existential or metaphysical sense, until modern science came along.

8.7.9 Curve Fitting

Suppose we have an experiment with n initial parameters that we can set. Suppose we run the experiment n times, setting the initial parameters differently each time, and measure the results each time. Then we can concoct an nth-degree polynomial, of the initial parameters, that exactly fits all the results. Does that mean that the polynomial will exactly fit the results of the next run of the experiment with probability greater than or equal to $n/(n+1)$?

Of course not. The error here is similar to the error of ascribing causal efficacy to a specific time. (See the discussion of Humean skepticism in Section 8.7.1.) We have good reason to believe that the results of the first n runs would more closely fit the polynomial, because we concocted the polynomial for that purpose. My probabilistic argument would apply only to the ensuing m runs. That is, after m additional runs, the probability that the results of the next run would yield the greatest deviation from the polynomial is greater than or equal to $m/(m+1)$. However, if no thinking went into the polynomial hypothesis except the intent to fit the curve, then this greatest deviation will almost certainly be so great as to be uninformative. Considering the matter from another perspective, such a non-causal hypothesis will be contrary to the kind of integration to be discussed in Chapter 9. Furthermore, the "Occam factor" (discussed in Section 9.7) will penalize the curve-fitting solution compared to other solutions that explain the data.

8.8 HISTORICAL CONTEXT AND TECHNICAL ELABORATION OF THE $n/(n+1)$ METHOD

I arrived at the $n/(n+1)$ method independently, inspired by Ayn Rand's idea of a characteristic as a range of measurement. But the method has a history in the literature, long preceding me. The origin of this line of thinking, as far as I know, is from Jeffreys (1932), who writes, "Two measures are made: what is the probability that the third observation will lie between them? The answer is easily seen to be one-third." (Jeffreys then derives the Jeffreys prior as the only probability distribution that satisfies this simple, "easily seen" condition; but the Jeffreys prior is another story.) Hill (1968, 1988, 1993; see also Fisher 1939 and Dempster 1963) generalizes Jeffreys' premise as follows: Given n exchangeable observations ordered by value (with no ties), the probability that the next observation will be in the interval between a given consecutive pair of the n past observations is $1/(n+1)$. Hill calls this idea $A_{(n)}$. Coolen (1998, 2011) has further developed and applied this method, now known as "nonparametric predictive inference," to many real-life problems.

Let us examine Hill's $A_{(n)}$ idea. Suppose that all we know about a phenomenon is 49 measurements that we have taken of it. Suppose the 49 measurements are distributed as follows:

This distribution of measurements is uneven and asymmetrical, reflecting an underlying probability density function that is probably uneven and asymmetrical. By means of the different widths of the 50 intervals created by the 49 measurements, the $n/(n+1)$ rule accounts for that unevenness and asymmetry. Even though the intervals are of different widths, the 50th measurement is equally likely to fall within any of the 50 intervals.

In the present book, I employ the following special case: The probability that the next observation will be greater than all n previous observations is less than or equal to $1/(n+1)$, with the less-than condition accounting for the possibility of ties.

My specialized application of the general $A_{(n)}$ idea is particularly conservative, because I am interested only in the tails—the regions above the highest measurement and below the lowest measurement, and usually only the tail on the high side. For example, suppose I want to test the validity of some physics equation. Each measurement I take is the measurement of the deviation (suitably normalized) from what the equation predicts. I am interested in the largest deviation, because the $n/(n+1)$ rule predicts that there is only a $1/(n+1)$

chance that the next deviation will be higher. If the largest deviation is very low, then the $n/(n+1)$ rule tells me that the equation is a good predictor of the next measurement. Of course, common sense tells me the same thing, but the $n/(n+1)$ rule validates and quantifies this common sense.

I don't even need to know the probability density function of the deviation. Of course, if the equation is right, then the deviation is just the error in measurement, which is likely to be normally distributed. But I don't even need to know that.

That I don't need to know the underlying probability density function is very important. Another perspective on this important point is that I don't need to come up with a prior probability. The need for a prior probability is often the Achilles' heel of typical Bayesian analysis, because the prior probability must be supplied by a process of reasoning that precedes Bayesian analysis.

8.9 THE STANDARD OF CONCEPTUAL KNOWLEDGE

Comparison of Validity of Sense Data, Perception of Entities, and Induction

We have described various levels of knowledge: knowledge of the external world and our faculty of consciousness, which we get directly by sensory awareness and introspection, respectively; knowledge of entities, of which we are aware initially by our perceptual faculties' automatic integration and differentiation of sense data, and which we also know through inductive analysis of this sense data; and conceptual (including propositional) knowledge, which we obtain and validate by induction.

Knowledge at the first level we know with certainty. In other words, out of N possibilities, all N are instances of us knowing these facts. We also know with certainty the facts implicit in this sense data. For example, we know with certainty the axioms of existence and consciousness.

The knowledge we obtain by the method of induction described above is held in the form of a probability. For any item of knowledge so held, we can compare this probability to the probability of 1, which is the degree of probability for our basic knowledge of the world through our sensing and introspecting. Thus the basic, certain knowledge serves as a standard against which we compare our other knowledge in order to understand the meaning of probability for our other knowledge. The higher the probability for an item of non-axiomatic conceptual knowledge, the closer we are to knowing it as well as we know that of which we are aware directly from our sensing and introspecting.

We can define 'reasonable' or 'contextual' certainty to be any probability above some number, such that the probability we are wrong is so small that we have no practical reason to consider this small probability in our thinking or our actions. For example, if the probability of our having a certain illness is 1 in 10 billion, then we can say we are certain we do not have that illness, and we should not choose to incur an expense to take medication for it, because there are far greater dangers for us to spend our money on avoiding. The standard of contextual certainty should be different in different contexts. We need a higher standard before saying "I am certain he is guilty of murder" than before saying "I am certain the car keys are on my desk."

Observe how the method of induction I have presented comports with common sense. Every new observation consistent with a theory slightly improves the probability that the theory will correctly predict the future.

Observe also that this method of induction does not merely conclude that a certain theory is the best, and that errors are corrected with more knowledge. This method actually calculates a probability that the future will turn out as predicted.

For clarity, note what this kind of calculated probability is and is not. The calculated probability is not a probability that the theory is universally true, but is rather a probability that a given set of future instances will be consistent with the theory.

Now that I have identified and validated my method of induction, let us see how we can make the method more powerful.

9 MAKING OUR INDUCTIONS MORE POWERFUL AND ROBUST

9.1 GREATER ENUMERATION THROUGH INTEGRATION

In this book, we have encountered various forms of integration. In Chapter 6, we considered the narrowing, intensive integration performed by phrases and propositions. In the present chapter, we will consider a form of integration that aggregates groups of instances into a larger group over a wider range of measurement. As an example, let us see how one would make an inductive proof of the following statement: Food is necessary for a person's survival.

9.1.1 Basic Integration

To begin, observe all instances that you can think of involving a man surviving for some duration of time. Think of people you know, like the man next door, or somebody you read about in a book, or Socrates, or your uncle; and then ask, "Did they eat food?" And you might conclude, "I just examined 20 or 2,000 lives and, yes, they all *did* eat food." Then you can think of people who stopped eating food, and you ask, "Did they survive?" And you can observe that they all starved and died.

Then you think of examples of prisoners that are given only water and not food, and they die. We also know of famines in which people without food died. And we see that in perhaps many thousands of instances, say 100,000, whenever people did not eat, they died.

In addition, we find instances spread over wide ranges of measurement; these instances include people living in America, in Japan,

China, Russia, etc. They include people from every era, over a wide range of conditions, from every walk of life.

It is straightforward to apply our $n/(n+1)$ argument. All we need do is ask: What is the probability that the next man who does not eat food will have the highest measurement of being alive compared to the n starved men before him? The answer is less than or equal to $1/(n+1)$. The less-than condition applies because of the possibility of ties—actually, a high probability of ties, because all of the men will have their aliveness measured as zero. Therefore, the probability that the next starved man will die is greater than $n/(n+1)$.

We could thus conclude with reasonable certainty that food is required for survival.

But we can come up with billions or trillions of instances—even more instances than there are people. Let us see how.

One simple thing we could do is observe the same phenomenon in animals, which have many physical similarities to humans, and which also die if they don't eat. Suppose we observe 50,000 instances of animals dying if they don't eat.

Next, to consider the instances of animals as valid for our induction for humans, we have to know that food works for animals as it does for humans. Suppose we dissect some animals and discover that their food travels through a similar path as does food in humans—to a stomach and through intestines. And suppose we observe that the development of muscles in animals correlates to the animals' eating of food, as it does in humans. Then we can consider our instances of animals as evidence for our induction about humans.

By integrating our knowledge of animals with our knowledge of humans, we now have 150,000 instances. Note how integration increases the number of instances for our induction. Indeed, integration is a means of aggregating groups of instances into a larger group over a wider range of measurement. Integration, in this form, is building larger groups of interchangeable instances, or units.

9.1.2   Integration Using Causal Explanation

Let us go further with our example. What if we could figure out what food *does* for survival, how it is somehow a cause, or factor in the cause, for survival?

Let me explain what I mean by cause or factor in the cause. As discussed earlier, we know that every entity we can ultimately perceive exerts force(s) on us (often through intermediate entities) and on other entities; also, every entity has its own way of acting and its own way of reacting to the forces exerted by other entities. What happens (the effect) at any given time depends on how each entity acts and reacts to the *sum* of all the forces exerted. The effect is based on the mathematical relation among all the forces. *All* the entities involved constitute the cause, in this sense. But it is more useful, cognitively, to define the cause more contextually, in a way analogous to how we define a fundamental characteristic. What we usually call the cause is that combination of entities that constitutes the large or essential or decisive or pivotal or distinctive aspect of the cause in the given context. By 'decisive' I mean that which was different from usual, in an instance in which the effect was different from usual in an important respect. Maybe a better word is 'pivotal'—that is, the force that, whichever way it goes (other things being equal), so will go the effect. And we can call one aspect of this pivotal cause a causal factor.

Returning to our example of food and survival: What if we could understand the chemistry of the process and realize that the food contains stored energy, as there is stored energy in the fuel used by a car or any kind of motor? Also, we know that if we burn fuel, such as oil or gas, the burning fuel creates heat; and the heat is converted into energy (the ability to do work) by the engine or the motor. And we realize from our study of thermodynamics that for work to be done by any kind of machine, some kind of fuel is needed. And then we realize: *Food is an animal's fuel.* If we take a food such as sugar, and we try to burn it, it burns; it creates fire and heat. Then we realize by studying human (and animal) anatomy and physiology that some kinds of reactions take place that actually release heat—a form of energy—from the metabolism, from the chemical processing of food. And then we realize that, just as all these machines use fuel, so humans use food as their fuel, as their source of energy.

In other words, we know that all internally-generated action requires fuel as a source of energy for that action. And internally-generated action is necessary for the survival of a living being. Therefore, fuel is a necessary causal factor in the survival of man. Now we know that food is a man's fuel. We have determined that food, as man's fuel, is a necessary part of the cause of man's survival.

Thus we have found a deeper causal explanation. We started with the claim that food is a causal factor in man's survival. Our new, deeper causal explanation is that food is a causal factor in man's survival because food is man's fuel. This deeper causal explanation gives us more confidence in our original conclusion that food is necessary for man's survival. But why should it give us more confidence? The reason is that we have integrated our knowledge of man and animals needing food with our knowledge that all entities that internally generate action need fuel. But why should that integration give us more confidence? The reason is that we now have many more instances, more units, to support our induction. Our increase in confidence is an increase in probability, an increase in contextual certainty.

By seeing food as a cause, and by integrating this fact with what we know about fuel for motors, we have widened our groups of units, and we now have a group of units far more numerous than the one we started with. No longer are we looking only at instances of men and animals. We now include instances of every machine we have ever seen, of every physical process that requires fuel, and of every level of living organism. So we have multiplied the number of units greatly. And in every one of these instances, for every living thing surviving and being able to act, and for every motor or engine being able to do its work, the entity required fuel.

We can take this method of reasoning further. Chemistry and physics have found deeper physical laws that explain why fuel is needed. Again, this explanation widens our group of units more. The explanation might widen our group of instances to include all of our known instances of electromagnetic charges and gravitational forces according to known physical laws. We could see that an instance of fuel being needed is, more deeply, an instance of the applicability of known physical laws. Thus we have widened our group of instances to include every motion we have ever observed. In every such motion, certain physical laws have been observed to hold. Now we have a huge collection of observations that all confirm the same conclusion. Now we literally have billions or even trillions of instances to validate the induction that man needs food in order to survive.

Thus, when we find deeper causes or explanations, our induction is much stronger than a conclusion based merely on the simple enumeration of the narrower situation we began observing. Instead of finding thousands or millions of people who starved or did not starve depending on whether or not they ate, we now have trillions of instances of basic physical laws holding true, and each of those instances supports our induction that man needs food to survive.

In short, integration using progressively deeper causal explanation enables us to enumerate astronomically large numbers of supporting instances.

Of course, integration can work both ways, so to speak, either increasing or lowering the probability of a future occurrence. If I learn that an organism of a species I know nothing about has lived for ninety periods of time, without my knowing the duration of the period of time, then I can conclude that the probability that the animal will survive the next period is 90/91. But if I learn that the species is man, living now in the United States, and that the period of time is a year, then I can integrate this information with my knowledge of the millions of instances of the longevity of such men, and lower the probability accordingly. I can conclude that, from my new context of knowledge, the probability that the man will survive the next year is roughly 5/6, not 90/91. (See the actuarial table at Social Security Administration 2020.)

9.1.3   Integration Through Lawful Quantification of Differences

Consider this example. Each time a ball is hit by a bat, its flight appears different. Sometimes the ball flies high in the air, sometimes it travels close to the ground, and sometimes it bounces repeatedly. Sometimes the ball travels far, sometimes not so far.

But there is something the same in each different instance. There is something unchanging amid each change. What is unchanging is a certain mathematical relationship—the mathematical relationship between the forces acting on the ball and the change in momentum of the ball. This relationship is expressed by Newton's Second Law of Motion, which is a mathematical equation.

Thus, in this case, the use of mathematics takes seemingly disparate instances, instances that seem different in kind, and shows how they are similar, how they are all merely different in degree. Newton's equation accomplishes this end by lawfully *quantifying* the differences in each case. For example, a certain quantity of difference in the forces causes a certain predictable quantity of difference in the effect, the change in momentum.

Before using Newton's law, we had some instances of the ball bouncing, and some of the ball flying, with no clear pattern. After Newton's law, we have instances all of the same kind; all instances are confirming instances of Newton's law.

The same point applies to our earlier example of the horse and the saddle. The horse carries the saddle easily, must work harder to carry a person, and is unable to carry a saddle loaded with five hundred pounds of lead. All these instances are confirming instances of Newton's law.

A mathematical law, such as Newton's Second Law of Motion, describes a relation of measurements—for example, the measurement of force vs. the measurement of change in momentum. But because the law is a law—a principle—it has some omitted measurements. (Recall that the idea of ranges of measurement in concept-formation is another perspective on the idea of measurement-omission.) Newton's Second Law states that the ratio of force to change in momentum is constant. The omitted measurements are specific quantities of force and change in momentum. Therefore, the law applies to *any* quantity of force and change in momentum. Thus the law applies to a very wide range of measurement, and therefore a very wide range and very large number of instances. It applies not only to balls being batted, but also to any objects being batted, or thrown, or dropped. It also applies to rocks, boulders, grains of sand, and planets. The same mathematical law integrates all these instances that seemed before to be disparate, and shows how they are similar. All these instances are seen to be confirming instances of the same one induction. We have achieved integration, and many more instances for our induction, through lawful quantification of differences.

Given this understanding of mathematics in integration, let us revisit our example of food providing fuel. Prior to using mathematics, we could know that certain amounts, within certain ranges of measurement, of certain kinds of food led to healthy living. With further discoveries aided by mathematics, we could find more precise relationships; for example, the number of calories digested equals the number of calories expended in action plus the number of calories used to build proteins plus the number of calories stored in the body as fat. Then instead of having only the measured outcomes of ranges of measurement of healthy living and unhealthy living (plus death), we also have measured outcomes of calories used and stored. And we have another set of measured outcomes: the deviations from our mathematical formulas. If these deviations are small, then we know, with high probability, that the deviations in the next outcome will be small. That is, certain results—such as loss of weight—for an individual on a certain diet will be predictable.

9.1.4   Integration Through Discovering Elemental Particles

If I pour a cup of rice and watch the rice fall into a pot, I have made one observation of gravity. But if I look more closely and see the individual grains falling, I have in effect made thousands of observations of gravity. If, from other studies, I know that the grains are composed of molecules, and I calculate that each grain of falling rice is falling according to the law of gravity applied to each individual molecule in each grain of rice, then I have trillions of instances of gravity. Instances observed or inferred on smaller scales lead to a greater number of instances, and therefore stronger inductions. If the scale is much, much smaller, then the number of instances is much, much greater.

By simple combinatorial mathematics, there are far fewer kinds of particles—molecules, atoms, or sub-atomic particles—than there are kinds of combinations of particles (such as the millions of kinds of human-scale objects), and there are far fewer kinds of actions related to the particles (such as actions described by the laws of motion) than there are kinds of actions of combinations of particles (such as elasticity, tides, storms, sound, etc.). Therefore, the particles are more ubiquitous. They are also uniform. The combinations of these particles are less ubiquitous and more diverse. Therefore, any explanation in terms of the particles is going to be a wider integration with more numerous instances. For example, if I explain, in terms of molecules obeying laws of motion, the fact that mixing hot and cold liquid yields warm liquid, then I will have integrated my knowledge of liquid and heat with my wider-ranging knowledge of molecules and motion. Such an integration will be a far more cogent induction, because it integrates a far greater number and wider range of instances. Instead of having hundreds or thousands of instances, I will have trillions of trillions.

A key fact of nature that makes this method of thinking fruitful is this: Except in rare circumstances discovered by modern physics (such as nuclear reactions and the collisions of antimatter and matter), constituent parts retain certain fundamental properties—such as mass and electrical charge—regardless of how they are combined.

It is often necessary to deduce the macro or overall effect of a collection of many micro particles. This kind of deduction is what

Newton performed in calculating the behavior of planets. Using mathematics, he deduced that the gravitational effect of a body of mass is exactly the same as if the entire mass of the body were concentrated at a single point, the center of mass of the body. In other words, the gravitational behavior of the Earth, with all its particles distributed fairly evenly throughout this large spheroid, is roughly the same as if all the particles were concentrated at the Earth's center of mass. Thus, by making one observation of the behavior of the Earth, Newton was in effect making trillions of trillions of observations; he was making an observation of each of the trillions of trillions of atoms that constitute the Earth. Again we see a method of strengthening an induction—in this case, the inductive conclusion is Newton's law of gravity—by increasing astronomically the number of observed instances.

Note the essential need for mathematics in this approach. The elemental parts are far too numerous to allow purely non-mathematical understanding of their aggregate behavior. Using mathematics, however, one *can* understand their aggregate behavior. The reason is that each elemental particle of a certain kind—such as a proton—exerts exactly the same quantity of gravitational force and resistance to that force. In other words, each unit of matter is uniform in its degree of gravity. And mathematics is man's means of measuring through enumeration of units of uniform measure. (See Chapter 7.)

That reality consists of many uniform instances of a few kinds of elemental particles is the cause of the pervasive practicality of mathematical measurement.

Taking further the example of Newton's law of gravity, note how finding an elemental material allows also for wider integration. Because all objects—Earth, all the other planets, a ball when thrown, a rock when dropped—are made of the same material (the same kinds of elementary particles), the same one law of gravity applies to all these types of cases. We don't need one law of gravity only for the planets, another law only for objects on the Earth's surface, another law to explain the tides, etc. We have one law for all these categories of instances—one law with many more confirming instances than any of the separate laws could have separately.

In summary: Discovering uniform elemental or micro particles or materials and then explaining observed instances in terms of those elemental particles leads to astronomically more instances over wider ranges of measurement. Often, it is necessary to deduce and apply mathematical laws describing the aggregate or macro behavior of these elemental particles. One can then observe the actual aggregate behavior to see that the actual behavior is consistent with the deduced behavior.

Thus the old pursuit of the ancient Greeks to find the one in the many, the one or few kinds of elements constituting all matter, has been vindicated in modern science when combined with mathematics. By discovering all of the world to be composed of a few kinds of particles that all obey the same laws, we are making one of the widest inductions possible. We are inducing that all of reality has the same nature in a fundamental way. Therefore, whatever we know about the nature of the particles we have observed—for instance, that they exert and react to certain exact amounts of gravitational and electrical force—is true of all the particles in reality. All that is left for us to do, it might then seem, is to deduce how combinations of these particles will act in a given situation. That is what Newton did in deducing that the entire Earth acts gravitationally (beyond its boundaries) as though its entire mass were at its center of mass.

In many situations, however, we have not discovered such simplifications in reasoning from individual particles to large groups of particles. For example, consider this problem: I inject 4.5×10^{24} molecules of inert liquid at an angle of 30 degrees from vertical, at a speed of 1 meter per second, into my mouth. Where will these molecules be in 300 seconds? We currently are unable to deduce the answer to this question simply from known physical laws of motion of individual particles.

Nevertheless, I could answer, "My kidneys." Why (or how) will molecular forces direct many of these molecules to my kidneys?

Because the molecules together act as a liquid, and the liquid is pro-
cessed by my digestive system and disposed of as waste. Instead of
deducing straight from laws of physics, biologists had to make new
inductions from observations of biological phenomena.

So we see that laws of motion (even when accounting for relativ-
istic effects), though fundamental, are not the final word in scientific
discovery. There are still plenty more inductions and deductions for
man to make.

The existence of uniform elementary particles, constituting all
matter, explains why some basic physical laws and formulas are linear (or approximately so in familiar contexts). For example, gravitational force is proportional to mass, and electrical charge is proportional to the number of electrons or protons.

Why do some formulas have powers, such as squared or cubed
terms? Some formulas are cumulative. For example, distance traveled is an accumulated value based on time elapsed. Also, there are
three dimensions of physical extension, and entities behave the same
along all three dimensions. Consider this sequence of examples.
Light disperses equally in all three dimensions. As a sphere grows, its
volume grows as the cube of the radius. Its surface grows as the
square of the radius. The amount of dispersed light hitting a certain
amount of surface area on the inside of such a sphere is therefore
reduced according to the inverse of the square of the radius. But if
each particle within the sphere emits a certain amount of light, then
the total amount of light hitting the total surface will be proportional
to the cube of the radius.

Although force is often proportional to the amount of matter being considered, the location of the matter is often much more important, because force varies with a power of distance. For example,
a two-pound weight falling on your foot exerts twice as much force
as a one-pound weight would, but moving your foot out of the way
of the falling weight results in no force at all on your foot.

Why do some formulas have exponential factors? Some forms of
growth and decay are caused internally, and each part grows or

decays independently of each other part, but according to the same uniform formula. The resulting aggregate formula is exponential.

Thus even powers and exponential terms in physical formulas are the result of uniform elemental particles.

Objectivity of Similarity, Difference, and Range of Measurement Revisited

The discovery of elemental particles—such as a hundred kinds of atoms that constitute millions of different substances, and relatively few kinds of subatomic particles that constitute all atoms—sheds light on why similarity and difference are caused by differences in degree of measurement. We see that differences in effects are based on quantitative differences either in the number of elemental particles or in the spatial location of these particles. In general, the more similar the total number of particles in question, the more similar the total amount of effect of those particles: An increase in the number of particles causes a proportional increase in mass, weight, force, etc.

Another perspective on this line of reasoning is that effects generally vary in a continuous or granular way within a range of measurement. If, in a given context, the effect of a 100-pound weight is similar to the effect of a 102-pound weight, then the effect of a 101-pound weight generally will be similar to these other two.

Now that we have explored the concept of integration, and how we can use integration to obtain astronomically many instances for our inductions, let us explore methods for leveraging our powers of integration and induction.

9.2   Leverage Arising from Volition

9.2.1   Pivotal Human Force

The existence of our free will greatly accelerates and improves our ability to observe causal laws. We can manipulate factors to discover what is pivotal and what is not. We can experiment: set up repeating sequences, varying one factor at a time. The most basic examples of experiment are of a young child experimenting with common objects, such as his pushing a ball and observing it roll when he pushes.

Our free will gives us discretion over very small forces, the ones we can exert through our muscles. But using our knowledge, we can exert these forces in strategic, highly-leveraged places to cause effects that normally require huge forces. We exert the forces in places where existing large forces are closely balanced, or in unstable equilibrium, so that our small force is pivotal. For example, the earth's gravitational force exerted on a boulder on a cliff is offset by the cliff's upward force on the boulder. But our meager strength, not enough to lift the boulder, is enough to roll the boulder until it rolls off the cliff—that is, until we have altered the relation of the large forces enough for one of them to overcome the other. All of our technology rests on the fact that we can exert the small forces of our meager muscles in highly-leveraged circumstances in which those small forces are pivotal. For example, we rub two sticks to create barely enough heat to create a spark. That spark would have little effect in most circumstances, but we have placed a dry twig near the spark, and the spark adds a little more heat to the heat of the twig. That extra little amount of heat is enough to ignite the twig; the twig catches fire, unleashing a large amount of energy stored in the twig, lighting a big fire. And so on to nuclear power plants.

9.2.2   Controlling the Future vs. Trying Passively to Predict It

In a section above (9.1.4 Integration Through Discovering Elemental Particles), I explained that it is often not feasible to deduce the behavior of complex systems of entities simply from basic laws of physics such as Newton's laws of motion. Moreover, the aggregate effect might not be linear with variations in causal factors; that is, the outcome might vary greatly with a small change in initial conditions. Classic examples of such phenomena concern the weather. It is not feasible to predict where lightning will strike, or where a hurricane will be two months hence. Similarly, two similar rafts left adrift at sea might start side-by-side but end up in very different places, neither place predictable.

The study of such complex and difficult-to-predict systems is sometimes called "chaos theory."

Suppose we set ten rafts adrift, and they end up washing ashore at various points along a coastline. By the probabilistic reasoning we have been using, we could conclude that, with probability 9/11, the next raft we set adrift will wash ashore somewhere within the range of the first ten. Such a probability is unreliably far from 1, owing to few observations, owing in turn to an idiosyncratic situation that cannot be integrated with many other observations to increase the value of n (from ten). Moreover, the range of landing places on the coastline is likely to be so wide as to be uninformative.

What is man to do in the face of such apparent unpredictability? Is the quest for knowledge in these cases impossible? Is man impotent in the face of such seeming chaos?

Quite the contrary. The fact that small changes in causal factors can have large effects is the reason that man—with his meager amount of muscle power—can move mountains.

The key philosophical and practical issue is that man must be active, not passive. If man tries passively to predict where lightning will strike, he will fail. But if he erects a lightning rod or, better yet, builds an electric circuit, sending electric power exactly where he wants it to go at the flick of a switch, then he will succeed. A raft might drift unpredictably, but man can steer a ship—or a spaceship—across a great distance to a precise destination. Man can even steer a raft with paddles and sails.

Making slight changes in location can cause large changes. A man can design his machines so that a slight change in location or position of some part—such as a switch or a steering wheel—can have very large effects, and precisely the effects the man wants.

9.3   LEVERAGE FROM PREVIOUS INDUCTIONS

Sometimes one new observation can be enough to make what seems like a new induction. As shown in the example below, such a conclusion is really a new deduction from many observations of wider phenomena, including the phenomenon of consistent causal laws.

9.3.1   Conclusions from One Instance

Suppose I form a new chemical compound and place a brick of it in a tub of pure water, and the brick sinks. Then I know, from this one observation, that this compound is denser than water, and that any brick of this compound will sink when placed in any body of pure water. Indeed, if I can measure the volume and weight of the compound, then I know—even without an observation of the compound in water—whether the compound will always sink or always float.

I know this conclusion because I can bring to bear billions of confirming observations that were used in previous inductions. I know that the density of any chemical compound—including water and this new compound—is consistent, that a compound denser than a liquid will sink in that liquid, and that a less dense compound will float. More broadly, I know from a previous induction that a compound's mass, weight, and density are consistent.

In other words, this new induction about how this new chemical compound will sink or float in water is really a deduction from wider inductions. All compounds denser than water will sink in water. This piece of this compound sank in this tub of water. Therefore, all pieces of this compound will sink in all bodies of water.

Now consider an example from the history of science: the famous experiment by Benjamin Franklin, in which he used a kite to capture the electricity from lightning into a key and then into a Leydon jar. Harriman (2010, 31–34) recounts this experiment and concludes that Franklin was able to make a wide induction—that lightning is electrical—from this one instance.

But let us use our theory to explain the actual steps in this induction. Recall the notation, for Bayes' Theorem, that we used in our example of the horse carrying the saddle (in Section 8.3.1):

$$P(H|DX) = [P(H|X)P(D|HX)]/P(D|X).$$

In that example, H was the hypothesis that the horse exerts causal force on the saddle, as the horse exerts causal force on me.

As Harriman reports, Franklin held an extensive theory, using many advanced concepts, predicting that the lightning striking the kite would cause an electrical charge to gather in the Leydon jar. So in the case of Franklin's experiment, let H be the hypothesis that Franklin's theory correctly predicts that the electric charge is deposited in the jar just when the lightning strikes.

Franklin's extensive theory was based on a very large number of prior observations. As Harriman (2010, 34) notes, "Franklin found data everywhere suggesting that lightning was electrical." Already it is clear that Franklin's inductive conclusion was based ultimately on many observations, not just one.

In the example of the horse and the saddle, we had $P(H|X) = 1/2$ as a lower bound. That is, our prior probability that the horse exerts causal forces on the saddle was 1/2, based on the prior information (denoted by X) that the horse exerts causal forces on our consciousness. For Franklin's experiment, we do not know the precise prior probability given the prior information X; but given that X was that "Franklin found data everywhere suggesting that lightning was electrical," it is reasonable to assume that $P(H|X) = h$, where h is some proper fraction significantly greater than zero.

Another key fact of Franklin's experiment, as identified by Harriman (2010, 32), is that "nothing else known explains the observations" made by Franklin in the one instance of his experiment. The significance of this fact according to my theory is as follows: If lightning were not electrical, it would be extremely improbable that the Leydon jar would end up charged at just the moment that lightning struck the kite—just as it would have been extremely improbable that the saddle would remain on the horse if the horse did not exert causal force on the saddle throughout the horse's travel.

Thus the case of Franklin's experiment is parallel to our example with the horse and the saddle, and we end up with the following equation, after only one experimental instance by Franklin: $P(H|DX) = h/(h + \varepsilon)$, which is just a little less than 1. That is, with the benefit of probability theory, we are virtually certain that the lightning caused the electrical charge in the jar.

What about the conclusion that lightning will always—under a certain range of conditions—cause an electrical charge? Here we use the same reasoning that we used to conclude that a certain compound will always sink in water. We have billions of known instances that led us to the prior inductive conclusion that causal forces are regular and will continue to be regular in the future. From this wide induction, we can deduce that the action of lightning is regular and will continue to be regular in the future.

In short, Franklin's conclusion from one instance rests properly on probability theory and on prior inductions from astronomically many instances.

9.3.2   Deduction and Bayes' Theorem

The examples above illustrate the power of Bayes' Theorem as compared to conventional deductive reasoning. (See Jaynes 2003, 3–6, 35–37 for one such comparison.) The familiar deductive argument known as *modus ponens* takes the following form:

> If A, then B
> A
> Therefore B

In contrast, arguments such as the one in the Franklin example above take a form that is closer to the following:

> If A, then B (If Franklin's theory is true, then electrical
> charge collects in the jar.)
> B (Electrical charge collects in the jar.)
> Therefore A (Franklin's theory is true.)

Of course, by the rules of deduction, this argument commits the fallacy of 'affirming the consequent'. But adding one more premise (italicized below) would make the deduction valid, as follows:

> If A, then B
> B
> *If not-A, then not-B (If Franklin's theory is false, then electrical charge does not collect in the jar.)*
> Therefore A

What Bayes' Theorem does is to allow the addition of a premise very close to "If not-A, then not-B," namely,

> If not-A, then B with very low probability. (If Franklin's theory is false, then it is very improbable that electrical charge collects in the jar.)

With the addition of this premise, Franklin can conclude,

> Therefore A (Franklin's theory is true) with high probability.

As powerful as Bayes' Theorem is, however, it is but a part of the overall method of inductive reasoning presented in this book. Moreover, when I have used Bayes' Theorem in this chapter and the previous one, I have preceded its use by the use of the $n/(n+1)$ rule, a rule for which I provided a philosophical validation. That is, the philosophically validated $n/(n+1)$ rule provided an objective basis for the prior probabilities in the Bayesian analysis. This idea can be stated more generally and more philosophically as follows: Applying Ayn Rand's principle that characteristics are ranges of measurement, I offer a philosophical validation of "nonparametric predictive inference" [which includes the $n/(n+1)$ rule], in turn providing an objective basis for prior probabilities in Bayesian analysis.

9.4   INDUCTION IN MATHEMATICS, REVISITED

The following is a very wide mathematical induction: One can keep adding units to a group so long as there are units to add, and so long as one's mind can hold the result. This induction is based on the fact that the units' only characteristic being considered is that they are units. Therefore, we know that each unit being considered is identical in the context we are considering. In effect, the only attribute we are considering for each unit is that the unit obeys the Law of Identity.

This line of reasoning—of being able to add another unit so long as there are units to add, and treating the difference between n and $n + 1$ as the same for any value of n—is the same line of reasoning we used in dealing with the difference between time t and time $t + 1$, regardless of the value of t.

In mathematics, we start with the condition that all the units are equal. That condition tells us that our measurement of the next unit will be exactly equal to the measurement of all the n units that preceded it. In our more general method of induction, we do not start with this condition. In the absence of such a condition, we do not know that the measurement of the next unit (or instance) will be exactly equal to the measurement of all the units that preceded it. What we do know is that, with probability $>= n/(n+1)$, the measurement of the next unit (or instance) will be less than or equal to the maximum of all the measurements that preceded it. Also, with probability $>= (n-1)/(n+1)$, the measurement of the next unit (or instance) will fall within the range of the n measurements that preceded it.

When we seek to discover the one in the many in physical reality—when we seek to discover some one class of particles that constitute all matter—we are seeking to approach the same degree of certainty we have in induction in mathematics.

9.5 AN EXAMPLE: PTOLEMY TO NEWTON

Let us see how my theory of induction applies to a historical example: the development of astronomy and kinematics from Ptolemy through Newton.

The geocentric theory of Ptolemy had the Earth at the center of the universe, with the other heavenly bodies—including the sun, moon, and planets—traveling around the Earth. According to this theory, however, the path traveled by the sun and planets was complex. For each body, a complex combination of eccentric circles, epicycles, and other devices was needed to describe the motion. These descriptions were limited to descriptions of the angular position of each body, and did not contain information about the distance of each body from Earth. One could say that these descriptions of motion were consistent with a theory of causality because these motions, so described, were the result of the combination of all causal forces involved.

But these descriptions did not integrate with each other, because the formulas for the motion of each body contained different values, and the descriptions certainly did not integrate with any other kind of motion known to man. Therefore, man's knowledge of the motion of Mars was limited to observations of the motion of Mars, which consisted of a very limited number of (apparent) full revolutions around the Earth. Therefore, any predictions about the motion of Mars would have to be of limited degree of certainty. Moreover, the ability to predict the motion of Mars did not carry over to an ability to predict the motion of other planets, which had to be described with their own formulas after observations of those bodies. Most importantly, the ability to predict the motion of Mars did not carry over to an ability to predict the motion of any object on Earth, and vice versa.

Then came Copernicus and his heliocentric theory, according to which the sun is the center of the solar system. This theory identified the distance of the sun and each planet along with their angular position. The theory also distinguished Earth's moon from the planets, as the moon was the one celestial body that did orbit the Earth. The theory also explained the apparent retrograde motion of Mercury and Venus—which were identified as being closer than Earth to the sun—thereby integrating knowledge of the motions of all the planets. In effect, this integration multiplied the number of all the observed instances of motion for each planet, because the evidence for the motion of one planet became evidence for a certain kind of motion of all six known planets. Nevertheless, the Copernican theory still used epicycles, which introduced non-integrated differences in the understanding of the motion of each planet. And the Copernican theory still did not enhance knowledge of motion on Earth.

Then came Kepler and his mathematical formulas for the motion of all the planets. Kepler recognized that the orbits of the planets were not circular, but rather elliptical. Moreover, his formulas identified precise mathematical relationships among speed, distance from the sun, and change in direction. These formulas more precisely conformed to observation, thereby decreasing the range of measurement within which future observations could be expected to fall. These formulas also were the same for all the planets. Thus Kepler's formulas not only integrated knowledge of motion of all the planets, but could be used to predict the motion of other bodies orbiting the sun. Still, however, this knowledge did not integrate with knowledge of motion on Earth. The causal explanation of planetary motion offered by Kepler did not explain any kind of motion on Earth.

Galileo studied motion of pendulums, falling bodies, balls rolling on inclines, and projectiles. By isolating horizontal and vertical motion, he was able to integrate all four kinds of motion, creating a single number of instances greater than each separate number of instances.

Then came Newton, who integrated the knowledge of Kepler and Galileo, and who identified his laws of motion and universal gravitation. With Newton's theory, the motion of the heavenly bodies was grasped to be of the same nature as motion on Earth. An apple falling from a tree and Mars crossing the sky some evening were confirming instances of the same simple causal theory. This integration increased astronomically (no pun intended) the number and scope of confirming instances of the theory, while also decreasing the range of measurement within which future actions could be expected to fall.

In hindsight, one can say that there was evidence all along that the laws governing planetary motion are the same as the laws governing motion on Earth and the motion of the Earth itself. That evidence was that the planets make our eyes see them, as entities on Earth make our eyes see them, and as the Earth beneath our feet makes us see it. But it is one thing to know that such common laws must exist, and another thing to discover them as Newton did.

Of course, Newton's laws still contained some inaccuracies, especially outside the ranges of measurement of daily observation—for example, at extremely high speeds. Awareness of these inaccuracies created an opportunity for scientists to make further discoveries.

Returning to the question from Laplace about the sun rising tomorrow, laws of motion and gravitation change everything. We have trillions of trillions of instances of these laws holding. The sun rising tomorrow is one such instance. Therefore, in our probabilistic formula $n/(n+1)$, n is no longer the number of days the sun has risen, but rather trillions of trillions.

9.6 THE LAW OF CAUSALITY

One of the most famous statements by Ayn Rand (1957, 1037) is the following:

> The law of causality is the law of identity applied to action. All actions are caused by entities. The nature of an action is caused and determined by the nature of the entities that act; a thing cannot act in contradiction to its nature.

Peikoff (1991, 12–17), reporting the position of Ayn Rand, offers a validation of this statement. Frankly, I do not understand this validation. Peikoff offers a clearer—and, in my judgment, much better but still unconvincing—validation, which he also attributes to Ayn Rand, in a subsequent lecture (1997, Lecture 1). Rather than criticize these validations in any detail, I merely refer the reader to them, to judge for himself. (Peikoff's explanation of Ayn Rand's account of

causality, in the references above, should not be conflated with Peikoff's own theory of causality expressed in Peikoff 2002, especially
Lectures 1 and 2, and Harriman 2010, especially 5–28. I also leave it
to the reader to judge Peikoff's theory.)

I do think that Ayn Rand's statement, as I understand it, is true
and crucial. But my own validation, presented below as a condensed
integration of previous content in this book, is significantly different
from anything I have read or heard from Ayn Rand, Peikoff, or any
other Objectivist philosopher. Therefore, I make no claim that my
own understanding of the statement is consistent with Ayn Rand's
intended meaning.

We know, from induction on astronomically many observations,
that entities exist and act—and will continue to exist and act—on our
consciousness in regular, consistent, and distinctive ways in accordance with scientific laws describable by precise mathematical statements. Also by induction on astronomically many observations, we
know that these entities act and will continue to act on each other
according to these same scientific laws. There is no dichotomy between the way entities act on us, causing us to perceive them, and the
way entities act on one another. We can even come to know how entities will act on one another by knowing how these entities act on
us—that is, by conceptualizing how we perceive them.

These regular and distinctive ways of acting can be conceptualized as characteristics that we can identify collectively as the *nature*
of each entity.

According to the philosophical hierarchy of knowledge developed in this book, the initial identification of a cause is of existence
exerting a force on our consciousness. But once we identify, by observation and induction, that these causal forces are regular and distinctive aspects of entities, and once we form the concept of 'nature',
then we can form a more advanced concept of 'cause'. A cause then
is a specific aspect and/or instance of an entity's nature, a specific
aspect and/or instance of an entity's regular and distinctive way of
acting.

For example, the cause of John's competence is his conscientious-ness, which is an aspect of his nature. The cause of the fire was a lighted match, which by its nature can burn and set other things on fire.

Here is another conceptual connection between entities and cau-sality. Causality is what is unchanging—what is the same or constant or similar—about change or action. The search for causality is the search for the unchanging, even if the only thing unchanging is a rate of change (such as velocity), or a kind of change (such as growth or decay), or a rate of a rate of change (such as acceleration), or a com-plex mathematical equation identifying the change. From our per-ception of entities, we know there has been something unchanging about how entities act on our senses. We also look for something un-changing about how entities act on and react to one another, such as the way an object falls when I drop it. What we discover to be un-changing about these actions of entities is what we characterize as causality. That is, "The law of causality is the law of identity applied to action."

9.7   THE QUANTIFIED BASIS FOR OCCAM'S RAZOR AND FOR REJECTING THE ARBITRARY

9.7.1   An Example: Knowledge of Other Minds

We have considered at least two cases in which we drew induc-tive/deductive inferences beginning with observations regarding a single entity. The first case (in Section 8.2) started with observations that entities act in a distinctive and persistent way on oneself, a single entity; then, using related observations and inferences, we concluded that all entities act in a distinctive and persistent way in relation to all other entities. (Recall our example of the horse acting on a saddle.) The second case (in Section 9.3.1) started with one observation of a new chemical compound sinking in water; then, using related observations and inferences, we concluded that this compound will always sink in water.

There is a very important inductive/deductive conclusion that follows the logical pattern of the cases above, especially the first case above. Start with the observation that one is conscious. Then, from related observations and inferences, one can conclude that other human beings are conscious. Going through the argument will reveal important philosophical principles.

The simplest form of evidence for this conclusion is the report of truthful people. They tell us that they are conscious. Let us do the math for this argument.

Suppose John has made many thousands of statements that have been directly confirmed as true. We can say that the truth value of all n of these statements has been 1. Therefore, by our $n/(n+1)$ argument, the probability that another statement by John—namely, that he is conscious—is true is greater than $n/(n+1)$.

Moreover, the statement that he is conscious is much less likely for John to be wrong about than are other statements by John. Our own consciousness is something we are aware of directly; indeed, it is axiomatic. Furthermore, there is no apparent motivation for John to lie about such a fact as his consciousness. Finally, as a solid behaves consistently regarding whether it floats in water, so a person behaves at least fairly consistently regarding telling the truth.

Continuing the argument, we have billions of examples of truthful individuals reporting that they are conscious. From this evidence, the probability that the next person we encounter is conscious, so long as the person exhibits conceptual functioning, is $n/(n+1)$ where n is some number in the billions.

9.7.2   Occam's Razor

But let us continue this example in order to get to the philosophical principles I have promised. Although numerous philosophers have written on this "problem of other minds," I find the work of some scientists in the Bayesian tradition more cogent. In particular, I recommend MacKay (2003, 343–356) and Jaynes (2003, 601–614). These references do not directly address the "problem of other minds"; they do address a more general idea: Occam's Razor. Indeed, MacKay and Jaynes provide a corrected and precise mathematical reformulation of Occam's Razor within a methodology they call "model comparison." (A better name might be "theory comparison.")

Let us use this method of "model comparison" to compare two hypotheses or theories or "models," H_1 and H_2.

Let X = the prior information that you are conscious.

Let H_1 = the hypothesis that other people are conscious.

Let H_2 = the hypothesis that other people are not conscious.

Let D = the fact that other people act in a way consistent with their being conscious.

Then the product rule of probability states that

$$P(H_1|DX)P(D|X) = P(H_1|X)P(D|H_1X),$$

and

$$P(H_2|DX)P(D|X) = P(H_2|X)P(D|H_2X).$$

Divide the first equation by the second, assuming that $P(H_2|DX)$ is non-zero. (If this term is zero, then we are done before we start.) The term $P(D|X)$ drops out, and we are left with

$$P(H_1|DX)/P(H_2|DX) = [P(H_1|X)/P(H_2|X)] \bullet [P(D|H_1X)/P(D|II_2X)]$$

The left side of the equation is the ratio of the posterior probabilities. The first bracketed factor on the right side is the ratio of prior probabilities, and the second bracketed factor on the right side is what is known in this context as the 'Occam factor'.

One statement by William of Occam of his famous razor is, "Plurality should not be posited without necessity" (Duignan 2018).

Such plurality can take the form of the positing of an unknown entity or an unknown causal factor. Jaynes (2003, 603) points out that some writers take Occam to be arguing for the 'simplicity' of a theory, although 'simplicity' and 'complexity' only approximate the proper meaning of the razor. A precise meaning of the razor is captured, according to Jaynes (2003, 601), by Bayesian analysis (as in the equation above).

Of the 'Occam factor', MacKay (2003, 343) writes,

> the second ratio, the data-dependent factor, embodies Occam's razor automatically. Simple models tend to make precise predictions. Complex models, by their nature, are capable of making a greater variety of predictions … . So if H_2 is a more complex model, it must spread its predictive probability $P(D\,|H_2)$ more thinly over the data space than H_1. Thus, in the case where the data are compatible with both theories, the simpler H_1 will turn out more probable than H_2, without our having to express any subjective dislike for complex models.

MacKay also writes (2003, 345),

> the complex theory … always suffers an 'Occam factor' because it has more parameters, and so can predict a greater variety of data sets.

The theory that other humans are conscious is the more "simple" theory, using MacKay's term, because we know that our being conscious is a major and obvious causal factor in our actions. (Not to belabor the obvious evidence for this knowledge, I will merely state that we make decisions and act based on what we perceive and conceive.) We observe also that other humans act consistently with their being conscious as a causal factor. The more "complex" theory would be that other people are not conscious and yet somehow act as though they are conscious, due to some other cause; that is, there is an as-yet unknown causal factor substituting for consciousness in the causal chain that goes from perceptual awareness to volitional conceptualization, to decision to act, to physical action (among other steps).

With this theoretical background, let us put in numbers for our equation. Let us start with $P(H_1|X)$. We have one known instance of consciousness, and no known instances of an absence of consciousness. Therefore, using our formula $(n+1)/n$, the probability that the next human will be as conscious is greater than or equal to 1/2. Let us be conservative and set $P(H_1|X) = P(H_2|X) = 1/2$.

Clearly, $P(D|H_1X) = 1$. Clearly, $P(D|H_2X)$ is less than 1. Thus we already have arrived at the conclusion that $P(H_1|DX) > P(H_2|DX)$. But let us go further, to see how very much less $P(D|H_2X)$ is than 1.

$D|H_2X$ can occur two ways. One way is that a person's actions would be consistent with his being conscious just by luck, as the saddle might move with the horse just by luck. Of course, such an occurrence is extremely improbable. The other way is for there to be a process that substitutes for consciousness in a causal chain terminating in the actions we observe being taken by other people.

Such a process that could substitute for consciousness would have to be very complex. The process would have to interact with all five senses and with memory, and would have to be able to perform something analogous to concept-formation. From our earlier treatment of the law of contradiction, we know that many characteristics preclude one another, and so we cannot know that such a process is even possible. But leaving aside that caveat for now, the genetic basis for such a process would have to be a fairly long sequence in the human genome. The full human genome contains about 750 megabytes of information, which is roughly two thousand times the size of this book. The average length of a single protein-encoding gene is roughly the length, in amount of information, of a six-page synopsis of Shakespeare's play *Hamlet*. (I am using a synopsis to capture the idea of not having to be word-perfect.) What is the probability that a six-page synopsis of *Hamlet* appears within three thousand books of random text? To offer perspective, there is about an even chance that the word "Hamlet" would appear in such a collection of books. The chance of the synopsis appearing is easily less than randomly picking the same atom in the universe ten times in a row.

Therefore, $P(D|H_2X) \approx 0$, and so $P(H_1|DX) \approx 1$. That is, the Occam factor is astronomical. That is, other people are conscious.

We can perform a similar analysis with other, even more fantastical theories, such as that a mastermind consciousness is using a machine somewhere to control other people, or that you are a "brain in a vat" (which of course must be engineered by an advanced mind). The even more fantastical notion that a computer simulation can be conscious is not, in my judgment, science fiction but rather fiction.

We could have used the above method of "model comparison" to analyze our previous examples of the saddle on the horse and of Franklin's experiment. We could have made H_1 the hypothesis that Franklin's theory is true, and H_2 the hypothesis that lightning has no bearing on electricity. Then the Occam factor would have been $1/\varepsilon$. That is, the probability that the electrical charge ends up in the jar, given that Franklin's theory is true, is 1; whereas the probability that the electrical charge ends up in the jar, given that lightning has no bearing on electricity, is ε. Because $1/\varepsilon$ is a very large number, the probability that Franklin's theory is true increases by a very large multiple after Franklin's experiment.

Now we are ready to identify some philosophical principles from our example.

9.7.3   The Arbitrary

The extreme limit of "complexity" of a theory is reached when the theory is fantastical, that is, not based on any evidence at all—as in the theory that other people are not conscious even when behaving as though they are. A more philosophical word for "fantastical" is 'arbitrary'.

It is a well-known epistemological principle that arbitrary assertions have no cognitive weight, and we should not consider even the possibility of their stating an actual fact. The reason for this principle is that there is an astronomically large number of arbitrary assertions we could make that are disjoint from one another, and, because there is no evidence for any of them, they are equally likely. Because each such assertion asserts one of astronomically-many equally likely possibilities, the probability of any one of them stating an actual fact is minuscule.

Here is another perspective on the same principle. Any entity that has a complex function will have some sizable number of parts. A human being has thousands of parts. Even something relatively as simple as a semi-automatic pistol with its ammunition has at least thirty parts. Such parts must work together in a very specific way, and each part has numerous essential characteristics regarding material, shape, and connection with other parts. Taking just the number of possible connections of k parts to one another, we get $(2^{k-1})^{k/2}$ possibilities. Then take the number of possible orderings of the parts if we take one part arbitrarily to be the first; that number is $(k-1)!$. Multiplying these numbers yields $(k-1)!(2^{k-1})^{k/2}$. For $k=30$, that means more than 10^{160} possibilities. That number of possibilities is many trillions of times more than 10^{100} times the number of entities the size of a pistol that can fit in the solar system, out to Neptune, if packed tight. Then suppose very conservatively that there are a thousand different materials and, for each part, a thousand different shapes. For the thirty parts, that makes 10^{90} possibilities. That means that if you dream up a thirty-part entity with no evidence of it existing, the probability that such an entity exists in the solar system is less than 10^{190}. Of course, an entity outside our solar system cannot exert moment-by-moment forces in synchronicity with our own chosen actions here on earth.

What is the philosophical point of the above indulgence of arbitrary assertions? The point is that if you fantasize, without evidence, that a certain kind of entity of any complexity exists, then there is essentially a zero chance that such an entity really does exist anywhere near enough to have causal efficacy.

Thus we see another kind of error caused by sensualism. Earlier (see Section 8.7.1), we saw that sensualism rejects causality on the (invalid) grounds that we *cannot* form an impression or image of causality. Now we see the sensualist premise that we should entertain a fantasy on the grounds that we *can* form an impression or image of such a fantasy. Once we reject sensualism as absurd, we are free of the errors of rejecting causality and of entertaining the arbitrary.

For the standard Objectivist treatment of the arbitrary, see Peikoff 1990, 163–171 and Binswanger 2014, 278–292. The essence of Peikoff's treatment is contained in the statement (1990, 164), "An arbitrary statement has no relation to man's means of knowledge." My treatment above, however, does indeed relate the arbitrary to man's means of knowledge, by showing the relationship between an arbitrary statement and reality. Therefore, my treatment above—including my reason for rejecting the arbitrary—is more in keeping with the primacy of existence, in the following respect: My treatment not only recognizes the nature of man's consciousness, but also shows that this nature is, in the current context, sufficient for knowing reality.

9.8   A WORD ON ETHICS

An in-depth treatment of induction in ethics and derivative fields is beyond the scope of this book. But I would like to touch on this subject through the following brief example.

Suppose I observe numerous instances of my using reason to make a decision, and numerous instances of my using emotion to make a decision. Suppose that my reason-based decisions result in the achievement of my goal 99% of the time, and my emotion-based decisions result in the achievement of my goal 5% of the time. Then I can conclude that, in the next instance, a reason-based decision, instead of an emotion-based decision, is more likely to result in the achievement of my goal. If I use some of the methods in this chapter to multiply instances, and I then observe the same percentages of outcome, I can conclude that a reason-based decision will be more effective in the next large batch of instances. That is, if I want to achieve my goal, I should decide according to reason. I know this conclusion with certainty, because I know that 99% is greater than 5%.

Thus, we can be certain that rationality is a virtue, even if we are uncertain as to whether rationality will lead to success in a given instance. More generally, we can attain certain knowledge that a normative principle is true, even though we have only probable knowledge regarding the outcome of applying the principle.

This conclusion comports with common sense, which tells us that rationality does not guarantee success, but is the policy most likely to lead to success.

9.9   APPLYING THE $n/(n+1)$ METHOD TO ITSELF

How well will the $n/(n+1)$ method work in practice? One way to find out would be to apply the $n/(n+1)$ rule to itself in an nested way: Look at how many times in n observations that we reached a new high (or a new low, or a new midpoint, etc.), and then compare that number to the number of times predicted by the rule itself: $(1/2) + (1/3) + (1/4) + \ldots + (1/n)$. If the number of new highs is close to the predicted number of new highs, then we have further validated our $n/(n+1)$ method for the given problem.

Indeed, we could apply the $n/(n+1)$ method in a nested manner on the entirety of our experience. That is, we could track how well the method has worked or might have worked in the m times we have or might have used it. Such an empirical study would be interesting. I think it would yield results favorable to the method, thereby further confirming its validity. Of course, for all known scientific laws, the method does work.

9.10   SUMMARY OF CAUSALITY AND INDUCTION

Here then is a summary of causality and my method of induction.

1. Causal interaction between existence and one's faculty of consciousness is a fact implicit in the facts of existence and

consciousness. Thus the existence of causal interaction is known to us based on experience.

2. The fact that one perceives entities demonstrates—with trillions of trillions of confirming instances throughout our entire range of experience—that these causal interactions between existence and one's consciousness are regular.

3. Because we are part of reality, it is a reasonable (non-arbitrary) hypothesis that there are regular causal interactions not only between external existence and consciousness, but also among all things that exist. This hypothesis is supported by astronomically many observations, just as is our perception of entities. We then introduce a probabilistic argument—which we call the $n/(n+1)$ rule—building on the work of Jeffreys, Hill, Jaynes, and Coolen; and we give the argument a philosophical basis from Ayn Rand's identification of characteristics as ranges of measurement. Based on our astronomically many observations, and applying the $n/(n+1)$ rule in combination with Bayes' Theorem, the probability that regular causal interactions—obeying causal laws identified by scientists and codified in mathematical formulas and equations—will continue for the foreseeable future is very, very nearly 1. Therefore, we know this fact to a degree of certainty that is very, very near to our degree of certainty of our basic sensory awareness of existence.

The pattern of thinking just described to validate causality is the pattern of induction we can employ generally. Our knowledge of the law of causality (validated above), combined with methods of integration, enable us to assemble astronomically large numbers of confirming instances for further inductions. Particularly powerful methods of integration include causal explanation, mathematical quantification of differences, and discovery and aggregation of elementary materials and particles.

The method of induction described herein provides a calculus for measuring the degree of certainty of an inductive conclusion as it applies to a given set of future instances.

Hill (1988, 227) writes of his assumption he calls "$A_{(n)}$," which is a seminal precursor to my probabilistic argument, as follows:

> Let me conclude by observing that $A_{(n)}$ is supported by all of the serious approaches to statistical inference. It is Bayesian, fiducial, and even a confidence/tolerance procedure. It is simple, coherent, and plausible. It can even be argued, I believe, that $A_{(n)}$, along with [a related function that accounts for ties in measurements of various instances], constitutes the fundamental solution to the problem of induction.

I agree that Hill's $A_{(n)}$, a precursor to the third step in my argument for induction summarized above, is a crucial step in a full solution to the problem of induction. In my judgment, my three steps taken together are the essence of a full solution.

10 CLOSING

We began our validation of knowledge with something we were conscious of. This something consisted of parts of a whole sensory field. We conceptualized the world as encompassing all that we would ever be conscious of. We grasped the relation of the world to our consciousness as a causal relation. We grasped this relation as regular when we perceived the world as consisting of entities.

We encountered three recurring themes to help integrate the numerous steps of our inquiry:
1. Axiomatic concepts and their role in cognition.
2. Similarity, difference, and range of measurement.
3. Integration.

We then understood more fully our conceptual faculty—which we had already understood to some degree and had already been using—and began volitionally to organize our perceptions into concepts according to perceived similarities and differences. We then understood our ability to form propositions. We used propositions to put the content of our concepts into logical order. We identified the Law of Non-Contradiction and a method of induction to validate and calculate the reliability of each of our propositions, so that we could reliably predict and change the course of the future according to our purpose.

Using the epistemology in this book, we have an organized corpus of knowledge, based entirely on our sensory awareness of reality—a corpus of knowledge that is true, readily applicable to new situations, and conducive to the discovery of new knowledge—for the purpose of making the most of reality.

Appendix: Supplemental Material on Mathematics

This appendix is a lightly edited version of Pisaturo 1998 and a section (on infinity) of Pisaturo 2001.

A.1 Further Applications

A.1.1 Multiplication

Let us begin by contrasting multiplication to addition. Consider the phrase "2 + 3." We know that this phrase does not refer to abstract number-objects in a non-real "world." We know that "2" means "2 (uniform) units." The phrase "2 + 3" means "2 units of some kind plus 3 units of the same kind." The units might be "beans," for example; then we would have "2 beans + 3 beans."

The word "plus" means "with the addition of." Addition is a mental operation whereby the uniform units of each group are considered to be uniform units of a single combined group. (This mental operation may or may not be accompanied by a corresponding physical operation.)

Now consider the phrase "2 x 3." We know that "3" still means "3 units." But does "2 x 3" mean "2 units of some kind times 3 units of the same kind"? It would make no sense, for example, to talk about "2 beans times 3 beans."

What, then, does "2 x 3" mean? It can mean "2 groups of 3 units each," or "3 groups of 2 units each." It can mean either of those things, because each of those things is equal, as we will now show.

245

Let us take 2 x 3 to mean "2 groups of 3 units each." For example, we might have "2 plates of 3 beans each." (See Figure A.1.)

Figure A. 1. Two plates of three beans each.

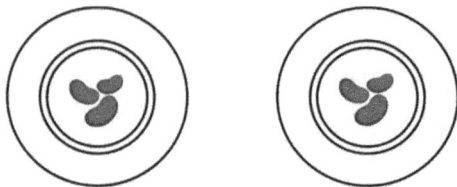

If we then count out the total number of beans in both plates, we see that we have a total of 6 beans. Applying the same inductive method used in the earlier chapter on mathematics, we then can show that 2 x 3 is *always* 6; and, in general, we can prove the entire multiplication table.

Whereas addition is a mental operation of combining groups of units, multiplication is a mental operation of replicating or repeating—that is, multiplying—*groups* of units, and *then* combining them. For addition, the units of each group must all be uniform, within each group and across both groups. For multiplication, the *groups* (as well as the units) must be uniform.

Now let us relate the concept of multiplication to the concepts of quantity and number. Even a single number can be thought of as a multiplication. For example, the number 3 can be understood to be a unit multiplied to make 3 units. From this perspective, one can think of an expression such as 2 x 3 as entailing the same kind of operation (multiplication) performed twice in succession—performed first on a unit, and then again on a group of units. The expression represents a quantity of quantities of units. The expression uses two levels of uniform units; in our example, the first level of uniform units is beans, and the second level of uniform units is groups of 3 beans each. (In other words, the expression is a nesting, or iterative use, of the concepts of unit and number.) In short, we have a 2-group of 3-groups of units (beans).

Using our mathematical condition of uniform (and therefore interchangeable) units, we can prove by our inductive method that 2 x

3 = 3 x 2, or, more generally, that *ab* = *ba*. Start with *a* groups of *b* units each—in this case, two groups of three units each. (See Figure A.2.) Form a new group of *a* units by taking the first unit from each group. Do the same for the second unit of each group, and so on. At the end of this process, you will have *b* groups of *a* units—that is, three groups of two units each. This fact is known as the *commutative law* of multiplication. One immediate benefit of knowing this law is that it allows us to halve the size of the multiplication tables we must memorize.

Figure A. 2

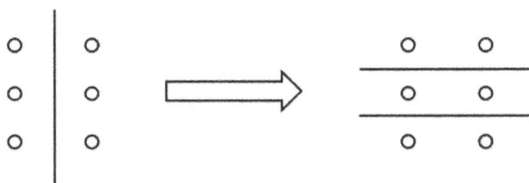

As multiplication is an iterative use of the process of grouping uniform units, we can increase the degree of iteration. For example, we can multiply our 2-group of 3-groups by 4, giving us 4 x 2 x 3.

Again, we can prove that the order of numbers does not change the final result. Or, equivalently, the order of the performance of the two distinct operations of multiplication does not change the result. Draw a picture of our example: 4 groups, each containing a 2-group of 3 units each—that is, each containing 6 units. (See Figure A.3.) The same picture also shows a 4-group of 2 groups each—that is, 8 groups, each containing 3 units each. In other words, we get the same result if we multiply 2 times 3, then multiply the result by 4, as we do if we multiply 4 times 2 and then multiply the result by 3. This fact is the *associative law* of multiplication.

Figure A. 3: (4 x 2) x 3 = 4 x (2 x 3).
More generally, (a x b) x c = a x (b x c).

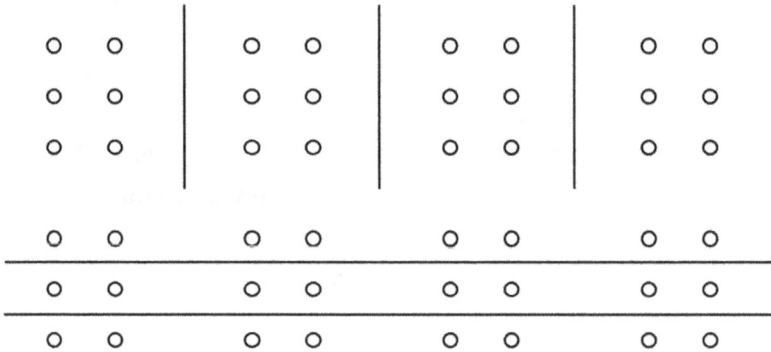

The commutative and associative laws of multiplication, along with the other laws of arithmetic, are very useful for performing the operations to arrive at a single-number result. More importantly, these laws are indispensable for the method of algebra. (In the earlier chapter on mathematics, we explained how the interchangeability of units leads also to the commutative and associative laws of addition.)

Thus we have described multiplication of units, such as beans, rocks, etc. But what about when we multiply physical measurements such as *feet* x *feet* to get *square feet*? We noted above that we cannot multiply beans by beans; how, then, can we multiply feet by feet?

We are not literally multiplying feet by feet. Here is what we are doing. Through observation of the physical world, we learn that area is an attribute that can be measured by the standard unit of a square foot—which is a square with each side one foot long. We can measure an area by using an object such as a flat piece of wood in the shape of a square with each side one foot long. We can place this "square ruler" on a part of the area we are measuring. We can then mark off the part of the area that is covered, and then place the ruler on another part. If we count up the number of parts we mark off in this way, we have measured the whole area as a number of square feet.

But there is an easier way, especially if the shape of our whole area is regular. Suppose the shape is a rectangle. (See Figure A.4.) Suppose we measure the rectangle to be 10 feet wide and 15 feet long. Let us then mentally divide our rectangle into 15 strips, each 10 feet wide. Each strip can be divided into 10 squares, each a square foot in size. Thus, each strip is a 10-group of square-foot units. And we have 15 of these 10-groups. In other words, we have 15 x 10 square feet. (Equivalently, if we had divided our area into 10 strips, each 15 feet long, we would have 10 x 15 square feet.)

Figure A. 4: A rectangle 10 feet wide and 15 feet long is 15 x 10 square feet.

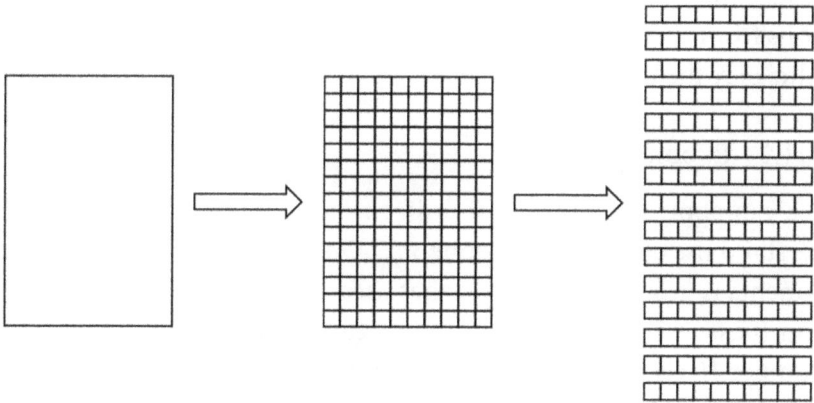

What we did was the following: For each foot of the rectangle's length, we associated a uniform-sized strip (group) of square feet, and we also observed that the quantity of square feet in each strip was the same as the number of feet in the width of the rectangle being measured. In other words, we made a unit-to-unit correspondence between units of width and units of square feet in a strip, and we also made a unit-to-*group* correspondence between each unit of length and each strip of square feet. Thus, we did not multiply feet by feet; we multiplied the number of square feet per strip by the number of strips.

This kind of unit-to-unit or unit-to-group correspondence must be made and understood before one can multiply two measurements in reality—measurements such as time and speed, mass and acceleration, etc. If this fact is not understood, one may end up multiplying beans by beans and getting square beans, clearly nonsense.

But if proper care is taken, multiplication adds great efficiency—because of an important property of uniform units: Once you know the size of one uniform unit, you know the size of each of them. In our example, once I counted how many square feet were in one strip, I knew how many square feet were in each strip.

In summary, multiplication makes use of the concept of the uniform unit with further ingenuity: It uses nested levels of uniform units—that is, numbers of numbers of units (analogous to abstractions from abstractions). In so doing, multiplication achieves further efficiency through unit-economy.

A.1.2 Exponents

We can apply the concept of uniform units in a related way to understand the concept of "exponents." One of the simplest uses of exponents is in a number system that uses a base, as in the decimal system (base 10). The number 1 refers to 1 unit, such as 1 bean. The number 10 refers to 1 group of 10 (uniform) units each. The number 100 refers to 1 group of 10 (uniform) groups of 10 units each. The number 1000 refers to 1 group of 10 (uniform) groups of 10 (uniform) groups of 10 units each. For the number designated by a 1 followed by 50 zeroes, we would have 50 nested iterations of groupings. One way to abbreviate this number is to use the notation of exponents: We write 10^{50} or "10 to the 50th power." The number "50" in this example is called an "exponent."

Thus, every one of the 50 iterations of multiplication by 10 is itself a uniform unit in the group of 50 such operations! Each such operation is interchangeable with each other one. Once you understand one of them, you understand all of them. Thus, by the use of exponents, which is the application of the uniform unit to repeated multiplication, even further unit-economy is achieved.

The relation of exponents to multiplication is analogous to the relation of multiplication to addition. As exponents count iterations or repetitions of uniform multiplications, multiplication can be thought of as counting iterations or repetitions of uniform additions.

Notice again the importance of knowing what kind of uniform units are being referred to by each number in a mathematical expression. In the expression $2 \times 3^5 \times 4$, each number counts a different kind of uniform unit.

A question that often arises is, what is the meaning of 10^0? If there are no 10s at all to multiply, what meaning could this expression have? The meaning is clear if we examine the nature of the uniform unit from another perspective.

What the expression 10^0 means is a unit not multiplied at all. That is why $10^0 = 1$, meaning 1 unit. In fact, n^0 is 1 for *any* value of n.

Let's take an example. Suppose I have a dollar in the bank, and the dollar multiplies in value 10-fold every generation (say, 25 years). How much money will I have in 3 generations? The answer is 10^3 dollars, because I multiply my dollar by 10 in the first generation, then multiply that amount by 10 in the second generation, and again a third time. How much money will I have in 5 generations? The answer is 10^5 dollars. How much money will I have in 0 generations? The answer is 10^0 dollars, because I am not multiplying my dollar at all. I just have my 1 dollar.

In other words, if we don't multiply by any 10s, the unit stays as it is. We *started* with the unit alone. Multiplication is multiplication of units. If we don't do any multiplications, or if we undo them, we are still (or again) at the starting point: the unit.

This approach can be extended to answer the following question: How much money did I have one generation ago? But first we must understand negative numbers, which will be covered in Section A.1.4. But there is another extension of this approach we can examine now to answer another question: How much money will I have in half a generation? To help us answer this question, let us consider another kind of example.

Suppose we draw an isosceles right triangle (Figure A.5)—that is, a right triangle with legs of equal length.

Figure A. 5: Isosceles right triangle.

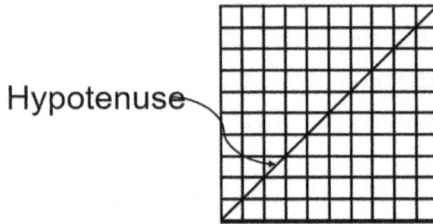

Now let us take the hypotenuse and draw another isosceles right triangle, this time using the first hypotenuse as one of the legs of the new triangle. (See Figure A.6.)

Figure A. 6: Hypotenuse of hypotenuse (hypotenuse squared).

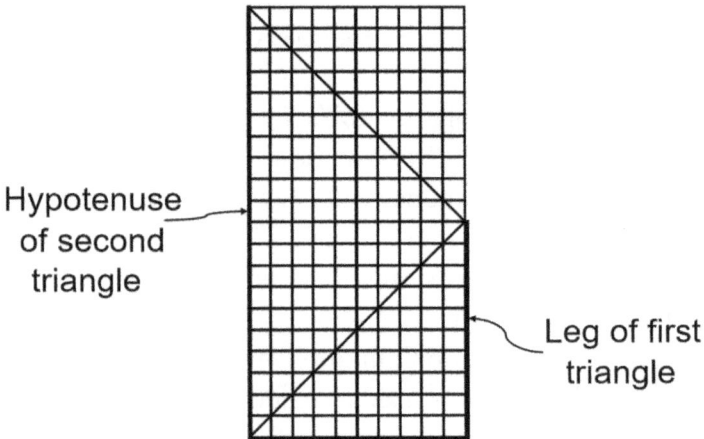

We can see from the figure, and from elementary geometry, that the hypotenuse of our second triangle is exactly twice the length of a leg of the first triangle.

Let us take a mathematical perspective on what we have done: Let us look for another kind of uniform unit. We started with a line whose length was one unit—let's say one meter. We then constructed an isosceles right triangle, using that line as one of the legs; we thus ended up with a line (the first hypotenuse) of unknown length (call that length x). Then we repeated the whole process, this time starting with our result from the first repetition of this process. Though we do not know the result (the value of x) after the first repetition, we do know the result after the second repetition: a line twice as long as the line we started with.

Thus, we have achieved a doubling of length in two uniform steps. The uniform units are the *steps*! Each step, or operation, increases the length by the same proportion: It converts each unit to x units; therefore, each operation is a multiplication by x. Each operation of multiplication by x takes us half-way to multiplication by 2. In other words, each operation is multiplication by 2 to the 1/2 power! We can write this as $x = 2^{1/2}$. Alternatively, we could say that two iterations of multiplication of a unit by x yields two units. In other words, $x^2 = 2$; therefore, x = "the square root of 2," written as "$\sqrt{2}$," the number which when "squared" (taken to the second power) equals 2.

Recall our earlier example of our money increasing ten-fold every generation. How much would it increase in half of a generation? The answer is that it would multiply by $10^{1/2}$, the square root of 10. How much would our money increase after only one year? The answer is that it would multiply by $10^{1/25}$, the number that would yield 10 if it multiplied a unit through 25 iterations.)

This line of thinking leads us, however, to an important new issue. "The square root of 2" is a mathematical expression, but it is not a number—because it does not yet bring the measurement of an attribute (in this case, the length of the hypotenuse) into full mental grasp. Suppose you needed to put a strip of gold plating along the hypotenuse of the triangle. You could not just order $\sqrt{2}$ meters of gold plating, unless either you or the merchant knew how to convert $\sqrt{2}$ into a *number*. Only then can you grasp whether, for instance, $\sqrt{2}$ is greater or less than 1, than 2, than 1.5, etc.

A.1.3 Irrational Numbers

What exactly is this number that when squared equals 2? We find that 1.5 squared is more than 2, and 1.4 squared is less than 2, so the number is between 1.4 and 1.5. We find also that the number is between 1.41 and 1.42, and between 1.414 and 1.415. That is, if we divide a leg of the triangle into 10 equal parts (tenths, as in Figure A.5), and we then use these tenths as a unit of measure to measure the length of the hypotenuse, we would discover that the length of the hypotenuse is a little more than 14 of these tenths, and a little less than 15 of these tenths. If we divide a leg into 100 equal parts (hundredths), then the length of the hypotenuse is a little more than 141 of these hundredths, and a little less than 142 of these hundredths. Using simple math, it can be proved that no matter how many tiny pieces we divide a leg into, if those pieces are uniform, no count of them will give us the exact length of the hypotenuse. Moreover, no fraction of *any* kind (thirds, tenths, thirteenths, etc.) is equal to $\sqrt{2}$. In other words, $\sqrt{2}$ is *irrational*.

The term "irrational" in this context does not mean unreasonable. It means not expressible as a ratio of two whole numbers—or, using the language of uniform units, not expressible as a fraction (a fraction being a count of uniform-sized pieces).

Now let us state this example more generally. Suppose we have two lines of different length. Suppose we take one of the lines—for instance, the shorter one—and divide it into uniform sections, that is, fractions. Then suppose we try to measure the length of the longer line as a count of the fractions of the shorter line. Usually, no whole count of the fractions will exactly equal the length of the longer line. But suppose the following fact is also true: No matter how many equal pieces we divide one line into, if we try to measure the second line as a count of uniform pieces of the first line, we will never get an exact whole count. To use the traditional mathematical term (which may not be the best term), these two lengths are "incommensurable"; and when one length is measured as a count of some other, incommensurable length, the measurement is an irrational number of units.

This possible fact of "incommensurability" seems to present a problem. The counting of uniform units is the fundamental method of mathematics—but here we have a case in which no number of uniform units can be used to count the length of both lines. But we must remember that the concept of number, like all concepts, is objective and not intrinsic. Numbers are not immutable objects inherent in reality, independent of consciousness and the requirements of cognition. There is nothing to say that numbers as initially conceived would apply unaltered to our new range of examples. Rather, we must amend our concept to deal with our new, wider context of knowledge.

Our amendment is as follows. The hypotenuse in our example is equal to 141 uniform hundredths *plus one extra little unit that is smaller than a hundredth*. If this measurement is not precise enough for our purpose, then we can get more precise: The hypotenuse is equal to 1,414 uniform thousandths plus one extra little unit that is smaller than a thousandth. If this measurement is still not precise enough, then we can get more precise still.

Thus we can write our irrational number like so (this is my notation):

$$1.414 \dashrightarrow \sqrt{2},$$

meaning that our irrational number is equal to 1 plus 414 thousandths plus one unit smaller than a thousandth that would make the number exactly equal to $\sqrt{2}$.

This irrational number is indeed a number, not merely an expression, because it brings our measurement within our perceptual grasp. We could now order just the amount of gold plating we need for our hypotenuse.

Note the objective bounds on that extra little unit in an irrational number. It cannot be of any size. It must be smaller than the uniform unit. And because of that fact, we know that our irrational number is a little bigger than the rational number we would have without the extra little unit, yet smaller than the rational number we would have if the little extra unit were as big as the uniform unit. Therefore, the uniform unit is still the guiding principle of measurement, but in a way dictated by reality.

Square roots (and cubed roots or nth roots) are only one kind of irrational number. Other kinds are beyond the scope of this book. But the principle is the same. Irrational numbers make use of a single unit which, being smaller than the uniform units, thereby assures that the degree of precision as measured by the uniform units is within one uniform unit.

A.1.4   Negative Numbers

What gives rise to the need for the concept of negative numbers? Let us take an example. A man drives east on a road for 5 miles, then turns around and drives west for 8 miles, then turns around and drives east for 6 miles. Where is he in relation to his starting point?

In this example, what are the units? We find that we have two different kinds of units: "miles traveled east" and "miles traveled west." But in mathematics, all units must be interchangeable (by being uniform), so we have a problem. Note, however, the special relation between these two kinds of units: They are opposites in the sense that they cancel out, or negate, each other. That is, any one of either kind of unit followed by any one of the other kind has the same result as if there were none of either kind. This fact regarding the units can be identified in mathematical terms as follows: (one mile east) + (one mile west) = 0.

"One mile west" is a negating or negative unit of "one mile east." But observe that negation has the same effect as subtraction. In fact, subtraction is a kind of negation. Thus, adding a negative unit is the same as subtracting a base unit, with one significant difference: We can add a negative unit even when there are no base or "positive" units (the kind of units we started with). For example, we can add three negating units to one base unit, and we end up with two negating units. If one were then to add two base units, they would negate, and be negated by, the negating units. Thus, negation is a more general process than subtraction; it is an extension of subtraction that applies when there are two kinds of mutually negating units.

As mentioned earlier, the commutative and associative laws of addition and multiplication are extremely important for the ability to manipulate numbers algebraically. Because of our uniform-unit condition that any one positive unit plus any one negative unit always equals zero, the order of adding positive and negative units is irrelevant; therefore, these laws for addition are valid for negative numbers as well as positive ones. (We will discuss the laws for multiplication below.)

Let us define a symbol for the negating or negative unit: $\wedge$. Thus, $3\wedge$ means three negative units. Observe that, because each of the 3 negative units can negate a positive unit, our total of 3 negative units would negate a total of 3 positive units. Therefore, we could equivalently write $\wedge 3$, meaning the negative of 3 positive units. (For those versed in mathematics, we have just shown that taking the negative is distributive over addition, which is another very important property for being able to manipulate negative numbers algebraically.)

Suppose we start with $\wedge 3$ units, and then add 4 units to it. We then have 4 units + $\wedge 3$ units. Because there are units to be negated by the negating units, we have 4 units − 3 units, or 1 unit.

Now we can make one simple change in notation. We can replace the symbols "$+\wedge$" with "$-$" because adding a negative unit means the same thing as subtracting a positive one, when there are positive units to subtract; and when we have a term like $\wedge 3$ by itself, there would be no ambiguity in writing it as "-3" as long as we understand it means three negative units, or the negative of 3 positive units.

Thus we see that "-3 units" does not mean some quantity less than nothing, which would be an absurdity. It means three actual units that are negatives of the base or positive unit; that is, they would negate and be negated by the addition of 3 positive units. Thus "-3 units," while not less than nothing, is more negative than nothing.

In our example, we can define "one mile west" to be the "negative of" (that which would negate or cancel out) "one mile east." Then, everywhere that we have "one mile west," we can substitute "$-$(one mile east)." We have thus reestablished the mathematical condition that all units are uniform.

Thus the solution to our initial problem is: 5 east miles – 8 east miles is –3 east miles (because five of the eight negating units are used to negate the 5 east miles, leaving three negating units); then add 6 east miles, making 3 east miles.

Note that this approach works for units such as money as well, where there is no attribute of direction. In the context of figuring net worth, a dollar owed is the negative of a dollar owned.

As a further application, we are now able to answer the question we posed in the first part of this article: What does a negative exponent mean? For example, what does the -1 in 10^{-1} mean? It means a negative unit in relation to a positive unit in the exponent. A positive unit in the exponent is an iteration of multiplication by the base number (in this case, 10). A negative unit is an operation that would negate, or cancel out, such an iteration of multiplication. Therefore, a negative unit in the exponent is division by 10. Therefore, 10^{-1} means a unit divided by 10; that is, one tenth (1/10); and 10^{-2} means 1/100; and so on.

We can also think of the minus or negative symbol as an operator (as the multiplication symbol too can be thought of as an operator); the operation it performs is to replace positive units with negative units. Thus, in our initial example, the negative operator replaces a mile west with a mile east: (one mile west) ==> –(one mile east). Such replacements are often very useful in algebra. But here is a very important point: Because a positive unit plus a negative unit always equals zero, the relation between positive and negative is reciprocal! (Note that, in our example, we could have defined "one mile west" to be the positive unit.) This means that, just as the negative of a positive is a negative, the negative of a negative is a positive.

Now we are ready to consider multiplication with negative units.

What does "2 x (–3)" mean? It means 2 groups of 3 negative units each, and it is equal to –6, that is, 6 negative units.

What does "−2 x 3" mean? It means 2 negative groups of 3 units each. What is a negative group? It is a group that would negate a positive group. What kind of group would negate a group of 3 units? A group of 3 negative units. Therefore, "−2 x 3" equals "2 x (−3)", or −6 units.

What does "−2 x (−3)" mean? It means 2 negative groups of 3 negative units each. What kind of group would negate a group of 3 negative units? A group of 3 positive units. Therefore, "−2 x (−3)" equals "2 x 3", or 6 units.

Let us now take an example of multiplication with negative units. Suppose you think Acme company's stock, which is now selling for $25 per share, will be $30 by next year. If you buy 5,000 shares now, what will be your expected profit next year?

To get our answer, we use the following formula:
Number of dollars in Profit = (Number of shares you buy) x (next year's price − current price).
Therefore: Profit = 5,000 shares x ($30 − $25) per share. In other words, we have 5,000 groups of $5 each, and our total expected profit is $25,000.

But what if you are wrong in your expectation, and the price next year goes down to $12 per share? What would the result be? By our formula, we would have: Profit = 5,000 x ($12 − $25). The value in parentheses is −$13. Is there truly a unit that is negative to profit in this example? Yes. The negative unit is loss! Loss negates and is negated by profit. Therefore, in this case, we have: Profit = 5,000 x (−$13) = −$65,000, the negative of a $65,000 profit—a $65,000 loss.

Maybe instead you should sell short. That is, you accept someone's money today in payment—at today's prices—for shares that you agree to deliver next year; but you don't actually buy the shares until next year, at next year's lower price. To figure profit in this case, can we use the same formula we have been using? We can if a share sold short is simply the negative of a share bought. And this is the case. For every dollar that the price of the stock rises, you would have a profit of one dollar for every share bought and a loss of one dollar for every share sold short. Conversely, for every dollar that the price drops, you lose a dollar for every share bought and gain a dollar for every share sold short. Thus, a share sold short negates and is negated by a share bought. Identifying a "share sold short" as the negative of a "share bought" restores the condition of uniform units. (In order for this condition to hold, we must ignore any additional transaction costs or other expenses.)

Let's say you short 1,000 shares now, and then buy 1,000 shares back next year. Then we have: Profit = $-1,000 \times (-\$13) = \$13,000$ in profit (a positive number).

A.1.5 Complex Numbers

Complex numbers arose when certain mathematical equations called for taking the square root of a negative number. This operation can be performed only if there is a very specific kind of relation among the kinds of units being considered.

Complex numbers are complex in that they have two components, one that is an ordinary number and another that is called an "imaginary number" (an unfortunate term), designated by the symbol i. The "imaginary number" i is an operator that must be applied to a unit not once but twice in order to yield a unit that is the negative of the original unit—that is, $i^2 1$ units $= -1$ units. When the operator is applied to a unit only once, the operation yields a unit that is not reducible to the original unit or its negative. Thus the operator i applies in cases in which there are kinds of units that bear such kinds of relations. One such case is units of length in a two-dimensional plane, where the operator i is analogous to a right-angle rotation. For example, if the base unit is a mile east, then i operated on that unit is a mile north; i operated on a mile north (which is like operating twice on a mile east) is a mile west, which negates a mile east; i operated on a mile west is a mile south, which negates a mile north; and i operated on a mile south is a mile east again. Each of these four types of units is negated by the type of unit produced with two successive operations of i.

Just as the negative operator allows us to express two kinds of units—positive and negative—in terms of one kind of unit, the i operator lets us express four kinds of units in terms of one kind of unit. For example, if 1 mile east is our base unit, then 3 miles north can be expressed as i3 miles east. Just as with the negative operator, the i operator achieves the result of restoring the condition of the uniform unit.

Note also the similarity to our explanation of the square root of 2. Just as we broke multiplication by 2 into two uniform steps, we have now broken multiplication by -1 into two uniform steps. Each uniform step is multiplication by i. Hence, $i^2 1 = -1$.

Some inconsistent and confusing conventions of notation should be explained. With the negative operator, the negative symbol precedes the number symbol, as in "-3"; with the i operator, however, the i symbol follows the number symbol, as in "$3i$." More confusing, whereas a negative unit is written as "-1," an "imaginary" unit is written as "i," with the "1" omitted, instead of as "$i1$." Don't let these inconsistencies in notation confuse you. The i operator works the same way, is just as valid, and designates relations just as real, as does the "$-$" operator. The fact that $i^2 1 = -1$ is just as real as the fact that $(-1)^2 = 1$. If you get an "imaginary" number as part of the solution to a problem, it tells you that if there are, in reality, kinds of units and kinds of operations that satisfy the conditions above, then you have a valid solution. If there are such units and operations, then the number is not imaginary at all.

Many oscillating or rotating systems bear this kind of relation between units. For example, in an oscillating spring or pendulum, velocity and distance, from equilibrium, bear this relation (with multiplication by the operator i corresponding to the passage of a uniform interval of time). So do current and voltage in an alternating-current circuit. So do force and momentum in a revolving body. So do lateral distance and vertical distance in a revolving body. In general, these two kinds of units are mutual actualities and potentialities of each other. In a pendulum, velocity is potential distance, and vice versa;

voltage is potential current, and vice versa; and so on. In fact, what makes such systems continue a set pattern of action is that a certain type of summation of actuality and potentiality maintains a constant total quantity. This constant quantitative relationship is expressible with complex numbers.

Consider an example of complex-number solutions. Suppose we have a compass-like dial whose needle is spinning counter-clockwise at a constant speed. (See Figure A.7.) Suppose the needle is pointing east at noon, and is pointing west at 3 seconds past noon. In which direction was the needle pointing at 1 second past noon?

Figure A. 7: A dial spinning counter-clockwise.

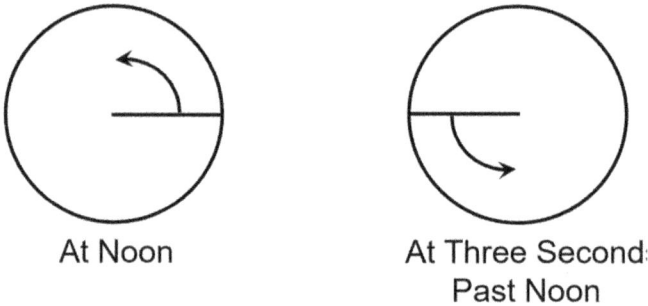

At Noon   At Three Second
                                 Past Noon

At noon, we could say the tip of the needle was positioned at 1 unit east. At 3 seconds past noon, it was positioned at 1 unit west, which is −1 unit east. Each second, the needle undergoes a rotation r. (A rotation is a kind of operation, and r is a measurement of uniform units of this operation.) After 3 seconds, the needle has undergone 3 uniform rotations r. We thus have the equation: $r^3 1$ unit = −1 unit. We must find out what one rotation r is. We must solve: $r^3 = -1$.

The methods of algebra tell us that such an equation, a "cubic," has three solutions. Using known formulas of algebra, we can identify the three solutions of this equation as follows:

$r = -1$
$r = \frac{1}{2} + \frac{1}{2}\sqrt{3}\, i$
$r = \frac{1}{2} - \frac{1}{2}\sqrt{3}\, i$

Each of the numbers on the right side of these equations, when raised to the third power, is equal to -1. Is the first solution the only "real" solution? Certainly not.

The first solution (see Figure A.8) tells us that after 1 second, the tip of the needle was at $(-1)(1)$ units east, that is, -1 unit east, that is, 1 unit west. Let's check to see whether that is a valid solution. According to this solution, the needle would be back at 1 unit east after the second second, and back at 1 unit west, that is, -1 unit, after the third second. Therefore, this solution is valid, and the needle may have been pointing due west after the first second.

The second solution says that after one second, the needle was at ½ unit east and $\frac{1}{2}\sqrt{3}\ i$ units north. This is equivalent to a 60-degree rotation. Thus, after 3 seconds, the needle would have rotated 180 degrees, and would be pointing due west. Therefore, this solution is just as valid as the first one!

Figure A. 8: The three solutions.

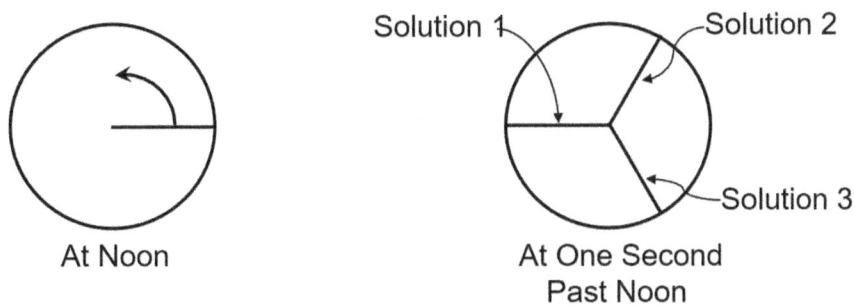

At Noon

Solution 1   Solution 2

Solution 3

At One Second
Past Noon

The third solution says that after one second, the needle was at ½ unit east and $\frac{1}{2}\sqrt{3}\ i$ units south. This is equivalent to a 300-degree rotation. Thus, after 3 seconds, the needle would have rotated 900 degrees, and would be pointing due west. Thus, this solution is just as valid as the first two.

Therefore, all three solutions are equally valid possibilities. (We would need more information to determine which one of them is the solution to our original problem.)

Another remarkable fact is the following: Even when there do not seem to be kinds of units that fit the relations required by complex or imaginary numbers, these numbers can be very useful in calculations. Sometimes, mathematicians and scientists use these numbers in intermediate calculations, but the imaginary numbers do not turn out to be part of the final solution. In many circumstances, this technique is perfectly valid! How can this be?

One way to understand how this can be is to recall the law of transitivity, which tells us that what is true of one kind of uniform units will be true for all kinds. If we arrive at a valid solution regarding our pebbles that we count, that solution will also apply to the sheep that our pebbles stand for. Likewise, for example, if we arrive at a valid solution for units of length along the east-west directions, that solution will also be valid for units of weight—*so long as the proper correspondence is made between units of length and units of weight.*

"Imaginary" units are not imagined; they are chosen or constructed selectively based on an objective purpose. The great 19th-century mathematician Gauss suggested that, instead of "imaginary," we use the term "lateral," drawing on the application to direction. Thus, instead of the symbol i, a better symbol would be L for "lateral" because its shape reminds us what the operator does. Another possible term is "potential." Operating by i converts a positive to a potential negative. Operating again converts the potential negative to a negative; the next operation converts the negative to a potential positive; the next operation gives us a positive again.

Once again, the principle of the uniform unit explains not only why and how mathematical techniques like complex numbers are valid, but also the conditions required for their valid application.

A.1.6 Calculus

In this section, I present the philosophic foundation of calculus using an example from differential calculus; the same philosophical ideas apply to integral calculus as well. I assume the reader already has a thorough knowledge of the concepts of limit, continuity, and derivative as they are usually taught.

Before presenting my example, I must address some philosophical controversies regarding ideas that would be implicit in any example.

The first controversial issue regards approximation, precision, exactness, and perfection. For example, is there such a thing as a perfect cube? Or are there only approximate cubes, or cubes that are cubes when considered in the context of a certain degree of precision?

The answer to these questions, in my judgment, requires adherence to Ayn Rand's principle of the primacy of existence over consciousness. Existence exists independent of consciousness. In the context of our questions above, the primacy of existence tells us not to confuse existence with our means of measuring existence. In this context, existence has primacy over measurement.

We do not know whether physical extension is continuous or discrete. We do not know whether, at some tiny size, physical extension is "granular." If physical extension is not granular, and if the physical world is a plenum (that is, if it has no spatial gaps), then perfect cubes certainly do exist; indeed, they exist all over the place. (They may exist even if physical extension *is* granular.) We may not be able to know, by our current means of measurement, whether some object we are observing is a perfect cube or not, but it either is or is not. The same is true of spheres, pyramids, squares, circles, etc.

Here is a simple analogy. Before Michelangelo sculpted his David, the part of the marble slab that ultimately would be the David existed. But no one, not even Michelangelo, could have measured that part exactly. In the same way, perfect shapes exist even though we may not be able to measure them exactly. What exists exists, whether or not we are conscious of it.

Is the length of an object exact, or is it an approximation to a certain degree of precision? Of course, it is the former. The Law of Identity states that A is A. That means that A is exactly A, not that A is A within some degree of precision. The length of a ruler is exactly what it is. If that ruler is the standard for a meter, then that ruler is one meter long, exactly. Twice the length of that ruler is two meters, exactly.

The concept of length, like all concepts, is open-ended. It is likely that, as measurements become more precise, the concept of length itself will be refined and might itself include (depending on the context in which the concept is used) more than one characteristic and consequently more than one measurement. For example, because the edges of many objects are jagged, length might include the minimum and maximum lengths, and/or some kind of average, and/or some kind of range, etc. But however the concept of length is refined, an object's length is its length.

Now, if we measure the length of another object with that ruler, we are not able—given current knowledge and technology—to identify the exact length of that other object. But the length of that object is exactly what *it* is. Whether or not we are conscious of the exact length, the exact length exists. A is A. (Moreover, there is no philosophical reason to believe that length will never be exactly measurable. Certain attributes today are exactly measurable. For example, one can measure exactly how many apples are in a barrel.)

The next controversial issue involves lengths, or intervals or lines, vs. points; and durations of time vs. points in time.

Consider an object such as a ruler. Suppose the ruler is our standard for one meter of length. Now consider the left end of the ruler. That end is a point. Let us assign that point the value of zero. Now consider the right end of the ruler. That end is another point. We can assign the value of that point the value of 1 meter.

Now, what is the length of each of these two points? Are the points of zero length? No, the attribute of length does not apply to points, any more than the attribute of weight applies to points. A point is a point, not an interval.

Is a point on a line a line of zero length? No. A point on a line is a point, not a line. A point is not an interval. The attribute of length does not apply to a point. A point is an *attribute* of an interval, but it is not a *part* of an interval; it does not *constitute* an interval. An interval *has* points (as its ends), but it does not *consist* of points.

The concept "point" subsumes two kinds of units: beginnings and ends. An end of an object is not *at* a point; the end *is* a point. Likewise, a point is not *at* a beginning or end; a point *is* a beginning or end. In our example, the points of the ruler are the left and right ends. If the point at the left is exactly location zero, then the point at the right is exactly location 1.

The same ideas hold for *ranges* of length. For example, suppose my measuring tells me that a stick is one meter long, give or take one millimeter. Then the length of the stick falls within a range whose length is exactly two millimeters, and the endpoints of that range are exactly the locations .999 meters and 1.001 meters.

The analogous facts apply to time as well as to length. Consider a duration of time. That duration is exactly what it is. Let us call that duration a "second," for example. Then we can call the beginning of that second "time zero," and the end of that second "time 1." Times 0 and 1 are then points in time. They are not durations; they are points. They are *attributes* of a duration, but they are not *parts* of a duration; they do not *constitute* a duration.

Is a point in time an instant? It depends what is meant by "instant." Sometimes the word "instant" is intended to have the same meaning as "point in time." But sometimes "instant" is intended to mean a very short duration. By this second usage, an instant of time is not a point in time. A duration is not a point, and a point is not a duration.

Is a point in time an instant of zero duration? No, a point in time is not a duration. It is the beginning or end of a duration. For example, noon today is a point in time; it is, for example, the end of the hour that began at 11:00 a.m., and the beginning of the hour that began at noon.

Note that every interval of time has a beginning and end, and every beginning or end has to be a beginning or end of some duration. Therefore, a point in time cannot exist without a duration of which the point is an attribute; and a duration cannot exist without the attributes of a beginning and end, which are points.

Now we are ready to "begin" with an example. Suppose we apply a gradually increasing force to an object initially at rest and notice that the distance d that the object travels obeys the equation $d = 5t^3$ meters East, where t is the number of seconds since the object was at rest. Let us assume that the object obeys this equation exactly. For example, at the end of exactly 4 seconds (that is, at the point $t = 4$), the distance traveled by the object is exactly 320 meters East. Now suppose that, after 4 seconds, the gradually increasing force ends, and no additional net forces act on the object. (In other words, after the initial 4 seconds, the total net forces—including frictional forces—acting on the object remain at zero.) Therefore, after the initial 4 seconds, the object travels thereafter at a constant velocity. What is that constant velocity?

We can use calculus to arrive at the answer. The velocity is the derivative of the distance d with respect to time t. Therefore, $v = 15t^2$ meters per second for $t = 0$ through 4 seconds, and constant thereafter. We plug in the value 4 seconds for t, and we get $v = 240$ meters per second for $t = 4$ seconds and thereafter. Therefore, the answer to our question is: The constant velocity of the object after the initial 4 seconds is 240 meters per second East.

Let us now alter our example slightly. Suppose the gradually increasing force does not end after 4 seconds. Suppose instead that it continues to increase gradually so that the distance d that the object travels continues to obey the equation $d = 5t^3$ meters. What then is the velocity of the object at the end of exactly four seconds?

The answer is the same: 240 meters per second East. We arrive at the answer the same way: we take the derivative of the equation $d = 5t^3$ meters, and we plug in the value $t = 4$ seconds.

Notice that our alteration to the example did not alter anything about what occurred in the first four seconds; what was altered was only what occurred *later than* the first four seconds. Therefore, the behavior of the object over the first four seconds was identical in each case, and the state of the object at the end of four seconds was identical in each case. (In each case, the state of the object was that its velocity was 240 meters per second.) Nothing about the forces acting on the object *beyond* the first 4 seconds could affect the state of the object at the *end* of the first four seconds. The future cannot affect the past or the present.

Let us now elaborate on what we mean by the concepts "time" and "velocity."

In standard usage, time can mean either a duration of time or a "point" in time. For example, "5 seconds" can mean a duration of five seconds; but "Time $t = 5$ seconds" means the point in time that is the end of a duration of five seconds, and "the time 5 o'clock" means a point in time. "Five hours" means a duration of time; but "the time five hours past noon" means the point in time that is the end of the five-hour duration that began at noon

Time, in the sense of a duration of time, is a certain kind of measure of motion. It is a count of completed uniform, standard motions. For example, 5 days is a count (5) of completed rotations of the earth; 20 seconds is a count of ticks moved by a second hand of a standard clock.

It follows that time, in the sense of a "point" in time, is the point in time that is the end of some count of uniform standard motions. Thus, 9 o'clock a.m. is the point in time at the end of 9 hours from the beginning of the day.

In contrast to time, velocity is another kind of measure of motion. It is a measure of a *state* of motion, or a *potential* for motion, as opposed to being a count of uniform complete motions. But we do not have a direct way to measure a state of motion or potential for motion; therefore, we measure a state of motion or potential for motion indirectly, by directly measuring a *ratio* of counts of complete motions. For example, suppose we want to measure the state of motion of a moving train. We observe the moving train while we observe a ticking clock. While the clock engages in one complete motion of ticking a minute, the train engages in two complete motions of traveling a mile. That is, the ratio of counts of completed motions is two miles traveled by the train compared to one minute ticked by the clock.

Then we make a big assumption. We assume that the train's state of motion, like the clock's, is constant. By making this assumption, we can make an inference from what we are measuring directly (the ratio of completed motions) to what we want to measure indirectly (the train's current state of motion). Based on the assumption that the train's motion is constant, we infer that the train's current state of motion is such that, if its motion remains constant, then it will travel 2 miles every minute.

When we say that the velocity of an object is 240 meters per second East, we mean that the current state of the object is such that, in the absence of any change in the object's state of motion in the future (or, equivalently, in the absence of any net forces acting on the object in the future), the object will travel 240 meters per second East.

We are now ready to define "velocity." Velocity is a measure of an entity's state of motion, or potential for motion, such measure being expressed indirectly as a ratio—directional distance traveled per unit time elapsed—under the assumption that the entity's state of motion or potential for motion will remain constant (or under the equivalent assumption that constantly zero net forces will act on the object in the future).

Now, what if an object's state of motion or potential for motion is *not* constant? Then, what we measure directly—directional distance traveled per unit time elapsed—will yield only an *approximation* to actual velocity. We measure the distance traveled by the object over an interval of time (or, equivalently, at two points in time), and we divide the distance by the interval of time to yield an *average* velocity. In general, the shorter the interval of time, the closer the average velocity will be as an approximation of the actual velocity at either the beginning or end of the interval of time.

Now we come to the genius of calculus. *Without* calculus, we measure average velocity over a *short interval of time* in order to infer an *approximate* actual velocity at a point in time. But *with* calculus, we measure average velocity over a *sequence of progressively shorter intervals of time* in order to infer the *exact* actual velocity at a point in time. We do this by observing a *pattern* in the sequence of approximations; this pattern enables us to identify the error inherent in using average velocity to approximate actual velocity; then we discount that error and arrive at the exact actual velocity.

To elaborate, let us return to our example equation: $d = 5t^3$. To avoid notational confusions, let us use the variable letter y instead of d. Thus we have $y = 5t^3$. Let us follow the usual, correct steps of the standard "epsilon-delta" technique. We have

$$\Delta y/\Delta t = [(y + \Delta y) - y]/ [(t + \Delta t) - t]$$
$$= [5(t + \Delta t)^3 - 5t^3]/\Delta t$$
$$= [5t^3 + 15t^2\Delta t + 15t(\Delta t)^2 + 5(\Delta t)^3 - 5t^3]/\Delta t$$
$$= [15t^2\Delta t + 15t(\Delta t)^2 + 5(\Delta t)^3]/\Delta t$$
$$= [15t^2 + 15t(\Delta t) + 5(\Delta t)^2]$$

From this result, we see that as Δt gets smaller and smaller (that is, as the interval $t + \Delta t$ is progressively shortened), $\Delta y/\Delta t$ gets closer and closer to $15t^2$. Indeed, from the theory of limits (which is essentially correct), we know that the limit of this expression as Δt approaches zero is $15t^2$. (The correct theory of limits does not, of course, assume that Δt becomes infinitely small or infinitesimal.) That is,

$$\Delta y/\Delta t \to dy/dt = 15t^2.$$

Thus the exact expression for the derivative is $15t^2$. But is $15t^2$ also the exact expression for the actual velocity? Or is that expression only an approximation, because Δt never actually reaches zero in the calculation of the limit?

My answer is as follows. If the distance y exactly obeys the equation $y = 5t^3$ meters, then dy/dt is the *exact* actual velocity, and the actual velocity *exactly* obeys the equation $v = dy/dt = 15t^2$. The term $15t(\Delta t) + 5(\Delta t)^2$ is an error term that is due to the fact that $\Delta y/\Delta t$ is a measure of *average* velocity, not *actual* velocity.

To prove my answer, that actual velocity is exactly $15t^2$, we need to make explicit one additional premise: Actual velocity can change only through the application of force over a duration of time. From this premise, it can be proved that actual velocity as a function of time is a continuous function; and from the continuity of actual velocity, it can be proved that the actual velocity at time t is equal to the limit of the average velocity over the interval of t to $t + \Delta t$ as Δt approaches zero. That limit of course is $15t^2$.

Because $15t(\Delta t) + 5(\Delta t)^2$ is the error term, a good alternative name for "limit" in this case and similar cases is "perfection." That is, $15t^2$ is the perfection of the expression $15t^2 + 15t(\Delta t) + 5(\Delta t)^2$, because it is that expression with the error term removed.

Note that when $\Delta t = 0$, we are unable to take a direct measurement of average velocity; if we try to take such a measurement, we get the answer 0/0. But by observing the general behavior of average velocity as Δt approaches zero, and by knowing that velocity is a continuous function, we are able to infer the actual (and the average) velocity when $\Delta t = 0$ *without* having to take a direct measurement.

Here is a rough analogy. Suppose we want to measure the weight of a cubic meter of water. We have a scale on which to place the water, but the water won't stay on the scale unless it is in a container. Therefore, we must put both a container and the water on the scale together. We will never be able to measure directly the weight of the water. But we know what the error will be when we weigh the container and the water; the error will be the weight of the container. Therefore, we subtract the weight of the container to infer the weight of the water without having to take a direct measurement of the water alone.

In conclusion, calculus is an exact method for measuring a real attribute. In our example, the answer 240 meters per second is as exact as the initial equation. In other words, if the distance y exactly obeys the equation $y = 5t^3$ meters, then at the end of exactly 4 seconds, the velocity is exactly 240 meters per second. If there is some error or imprecision in the initial equation, then there is no additional error due to calculus. Calculus itself incurs no loss of precision or exactness. Moreover, in our example, calculus gave us a measurement not merely of some mental construct (an esoteric "limit") but of a real attribute (velocity).

To arrive at our conclusions, we relied on the philosophical principle of the primacy of existence. We recognized the difference between what exists (in our example, velocity), and our consciousness of what exists (in our example, our measurement of average velocity). We also relied on the fact that A is A, meaning that A is *exactly* A, regardless of the imprecision of our *measurement* of A.

Observe, in the above example, the role of the uniform unit. Calculus is needed to measure motion that is not constant, not uniform. Velocity can be described mathematically only in terms of uniform units: a certain number of uniform units of distance traveled per uniform unit of time elapsed. Calculus solves the problem by considering progressively shorter intervals of time so that the assumption of uniform velocity becomes a progressively more precise approximation.

The uniform unit is a basis also for integral calculus (which we will not consider here in any detail). In Riemann integration, the x interval is divided into very small pieces so that the y value within each piece can be assumed to be uniform. In Lebesque integration, the y interval is divided into very small pieces so that the x value within each piece can be assumed to be uniform.

A.2 Concretizing Measurements

The key to applying mathematics to a particular science is finding the correct uniform units to count. In geometry, the uniform units include units of length (such as meters) and units of angles or direction (such as degrees). In mechanics, units include units of mass, speed, and time. In business, units include units of money and time.

Mathematics, as a science that applies across many sciences, is by its nature very abstract. Although numbers allow us to conceptualize relationships among measurements, such relationships can still be very abstract. Fortunately, just as philosophical abstractions can be concretized—that is, brought to the level of perceptual awareness—by art (see Ayn Rand 1975), so mathematical relations can be concretized by the technique of charts and graphs—thanks to the principle of uniform units.

Charts and graphs are not merely representational drawings. They are drawings that employ the logical method of analogy. They make it possible to express, in visual terms, measurements that may not themselves be visible.

Suppose we have gathered numerical data on the per capita Gross National Product for three countries—the United States, Sweden, and Communist China—for the year 1995. (World Bank 2020.) We may write down the dollar amounts for each country: United States, $26,980; Sweden, $18,540; Communist China, $2,920.

One way to help us see the relative magnitude of each of these income levels with the immediacy of concretes is by the use of a chart.

Because mathematics deals with units *qua* units (so long as they are uniform), the mathematical relations that we perceive by observing quantities of one kind of unit will also exist for the same proportions of any kind of unit. (We can validate this fact by recalling the law of transitivity, a law we proved in Section 7.1.) The technique of charting says the following: Instead of merely looking at the kind of units of your particular example, look at another kind of unit, an analogous kind of unit, that is simple to observe and that encourages new integrations. Whatever you observe about these analogous units will also apply to the units in your example. An excellent choice for these analogous units is units of length on a page—as exhibited in a chart.

Figure A. 9: A Bar Chart.

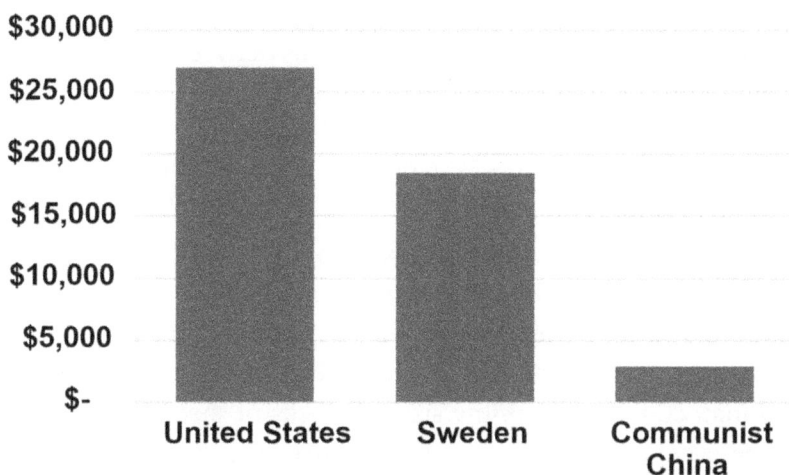

Figure A.9 shows one kind of chart—a bar chart—of the data we have mentioned. The proportional heights of the bars are analogous to the proportional amounts of the per capita GNPs. The proportions can be understood at a gross level by looking at the bars because we directly perceive the proportions. For example, by looking at our chart, we see instantly that the average American produced significantly more than the average Swede while both made much more than the average Chinese.

Units of length, as in a bar chart, are often a very good choice for a substitute, analogous unit. One main reason is that these units are easily put on paper. The other main reason is that our perceptual mechanism is very good at discerning small differences in length, and in observing proportions of length. For example, we can easily see a 5% difference in the height of two lines that are alongside each other. In contrast, it is not so easy to sense a 5% difference in such attributes as weight, color, or brightness. Moreover, it is easy to see that one line is about twice as long or three times as long as another. Such discrimination is very difficult for most other sense modalities.

Notice again the power of the principle of the uniform unit. When we write on our chart that one inch = $20,000, we have specified in one statement the relation between every inch and every other inch, between every dollar and every other dollar, and between every inch and every dollar. Consequently, the relations between measurements of length will be exactly analogous to relations between measurements of money. In contrast, if inches were equal to random amounts of money—some to $20,000, some to $35,000, etc., the chart would be meaningless.

Units of area, as in a pie chart, are another common choice of a substitute unit—again because of man's ability to see and compare relative spatial sizes. Before there was writing on paper, men relied on other substitute units with easily distinguishable size. For example, a man could compare the sizes of flocks of sheep by seeing the different sizes of groups of pebbles (where each pebble stood for one sheep and each group for a flock).

A graph (a plotted line connecting coordinates in two or three dimensions), like a chart, employs units of length on a page as a judicious, revealing choice of analogous units. Whereas charts are useful for revealing relations of size, graphs are most useful for revealing relative rates of change, because of another distinctive fact about the perception of spatial extent. Extent is dimensional, meaning that any location on a page can be reduced uniquely to two separate measurements of distance, and these separate measurements are directly perceivable simultaneously. Moreover, the relation between any two perceivable locations is also directly perceivable—as direction. This richness of visual information makes it possible for something as complex as a relative rate of change of two quantities (such as time and money) to be depicted visually—as the direction of a plotted line or curve on a graph. For example, if the quantity on the vertical axis (dollars) begins to increase more quickly compared to the quantity on the horizontal axis (years), the plotted line will become more vertical.

Note, however, how a graph's ability to convey information visually relies entirely on the uniformity of the units of length on the graph. For instance, on the horizontal axis, the distance between each year marker might be one centimeter; on the vertical axis, the distance between each incremental thousand-dollar marker might be two centimeters. What if these respective uniform distances were random? Then the directions of plotted lines would be meaningless, as would the relative heights of each plotted point.

There is a kind of graph in which the units of length on the graph are not uniform. For example, Wall Street stock analysts usually plot stock prices on a "semilog" scale. While the units of length on the x axis (representing time) are uniform, the units of length on the y axis (representing price) are not: they get shorter as they get higher. How can this be explained? Remember, when trying to understand a new mathematical technique, look for the uniform unit.

In this case, the uniform unit is the *exponent*, or *logarithm*, of the price. Consequently, every unit-of-length (such as centimeter) change on the vertical axis represents a standard *percentage change* in the price of the stock. For example, one centimeter = a doubling of price. Therefore, a change in price from $2 to $4 will look equally significant as a change from $20 to $40. This is just the kind of view the stock analyst wants, because both of these changes represent a doubling of the investment.

Uniform units of space, as in charts and graphs, are not the only examples of substitute units. In general, any kind of uniform unit may be substituted for any other, and the relations among the quantities will still hold. Thus, whereas altitude, speed, and level of fuel may be shown by gauges on a pilot's dashboard, the temperature of each part of the aircraft might be represented by a map of various colors or degrees of brightness; pressure may be represented by the pitch of a whistle, etc. These are all examples of analog measurements or representations, based on the principle of analogy.

Although there are many techniques of substituting one unit for another, there are none so popular as charts and graphs—because of the richness of our ability to perceive spatial extent.

A.3 THE UNIFORM UNIT REITERATED

Consider this mathematical expression:

$$-2 + 5[(\sqrt{3} + 1)/7 + 4(-6)(-7)i/12]^3$$

We know what this expression means, not because we know a list of rules for adding, subtracting, multiplying, and dividing "natural" numbers, exponents, negative numbers, fractions, complex numbers, etc.—rules that, according to the almost universal consensus among mathematicians, are "true" only because we define them to be so. We know what it means because one principle, the uniform unit, explains all the meanings and generates all the rules. Each number in the above expression counts some kind of uniform unit. A number by itself counts uniform "base" units. A number that multiplies is a number that counts uniform groups that it is multiplying. An exponent counts iterations of uniform multiplications. The denominator of a fraction counts the uniform pieces that constitute a whole unit; the numerator of a fraction counts how many of those uniform pieces we are considering. A negative sign designates negative units. An *i* sign designates "potential negative" or "lateral" units. And so on. All the rules for adding, multiplying, etc., follow logically from, and are determined by, the relations among each kind of unit. (My high school math teacher, Herbert Grossman, used to emphasize the importance of knowing the units being considered.)

Comprehending the principle of the uniform unit is the key to understanding every method of mathematics. Finding a uniform unit is the key to applying mathematics to a specific science. Finding a new kind of uniform unit, or a new way of dealing with uniform units, is the key to devising a new mathematical method.

To understand mathematics, remember this one principle: *the uniform unit.*

REFERENCES

Aristotle (1941), *Metaphysics*. Translation by W. D. Ross. In *Basic Works of Aristotle*. Edited by Richard McKeon. New York: Random House.

——— (1941b), *On Interpretation*. Translated by E. M. Edgehill. In *Basic Works of Aristotle*. Edited by Richard McKeon. New York: Random House.

——— (1984), *Physics*. Translated by R. P. Hardie and R. K. Gaye. In *The Complete Works of Aristotle*. Edited by Jonathan Barnes. Princeton: Princeton University Press.

Bacon, Francis ([1620] 2014), *The New Organon*. Translated by James Spedding, Robert Leslie Ellis, and Douglas Denon Heath. Originally published in *The Works* (Vol. VIII) in Boston by Taggard and Thompson in 1863. Adelaide: The University of Adelaide Library. Accessed on November 13, 2019 at <https://ebooks.adelaide.edu.au/b/bacon/francis/organon/complete.html>.

Barnes, Harry Elmer ([1937] 1965), *An Intellectual and Cultural History of the Western World*. Third revised edition. New York: Dover.

Binswanger, Harry (2014), *How We Know: Epistemology on an Objectivist Foundation*. New York: TOF Publications.

——— (2020), "Objectivist Workshop Participants Identified", *The Harry Binswanger Letter* January 20, 2020. TOF Publications.

Accessed on February 17, 2020 at <https://www.hbletter.com/objectivist-workshop-participants-identified/>.

Blumenau, Ralph (2001), "Kant and the Thing in Itself", *Philosophy Now*. Accessed on December 31, 2019 at <https://philosophynow.org/issues/31/Kant_and_the_Thing_in_Itself>.

Clawson, Calvin C. (1994), *The Mathematical Traveler*. New York: Plenum Press.

Coolen, Frank P. A. (1998), "Low Structure Imprecise Predictive Inference For Bayes' Problem", *Statistics & Probability Letters* 36: 349–357.

——— (2011), "Nonparametric Predictive Inference", *International Encyclopedia of Statistical Science*. Edited by Miodrag Lovric. Berlin: Springer, 968–970. Accessed on December 24, 2019 at <https://npi-statistics.com/pdfs/papers/Cool2011.pdf>.

Dempster, A. P. (1963), "On Direct Probabilities", *Journal of the Royal Statistical Society B* 25: 100–110.

Descartes, René ([1641, 1642] 1984), *Meditations on First Philosophy*. Translated by John Cottingham. *The Philosophical Writings of Descartes* Volume II. Translated by John Cottingham, Robert Stoothoff, and Dugald Murdoch. Cambridge: Cambridge University Press, 1–62.

Drake, Alvin W. (1967), *Fundamentals of Applied Probability Theory*. New York: McGraw-Hill. Accessed on September 17, 2019 at <https://ocw.mit.edu/courses/electrical-engineering-and-computer-science/6-041-probabilistic-systems-analysis-and-applied-probability-spring-2006/related-resources/>.

Duignan, Brian (2018), "Occam's Razor", *Encyclopedia Britannica*. Accessed on June 24, 2019 at <https://www.britannica.com/topic/Occams-razor>.

Euclid (2008), *Euclid's Elements Of Geometry*. The Greek text of J.L. Heiberg (1883–1885). Edited, and provided with a modern English translation, by Richard Fitzpatrick. Published by Richard Fitzpatrick.

Eves, Howard (1990), *An Introduction to the History of Mathematics*, 6th Edition. Orlando, Florida: Holt, Rhinehart and Wilson.

Fisher, R. A. (1939), "Student", *Annals of Eugenics* 9: 1–9.

Ghate, Onkar (2013), "Perceptual Awareness as Presentational", *Concepts and Their Role in Knowledge: Reflections on Objectivist Epistemology*. Edited by Allan Gotthelf and James G. Lennox (assoc.). Pittsburgh: University of Pittsburgh Press, 85–111.

Gibson, James J. (1986), *The Ecological Approach to Visual Perception: Classic Edition*. New York: Psychology Press, Taylor and Francis.

Goodman, Nelson (1946), "A Query on Confirmation", *The Journal of Philosophy*, 43 (14): 383–385.

Goodman, Steven N. (1994), "Future Prospects Discussed", *Nature* 368: 106–107.

Gott, J. Richard III (1993), "Implications of the Copernican Principle for our Future Prospects", *Nature* 363: 315–319.

——— (1994), "Future Prospects Discussed", *Nature* 368: 108.

Gotthelf, Allan ([1976] 1987), "Aristotle's Conception of Final Causality", *Review of Metaphysics* 30: 226–254. Reprinted in *Philosophical Issues in Aristotle's Biology*. Edited by Allan Gotthelf and James G. Lennox. Cambridge: Cambridge University Press, 204–242.

——— (2000), *On Ayn Rand*. Belmont, California: Wadsworth.

Harriman, David (2010), *The Logical Leap: Induction in Physics.* With an Introduction by Leonard Peikoff. New York: New American Library.

Herodotus ([449 B.C.] 2004), *The Histories.* New York: Barnes & Noble Classics.

Hill, Bruce M. (1968), "Posterior Distribution of Percentiles: Bayes' Theorem for Sampling from a Population", *Journal of the American Statistical Association* 63: 677–691.

——— (1988), "De Finetti's Theorem, Induction, and $A_{(n)}$ or Bayesian Nonparametric Predictive Inference", *Bayesian Statistics* 3, Edited by Bernardo J.M., DeGroot, M.H., Lindley, D.V. & Smith A.F.M. Oxford: Oxford University Press: 211–241.

——— (1993), "Parametric Models for An: Splitting Processes and Mixtures", *Journal of the Royal Statistical Society B* 55: 423–433.

Hume, David ([1777] 1902), *An Enquiry Concerning Human Understanding.* Edited by L.A. Selby-Bigge. Kindle Edition.

——— ([1739-40] 2019), *A Treatise of Human Nature.* Edited by Peter Millican and Amyas Merivale. Accessed on September 13, 2019 at <https://davidhume.org/texts/t/full>.

Jaynes, E. T. (2003), *Probability Theory: The Logic of Science.* Edited by G. Larry Bretthorst. Cambridge: Cambridge University Press.

Jeffreys, Harold (1932), "On the Theory of Errors and Least Squares", *Proceedings of the Royal Society of London* Series A, 138: 48–55.

Johnson, Scott P. (2010), "How Infants Learn About the Visual World", *Cognitive Science* 34 (2010): 1158–1184.

Joseph, H. W. B. (1916), *An Introduction to Logic.* 2nd Edition, revised. Oxford: Clarendon Press.

Kant, Immanuel ([1787] 1994), *The Critique of Pure Reason*. Second Edition. Translated and edited by Paul Guyer and Allen W. Wood. Cambridge: Cambridge University Press.

Klein, Jacob (1968), *Greek Mathematical Thought and the Origin of Algebra*. Translated, from the original German text published in 1934, by Eva Brann. Cambridge, Mass.: The M.I.T. Press.

Laplace, Pierre-Simon (1812), *Theorie Analytique des Probabilités*. Paris: Courcier.

——— ([1825] 1995), *Philosophical Essay on Probabilities*. Reprint. Translated by Andrew I. Dale. Originally published as *Essai philosophique sur les probabilite's* (Paris: Bachelier). New York: Springer-Verlag.

Laertius, Diogenes (2018), *Lives of the Eminent Philosophers*. Translated by Pamela Mensch. Oxford University Press.

Locke, John ([1690–1710] 1975), *An Essay Concerning Human Understanding*. Edited with an Introduction by Peter H. Nidditch. Oxford: Oxford University Press.

MacKay, David J. C. (2003). *Information Theory, Inference, and Learning Algorithms*. Version 7.2 (fourth printing) March 28, 2005. Cambridge University Press. PDF downloaded from <http://www.inference.org.uk/mackay/itila/book.html> April 8, 2019.

McGrath, Matthew and Devin Frank (2018), "Propositions", *The Stanford Encyclopedia of Philosophy* (Spring 2018). Edited by Edward N. Zalta. Available online at <https://plato.stanford.edu/archives/spr2018/entries/propositions/>.

Mill, John Stuart (1919), *A System of Logic*. London: Longmans, Green, and Co.

Norton, John (2018), *The Material Theory of Induction*. Draft of June 26, 2018. Accessed on July 1, 2019 at <http://www. pitt.edu/~jdnorton/homepage/cv.html#material_theory>.

Peikoff, Leonard ([1967] 1990), "The Analytic-Synthetic Dichotomy", *The Objectivist* 6(5)–6(9). Reprinted in *Introduction to Objectivist Epistemology*, Expanded Second Edition. Edited by Harry Binswanger and Leonard Peikoff. New York: Meridian.

——— (1991), *Objectivism: The Philosophy of Ayn Rand*. New York: Dutton.

——— (1997), *Objectivism Through Induction*. Audio recording of lecture series. The Ayn Rand Institute. Accessed on April 26, 2020 at <https://courses.aynrand.org/campus-courses/objectivism-through-induction/>

——— (2002), *Induction in Physics and Philosophy*. Audio recording of lecture series. Irvine, California: The Ayn Rand Bookstore. Available at <https://estore.aynrand.org/p/119/induction-in-physics-and-philosophy-mp3-download>.

Pisaturo, Ronald (1998), Mathematics in One Lesson, *The Intellectual Activist*, 12 (9): 13–22 and 12 (10): 11–23.

——— (2001), "Undermining Reason: The Assault on the Philosophy of Mathematics, Part 2," *The Intellectual Activist*, 15 (11): 22–39.

——— (2009), "Past Longevity as Evidence for the Future", *Philosophy of Science*, 76: 73–100.

——— (2015), *Masculine Power, Feminine Beauty: The Volitional, Objective Basis for Heterosexuality in Romantic Love and Marriage*. CreateSpace Independent Publishing Platform.

——— ([2011] 2016), *The Longevity Argument: The Doomsday Argument is wrong, and logical induction has a philosophical basis*. CreateSpace Independent Publishing Platform. Originally published by the author.

Pisaturo, Ronald and Glenn D. Marcus (1994), "The Foundation of Mathematics," *The Intellectual Activist*, 8 (4):1–15 and 8 (5): 1–14.

Plato (1994–2009), *The Republic*. Translated by Benjamin Jowett. The Internet Classics Archive by Daniel C. Stevenson, Web Atomics. Accessed on May 8, 2020 at <http://classics.mit.edu/Plato/republic.html>.

Rand, Ayn (1957), *Atlas Shrugged*. New York: Random House.

——— (1961), *For the New Intellectual*. New York: Signet.

——— ([1970] 1971), "The Comprachicos", *The Objectivist* 9 (8)–(12). Reprinted in *The New Left: The Anti-Industrial Revolution*. New York: Signet, 152–204.

——— ([1971] 1975), "Art and Cognition", *The Objectivist* 10 (4)–(6). Reprinted in *The Romantic Manifesto*. Second Revised Edition. New York: Signet, 45–79.

——— ([1973] 1984a), "The Metaphysical Versus the Man-Made", *The Ayn Rand Letter* 2 (12)–(13). Reprinted in *Philosophy: Who Needs It*. New York: Signet, 31–46.

——— ([1974] 1984b), "Philosophy: Who Needs It", *The Ayn Rand Letter* 3 (7)–(8). Reprinted in *Philosophy: Who Needs It*. New York: Signet, 1984, 1–15.

——— ([1966–1967] 1990), "Introduction to Objectivist Epistemology", *The Objectivist* 5(7)–6(2). Reprinted in *Introduction to*

Objectivist Epistemology, Expanded Second Edition. Edited by Harry Binswanger and Leonard Peikoff. New York: Meridian.

Salmieri, Gregory (2012), "Aristotle's Conception of Universality", Accessed on December 21, 2018 at <http://www.salmieri.org/research>.

——— (2013), "Conceptualization and Justification", *Concepts and Their Role in Knowledge: Reflections on Objectivist Epistemology*. Edited by Allan Gotthelf and James G. Lennox (assoc.). Pittsburgh: University of Pittsburgh Press, 41–84.

Social Security Administration (2020), "Period Life Table, 2017". Accessed on September 9, 2020 at <https://www.ssa.gov/oact/STATS/table4c6.html#fn1>

Warriner, John E. (1982), *English Grammar and Composition: Fifth Course*. New York: Harcourt Brace Jovanovich.).

World Bank (2020), "GDP per capita, PPP (constant 2011 international $)". Data converted to 1995 dollars. Accessed on May 8, 2020 at <https://data.worldbank.org/indicator/NY.GDP.PCAP.PP.KD?end=1995&locations=US-SE-N&start=1995&view=bar>.

Index of Persons

ABOUT THE AUTHOR

Ronald Pisaturo was a founder and President of American Renaissance School, a private high school with high academic standards. The school, located in White Plains, New York, operated in the 1980s. Mr. Pisaturo is also the author of *The Longevity Argument*, *The Merchant of Mars*, and *Masculine Power, Feminine Beauty: The Volitional, Objective Basis for Heterosexuality in Romantic Love and Marriage*. Articles by Mr. Pisaturo have appeared in *Philosophy of Science*, *The Federalist*, *Quillette*, *The Intellectual Activist*, *Barron's*, *Capitalism Magazine*, many newspapers, and his personal Web site at www.ronpisaturo.com. Plays by Mr. Pisaturo that have been produced include *Escape From Eden* and *Brothers, Not Keepers*.

www.ingramcontent.com/pod-product-compliance
Lightning Source LLC
Chambersburg PA
CBHW020847090426
42736CB00008B/265